C000281862

MotoGP
Season Review 2011

TISSOT
SWISS WATCHES SINCE 1853
INNOVATORS BY TRADITION

OFFICIAL TIMEKEEPER

MotoGP
Season Review 2011
Julian Ryder

Published in November 2011

A catalogue record for this book is available from the British Library

ISBN 978 0 85733 109 0

Library of Congress catalog card no 2011932704

Haynes Publishing, Sparkford, Yeovil,
Somerset BA22 7JJ, UK
Tel: +44 (0) 1963 442030
Fax: +44 (0) 1963 440001
E-mail: sales@haynes.co.uk
Website: www.haynes.co.uk

Haynes North America, Inc.,
861 Lawrence Drive, Newbury Park,
California 91320, USA

Printed and bound in the UK by Gomer Press Limited,
Llandysul Enterprise Park, Llandysul, Ceredigion SA44 4JL

Managing Editor Mark Hughes
Design Lee Parsons, Richard Parsons, Dominic Stickland
Sub-editor Kay Edge
Special Sales & Advertising Manager
David Dew (david@motocom.co.uk)
Photography Front cover, race action, bike side views and portraits by Andrew Northcott/AJRN Sports Photography; technical images pp22-29 and pp188-194 by Neil Spalding

Author's acknowledgements

Thanks to:

Toby Moody and Neil Spalding, my co-commentators on British Eurosport's MotoGP coverage; Nick Harris, Matt Roberts, Martin Raines, Andrew Northcott, Dean Adams, Kyoichi Nakamura, and everyone else who helped us get through the season

CONTENTS
MotoGP 2011

SHARK
PRAMAC
14

FOREWORD
CARMELO EZPELETA

The 2011 season has been another hugely significant one for the FIM MotoGP World Championship with the sport experiencing a continued growth in popularity and evolution on a technological front, as well as some fantastic racing throughout the year.

In MotoGP we witnessed the last year of the 800cc bikes as the premier class of the World Championship prepares for the return of 1,000cc machinery in 2012, and the Grand Prix Commission has been working tirelessly to finalise and define the technical regulations as teams, riders and fans anticipate an exciting new era. There was also the successful implementation of the engine usage limit rule this year, as our sport endeavours to adapt to the ever-demanding global economic climate by taking a number of measures.

In 2011 we also saw the final year of the 125cc two-stroke bikes, the category having been a World Championship class since the competition's birth in 1949. With the introduction of the new 250cc four-stroke Moto3 class, which will replace the 125s, the sport is taking another significant step forward in terms of technology and cost efficiency.

And of course 2011 was the second year of the hugely successful Moto2 class, a category that proved a massive hit upon its introduction in 2010 and that has continued to produce close racing of the highest calibre this year.

Within Dorna we continue to invest extensively in our television production facilities, improving our High Definition service and extending our coverage to ensure that fans around the world enjoy the MotoGP experience to the full.

Towards the end of the season we were confronted by tragedy when Marco Simoncelli lost his life at the Sepang circuit. MotoGP remains an innately dangerous sport and whilst we all accept this nothing can prepare us for such tragic losses as that of Marco. He remains in our hearts and memories and the tribute made to 'Super Sic' at Valencia by the MotoGP family was an emotional and fitting remembrance of him as a person, and of his contribution to the sport he loved.

In the *Official MotoGP Season Review* we will relive the final season of the 800s and see how Casey Stoner, in his first season in the factory Honda team, put on a show of supremacy that delivered him a second World title, how Stefan Bradl held off the challenge of Marc Márquez to become Moto2 World Champion, and how Nico Terol's displays secured him the last-ever 125cc title.

I hope you enjoy reading about the best moments of the past year and are already as excited about the forthcoming 2012 season as we are!

CARMELO EZPELETA

DORNA SPORTS CEO
NOVEMBER 2011

THE SEASON

MAT OXLEY

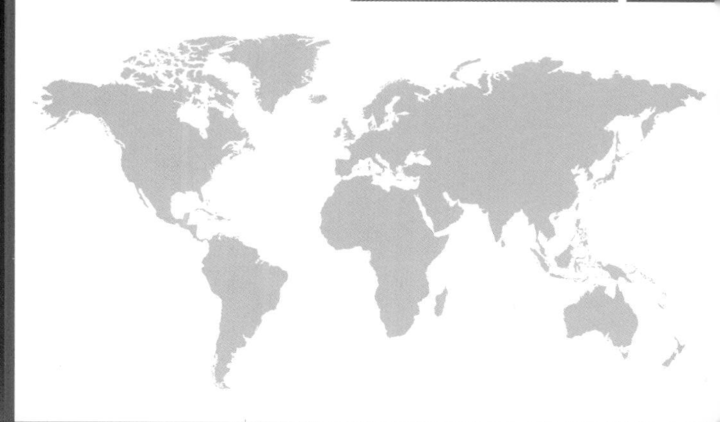

CHANGE ON THE HORIZON

MotoGP 2011 had many highs and one horrible low. It was also the last season of the unloved 800s, with the new 1,000s on their way and huge changes looming

Our memories of the 2011 MotoGP season will forever be dominated by two sights. We all delighted in watching Casey Stoner in full flight, released from the shackles of the evil Desmosedici. He was a wonder to behold, his talent to screw the maximum out of a motorcycle at least as remarkable as anything we've ever seen.

And then there was the horror of Sepang, witnessing bike racing's young lion lose his life. Marco Simoncelli might not have been the fastest or the most skilful MotoGP rider, but he was certainly the most exciting. He was the first superstar the sport has lost in a long time and he will be missed in all kinds of ways.

Simoncelli's passing reminded us of what we all already knew: that motorcycle racing is a dangerous, pitiless sport in which luck can sometimes be more important than talent.

Danger is an inevitable feature of racing bikes at high speed and it is the danger that gives the sport a greater sense of gravitas than most others. This is not football or cricket or tennis, this is a sport in which riders – willingly and eagerly – put their lives on the line every time they go out onto the racetrack; that is what makes it so different, what makes its greatest exponents such fascinating people. As Ernest Hemingway once said: 'There are only three sports: bull-fighting, mountain-climbing and motor racing. The rest are mere games.'

And this is what we should always remember when watching Stoner and the others do their thing. They are all thrill-seekers, but they are not reckless young men addicted to risk and danger. What attracts them to motorcycle racing is the thrill of speed, the rush of adrenaline and the complex demands of mastering a machine on the very edge

Above MotoGP had to come to terms with the loss of Marco Simoncelli at the Malaysian Grand Prix

of control. Of course, they are willing to face the danger and risk, but what really excites them is controlling that danger and risk with their own talent and skill. They know the cost of making a mistake can be very high, but they have to believe that they are better than that.

Stoner is certainly the greatest talent in MotoGP at the moment. He probably had been for the previous few years, but he was so busy fighting to keep the Ducati right side up that his skills weren't quite so obvious. Only in the light of Valentino Rossi's nightmare year with the Italian machine is his remarkable ability fully appreciated.

Stoner's unerring speed and consistency during 2011 stirred a sense of *déjà vu* in older fans: a feisty young Aussie on a Repsol Honda laying waste to his rivals. We had seen it before: a rider who's a pure racer, who doesn't go racing because he wants to be famous like a pop star, who doesn't hang around to make a race of it when he knows he's much better than that, a rider who rides his motorcycle with stunning aggression and who occasionally treats the press with a similar (and well-deserved) belligerence.

The comparisons between Casey Stoner and Mick Doohan are so obvious – from their dirt-track roots all the way to their domination of the class of kings – that it's tempting to overdo them. But Stoner is his own man, racing in a different era; it does him a disservice to proclaim him as a reincarnation of his childhood hero.

The genius of Stoner is that he can happily ride a motorcycle when it's shaking and bucking and tucking beneath him. It's something that great dirt-trackers learn: to wring the motorcycle's neck and then deal with the consequences, to let the bike find its own way, while adjusting body position, throttle opening and brake pressure to keep it between the kerbs.

Aboard Honda's RC212V, Stoner's talent was able to really flourish. The RCV wasn't the friendliest motorcycle out there – it's a snarling beast compared to Yamaha's burbling YZR-M1 – but after the Ducati it was like a magic carpet ride. Following his dominant victory at the season-opening Qatar GP, Stoner was moved to remark that he hadn't had one front-end lose all weekend, when during the previous few years he had had to get used to coping with such stomach-churning moments every few laps.

No longer haunted by such concerns, his talent was set free so he could be less defensive and more aggressive. He didn't need to keep half his race brain on constant alert to catch a front-end slide or save a rear-end wobble, so he could focus on the real business of going fast and working out new ways to extract another tenth or two from the RCV.

As the year went on Stoner turned down the traction control. The more comfortable he felt, the more he could revert to the style of riding he knows best: using the rear tyre to help steer the motorcycle. He was the first rider to do such a thing in the 800 era and none of his rivals seemed to have any answer to that. The 800s were supposed to be all about corner speed – big cornering arcs and keeping both wheels in line. But here was Stoner doing it old-school, using a bit of wheelspin to skew the bike mid-corner, then wrenching the bike upright and launching it out of the turn. There's no doubt he's ready for the new 1,000s, which should encourage riders to use the old point-and-squirt technique.

The Honda was certainly the fastest bike out of the

corners, but the Yamaha was still the smoothest going into them. Jorge Lorenzo exploited the M1's strong point to the absolute maximum and as a result he was the only rider who came close to Stoner in 2011. In fact, he had no choice, because that was the only weapon he had at his disposal: massive corner-entry and mid-corner speed. When the bike and front tyre were operating precisely as required, Lorenzo could be unbeatable. But Wayne Rainey and Mick Doohan used to tell us: relying on the front tyre is fine, until grip goes away, then you are easy prey for anyone who can ride with the rear and make a virtue of a degrading rear slick.

Yamaha's problem was the same as always – a lack of corner-exit traction and a lack of peak horsepower. Towards the end of the season it seemed like those disadvantages were starting to tell on Lorenzo and team-mate Ben Spies. Lorenzo had that horrible warm-up accident at Phillip Island, where he said goodbye to the title and goodbye to the tip of his left ring finger on the same day. Spies was going through a nightmare at the same time – three big crashes in just eight days forcing him to withdraw from both Phillip Island and Sepang. As Lorenzo had said following his dogged pursuit of Stoner at the opening race: 'If I have to ride like I rode at Qatar all year, I will crash for sure.'

Beyond Stoner and Lorenzo, the others were supporting actors. Spies didn't have the greatest of years to celebrate his promotion to factory status. He won at Assen, then seemed to find himself on a plateau. In the past the Texan has always been known for his ability for relentless forward progress. However, he's very close to the absolute pinnacle now, though those last few metres to the summit are always the hardest.

If Honda's RCV really was the best bike of 2011, it's worth remembering that the factory would still have lost the title if they hadn't had Stoner on their side. Stoner's Repsol Honda team-mates Dani Pedrosa and Andrea Dovizioso both finished behind Lorenzo following the kind of campaigns they're both well known for: Pedrosa's blighted by injury, Dovizioso's characterised by a nice consistency but lacking that winning punch.

Rossi's 2011 was like nothing he had ever known. This was the first season since he arrived 15 years earlier in which he hadn't won a race. If that was the worst thing about Rossi's season, it wouldn't have been so bad, but in fact it was much, much worse than that.

When everyone's favourite bike racer signed for Ducati in the summer of 2010, some journalists asked Ducati chiefs Gabriele Del Torcio and Claudio Domenicali whether they had considered the possible downsides of this most famous of racing marriages. If the nine-time World Champion and winner of 105 GPs fails to win on the GP11, won't it be a smirch on Ducati's brand image? No doubt Del Torcio and Domenicali had considered the possibility of failure, but the actuality of failure is something else. During 2011 we watched three motorcycling legends go down in flames: Rossi, Ducati and Jeremy Burgess.

Before 2011 most race fans and paddock people were prepared to consider Rossi the GOAT (Greatest Of All Time), but nowadays many fewer are prepared to confer that accolade upon him. Ducati's GP11 was the motorcycle that The Doctor couldn't fix. It's the machine that proved he's merely human after all.

But he's a human with a great sense of humour. Despite one gloomy result after another, one tumble after another, Rossi remained upbeat and philosophical throughout, always happy to make a joke at his own expense or at the

Below Honda finally won an 800cc title thanks to Casey Stoner's tyre-torturing riding and the forceful management of HRC by President Tetsuo Suzuki and Vice-President Shuhei Nakamoto

expense of his employers. At newly resurfaced Mugello, where he was a second off the pace, Rossi made everyone laugh with this quip: 'If we race with the new surface and the others race with the old surface then maybe we can win.' His future as arguably the greatest racer of all time now rests in the hands of Filippo Preziosi, who needs to build a great GP12 to keep Rossi in MotoGP.

No doubt thoughts of retirement must have flickered through Rossi's mind immediately after he lost his great friend Simoncelli at Sepang. But Rossi is intelligent: he knows that such things happen in racing and he knows it could so easily have been him on the ground and Simoncelli desperately trying to take evasive action. It underestimates the brainpower of racers to think that they would throw their hands up in horror and walk away, never to be seen at a racetrack again. In the backs of their minds, they're all prepared for such eventualities.

Simoncelli's death is a human tragedy. It's also a tragedy for the sport. The man was on the cusp of greatness. His brilliant ride to second at Phillip Island the previous weekend – resisting falling off in the squall of rain that claimed several other riders and then defeating Dovizioso in a last-lap slugging match – suggested that he had finally learned to ride the knife edge.

It had been a rollercoaster ride watching him get that far. He was a thrill to watch, that lanky body draped over the RCV, all knees and elbows, always pushing on, pushing on. Like so many great riders, he had been fast and wayward, but bit by bit he was learning to be straightforward fast. At Sepang all he lacked was some luck.

The controversy that dogged MotoGP's newest star earlier in the year – especially after his collision with Dani Pedrosa at Le Mans – became unseemly. Sure, Simoncelli made mistakes, but who in this sport hasn't? Let he who is without sin cast the first stone. Frankly, his treatment evolved into something reminiscent of schoolyard bullying, with only a few riders prepared to stand by the Italian.

When some riders suggested a new set of rules to govern overtaking, *à la* Formula 1, veteran Colin Edwards had this sneering response: 'You can't bring gladiators to an opera – we're here to fight.' Neither did Edwards agree with the penalty Simoncelli received at Le Mans. 'The ride-through they gave Marco was bullshit,' added the Texan. 'I don't think he's overly aggressive – he just enjoys the fight. They can shove their penalties up their arse – we're here to race motorcycles.'

Simoncelli wasn't the only rider embroiled in controversy during 2011. This was the year of MotoGP handbags, the summer during which petty disputes raged throughout the paddock, the fires always enthusiastically fanned by the media. Rossi and Stoner traded insults for much of the year, just as Simoncelli did with Pedrosa and Lorenzo. And when those fires died down, another blew up.

If nothing else, the Motegi debate kept the media in headlines for another few months. Most of the riders, including Stoner and Lorenzo, did their best to stay away from Motegi – concerned at the possibility of a meltdown at the earthquake-damaged Fukushima nuclear plant – but in the end they obeyed their contracts and raced. The paranoia didn't go away, however: the image of Lorenzo showering himself with bottles of French mineral water is one that will remain for a while.

In fact, the earthquake did affect Stoner's visit. He was

Right Try as he might, Valentino Rossi couldn't bend the Ducati to his will; more often than ever before in his career he was walking back to confer with his crew after a front-end crash

Far left Nico Terol became the last ever 125cc World Champion before the class transforms into Moto3

Near left Spain's new star, Marc Marquez, kept Stefan Bradl in the shadows for much of the year, but the German took the 125 title

Far left Dorna's top man, Carmelo Ezpeleta, has got heavy with the factories over costs

on his way to another runaway win at Motegi when his RCV flew out of control on some bumps, sending him off track and demoting him to third place. The bumps were a legacy of the earthquake.

MotoGP itself is heading for seismic change in 2012 and beyond. The 800s raced for the last time at Valencia and their departure was greeted with cries of 'good riddance' from most of the paddock. The new 1,000s, meanwhile, are being greeted with whoops of joy. The extra torque of the bigger engines should allow riders to use different techniques and racing lines, which in turn should lead to better racing than the dreary processions that had become the norm during the 800 era.

That's not the biggest deal in 2012, however. The real deal is the arrival of the so-called CRT (Claiming Rule Team) machines. But Dorna are now pushing the lower-cost CRT concept as something that's much more than just an exercise in providing a few extra bikes to fill the rear of the grid. Carmelo Ezpeleta quietly dropped the bombshell at Misano – in a few years he wants all bikes on the grid to be CRT bikes, not prototypes. In other words: no Honda RCVs, no Yamaha M1s, and no Ducati Desmosedicis.

It's not easy to argue with his logic. Times are hard and times are especially hard in the motorcycle business, with little prospect of much rosier times in the near future as the global economy lurches from one crisis to the next. The days of credit-fuelled booms and tobacco-funded riches are in the last past and the factories (with the possible exception of Honda) are struggling to justify the cost of limited-edition exotica, so it's time for a radical rethink. The present system is unsustainable and if a new and cheaper type of motorcycle is introduced, then why make that motorcycle just for the privateers at the back of the grid? Why not put everyone on that kind of motorcycle and let the racing commence?

It's a prospect that bothers the purists who believe that MotoGP should be about developing technology, but MotoGP is bigger than that now. It's a global TV phenomenon owned by a private-equity business, so it's the show – and the profits arising from that show – that matter more than anything.

So the next few years are going to be fascinating as a new-look MotoGP championship evolves. How many of the manufacturers will be running full-factory teams in five years' time? Will MotoGP be better or worse if there are no factories directly involved? Do traction control and other electronic rider aids have a long-term role in MotoGP? All these questions will be answered. And hopefully the racing will be thrilling – and safe – as well.

Below This was Yamaha's 50th year of racing, so they brought out the old corporate red-and-white colours, plus a few of their old bikes

OBITUARY

MATTHEW ROBERTS

MARCO SIMONCELLI

1987 – 2011

There can be scant higher praise to bestow on Marco Simoncelli than to say that he was the most exciting thing to happen to motorcycle racing since Valentino Rossi. As outrageous on the track as he was off it, his wild afro hairstyle and swashbuckling riding style won the hearts of fans all over the world. His death in Malaysia this year brought the sporting world to a stunned standstill.

Inspired by Rossi but quite evidently another maverick entirely of his own breed, Marco feared no rival and made no allowances for reputation, not even that of his great friend, the greatest of all time. His final act was a lap and a half of pure adrenaline, swapping positions with Alvaro Bautista with trademark panache: riding on the edge, the only way he knew, revelling in the one activity he loved the most.

His two race performances before that were arguably the best of his career, both of them breathtaking battles to the finish with his compatriot Andrea Dovizioso, another fierce rival. Marco won out on both occasions for fourth place at Motegi (despite a ride-through penalty) and second place – his career-best MotoGP result – at Phillip Island.

In those two races the signs were there that Marco had finally managed to curb the overly-combative style that had cost him further podiums or even wins earlier in the season and worked out how to channel his fearless aggression in the most productive manner. Up to then it had been the only chink in his armour.

Dovizioso and Bautista, like most of the current stars, both had 'previous' with Simoncelli from their days together in the smaller classes, when the gangly youngster was forced to compensate for his excessive frame by using it in body-to-body combat. A soaking wet race at Jerez in 2004 gave Simoncelli the level playing field he needed to fully exploit his raw potential for the first time with a maiden career 125cc victory that he managed to repeat one year later in the dry, following up with five further podiums that season.

The move up to the 250cc class didn't go as smoothly as many expected and it wasn't until the third race of his third season on the Gilera that he scored his first podium in the class. A first win came three races later and sparked a run of form and confidence that saw him crowned 2008 250cc World Champion. After narrowly missing out on the title in the final race of 2009 he made the step up to MotoGP for 2010 and battled with Ben Spies for Rookie of the Year.

His last ever Grand Prix season was the year of his confirmation as one of the sport's brightest talents and biggest characters. After a host of controversial incidents in the opening rounds, he came under intense pressure from his peers and from the media. Although his confidence took a beating, it didn't crack. His refusal to be intimidated by the establishment endeared him even more to his growing army of fans.

Born with talent but raised with humour, humility and good manners, Marco was a credit to the grief-stricken family left to mourn him. It's a common and bitter irony that our sport's greatest appeal is also its greatest pitfall. Motorcycle racing brought Marco Simoncelli to his death but it also brought him to life and you can rest assured that he wouldn't have lived it any other way. Ciao Marco.

TECHNICAL REVIEW

NEIL SPALDING

ROSSI GOES TESTING

It was supposed to be the Italian dream marriage, the combination of the rider many call 'the GOAT' (Greatest Of All Time) and Ducati, the factory responsible for the 2007 World Championship and the guys who built the bike on which Casey Stoner beat Valentino Rossi several times last year. Instead, it turned into a nightmare

Since the start of the 800cc version of the MotoGP championships in 2007, the Ducati has been a one-rider bike. Casey Stoner seemed to be the only man capable of getting the best out of the mercurial Ducati, as other riders managed just a smattering of podiums and there was just one other win – for Loris Capirossi at Motegi in 2007 – on the very day Stoner was crowned World Champion.

The bike has the same basic concept Ducati first brought to GPs in 2003: a 90-degree 'L' V4 with desmodromic valve actuation. Over the years it has been around in two basic versions, the steel lattice of the first six years and then the carbon-fibre 'stressed-airbox' design of the past three years. During Stoner's championship-winning year, when it still had a steel lattice frame, the bike acquired a reputation for being difficult to ride, a throttle with little connection to the rear tyre being the main rider complaint. That problem was forgivable as it seemed to be a side effect of Ducati's fuelling strategy, one that focused on super-lean performance in the twisty sections of the track while allowing the right levels for full power on the straights. Making the bike easier to ride became a priority for 2008, especially when new signing Marco Melandri found it simply too difficult to live with the vague-feeling throttle.

In 2009 the bike used a new 'stressed-airbox' design. This effectively took the carbon airbox and intake snorkel from the steel tube frame, reinforced them and made them do double duty as both air-intake system and frame. The 'box' section was bolted to the engine by means of three studs and bolts on the intake cam covers of each bank of the 'V'. From a packaging perspective, this design is simply superb: there are no cumbersome beams down either side of the

Above At the Estoril test a new engine with a higher inertia crankshaft joined the 'softer' chassis used in the race. It still wasn't enough, despite many different settings being tried. Here the swingarm pivots are being changed

engine, and there is far more space available behind the fairing for parts. On street bikes it would quite easily provide homes for ABS systems, ECUs and whatever emission equipment might be needed in the near future.

The trouble came when the same design was used on modern 800cc MotoGP bikes. The packaging advantages remain (although the Ducati doesn't seem to have got a lot smaller), but the carbon chassis now has to deal with the suspension compliance and the resulting grip issues that come with long corners taken at over 60 degrees of lean on Bridgestone's sublime but demanding control tyres. That's not something riders come up against anywhere else, even in Superbike racing. Add that to a design which already used the engine as a stressed member in the middle of the bike and that's where it all went horribly wrong.

Right By Misano the GP11.1 was settled in its peculiar 'nose up' stance, which rolled the 'vee' backwards and allowed the front forks to be put on an extremely 'vertical' position in the headstock, effectively moving the front axle backwards while keeping a reasonable rake

ROSSI JOINS DUCATI

Rossi started his first year with the GP11, basically the same bike as the GP9 and GP10, but with some 48mm Ohlins forks, a new fairing and a different top triple clamp.

Valentino had fought Yamaha to be released early from his contract, just to make sure that he could test and then have some development parts in the spring once his damaged shoulder had been fixed. In his very first outing at Valencia, the day after his last race on a Yamaha, he told Ducati that the front-end feel needed to change: he couldn't get the feedback from the front that he needed in order to allow him to go fast. It wasn't a good start – and after the test he went off to have his shoulder operation and couldn't ride hard for a few months.

While early-season testing was disrupted by the need to allow his shoulder to heal, Rossi nevertheless put the Ducati through all the set-ups that Jerry Burgess and his crew could think of. They weren't able to make the bike's behaviour change much – it seemed to have difficulties in the way it acted as it went through a corner, drifting wide pretty much regardless of settings – and there weren't many new parts to be seen.

The Desmosedici has always had a low centre of gravity to enable it to accelerate without wheelies, and a long wheelbase to keep it stable at high speeds. That direction, though, is the opposite to Rossi's preference for a high centre of gravity, which allows the bike to transfer weight back and forward to generate grip, and which flicks easily from left to right. Jerry Burgess started the winter by raising the bike over 20mm. He also evaluated a new progressive rear linkage to try and encourage the bike to pitch as he wanted it to. All these moves were an attempt to get the bike to change direction more quickly without sacrificing rear traction, something that has been a major strength of the Desmosedici.

Several different fairings were also tried, all with the Alan Jenkins-inspired winglets removed. Rossi prizes agility over everything else and the potential top-speed improvements offered by the larger slab-sided fairings are not as important to him. Their downside is a loss of agility and handling that Valentino refuses point blank to relinquish. The wings were removed because they seemed to make a bike that was already difficult to turn even more difficult, and because their fixed attitude interfered with Burgess's desire to raise and lower the front or rear of the bike as necessary

At the end of winter testing team manager Vittoriano Guareschi, who also doubles as a test and development rider, said: 'The bike is now almost on a standard setting. The big difference is that it's almost 20mm higher than we would normally have. Jerry works hard to make Valentino happy with his riding position. We need more turning ability in the second part of the corner, after the brake is off. Valentino feels it is heavy and this puts a lot of pressure on him in this position. But it also makes the front feel light on acceleration because the bike transfers the weight a lot. The higher bike moves more easily. We have a lot of rear traction but without the new anti-spin the bike is impossible to ride. Valentino also prefers the cut-away fairings. The bigger fairing is 2kph faster but he prefers the small fairing for agility. Nicky (Hayden) tried a 'softer' chassis at Valencia. It has the same stiffness in braking but more flex in the corners. We can see the difference on a measuring jig but the rider can't feel it.'

The bike's basic geometry had been developed for a riding style completely at odds with Rossi's. Stoner had found he had plenty of rear grip, and not enough front-end feel. He had also found that if he got the rear end spinning and drifting, and simultaneously slid the front, he could slide the bike through corners at 60-plus degrees of lean, while still being able to accelerate as hard as he wanted. That he crashed as infrequently as he did was a measure of his skill; his crew chief Cristian Gabbarini said it was quite common to see, on his data, the front end tuck two or three times a lap during a race, and for Casey to 'save' it each time. Under Stoner's input the bike was changed to fit with his style, one of the outcomes being that the front fork position was moved away from the bike, leaving even less weight on the front but possibly making it easier for Casey to drift controllably.

It was to be the third race of the 2011 season, at Estoril, fully six months after Rossi first sat on the bike, before a much softer chassis was available for him to try, and he used it to good effect in the race. In the test that followed he also tried a new engine with a much higher inertia crankshaft. This latter modification was to try to make the character of the engine much more controllable in corners, where Valentino's favoured style is to use the front brake simultaneously with the throttle to control the suspension's movement. Over the next few GPs Rossi tried several different versions of the 'stressed airbox' chassis, all with different internal constructions, but none gave the improvement in front-end grip and 'feel' that were desperately wanted. The problem now was that the sealed carbon box couldn't be made a lot 'softer' without it becoming dangerously weak, and the 'rider feel' wasn't really improving.

There were actually several different problems. The basic concept of a sealed box is pretty rigid, with the way it is mounted adding to the rigidity, and the box is very short. The long aluminium beams of the Japanese bikes stretch unsupported all the way from the steering head to the swingarm pivot; the Ducati uses the engine as a stressed member for the middle third of the bike. There are many things an engine is going to do well, but it is never going to allow flex and keep running. It increasingly looked as if the problem with the Ducati was not the material of the chassis, but that it could be the basic design concept – or even more likely, a mixture of the two.

Then, in mid-June, Rossi tested Ducati's 2012 challenger, the 1,000cc GP12, and he liked it. The bike had a different swingarm and linkage as well as the longer-stroke 1,000cc engine. The engine also had a new 'seamless shift' transmission, thought to have been made by British gearbox constructor Xtrac. The carbon 'box' chassis was also different, but only in detail to allow it to fit the larger and longer-stroke engine. The decision was quickly made to convert the engines to 800cc using short-stroke crankshafts and long connecting rods. It is a measure of how close the design of the new long-stroke '81mm' 1,000cc four is to the current 800cc version that the whole job took just six weeks to complete. The new bike debuted at Assen.

That's when they discovered that a short-stroke 800cc version of a 1,000cc bike handled completely differently. The weight of the crankshaft and the torque of the engine meant that the 1,000s are ridden very differently too. Critically, the bikes spend far less of their cornering time leaned right over, which is the Ducati's real weak spot.

The new bike had a far better rear suspension linkage, its movement was much more controllable for Rossi, and as a 1,000cc machine it seemed far easier to ride. The trouble was that the 800s need to maintain their speed in the

Below The GP11.1 'stressed-airbox' carbon frame was identical in concept to the previous version but accommodated the different mounting stud positions on the longer-stroke 1,000cc engine's cylinder heads

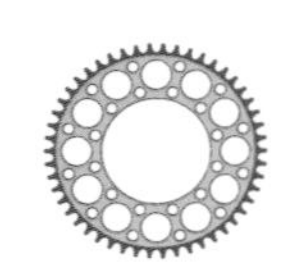

Right The aluminium 'interim chassis' moved away from the cylinder head mountings; at the front they had long drop-down hangers to the front cylinder bank

Below The 'interim' aluminium chassis (left) alongside its carbon predecessor at Aragon. The revised rear mounting system can be seen with small arms extending to the rear carbon seat sub-frame mounts

corners and therefore spend far longer over at maximum lean than the equivalent 1,000, and it was at high lean angles that Valentino found the new bike difficult to 'feel'. The result was a bike that in many ways was worse than the one he had used before. Nevertheless, the decision was made to persevere with the new bike, and to develop it, but that proved to be difficult.

At Mugello it was very good, but at the tight and twisty Sachsenring it was a disaster: the improved rear grip 'pushed' the front and the bike simply could not hold a line, and that's a big problem at the German circuit. A new set-up was found that lifted the front and allowed the forks to be swung backwards as far as possible, slightly shortening the front of the bike and rolling the engine backwards slightly. This put just enough weight on to the front tyre to allow Rossi to steer the bike around the Sachsenring's never-ending corners. The resulting bike looked strange – high at the front but with the rider repositioned so that he sat almost in the same relationship with the ground as before, his clip-on handlebars sitting 30mm down the fork tubes to achieve this. New chain pivot position was also needed to stop the bike jacking itself up every time Valentino touched the throttle. It wasn't until Brno that additional adjustment was found for the swingarm pivot, but by then Ducati had capitulated to Rossi's demands that they build an aluminium beam frame.

It is believed that British constructor FTR (previous builders of Kawasaki, KTM and Red Bull bikes) built and welded the frames to drawings prepared in-house at Ducati by some engineers recruited from Aprilia after the end of their Moto2 project. The first new frame – let's call it the 'stop-gap' frame – is an abbreviated unit that replicates the geometry of the carbon box but is made of machined aluminium welded together and which mounts differently to the engine. The front mounts are the old steel tube frame mounts (which are still cast into each engine but which are normally machined off) and the hard point at the rear of the rear cylinder head carries the front mount of the carbon rear sub-frame. This means the aluminium unit can flex more – it isn't a 'rigid by design' sealed box – but it still isn't a full beam frame of the type developed over the last two decades.

Rossi tested a new aluminium frame at Mugello, as part of Ducati's 1,000cc test programme. The same frame arrived at Aragon with an 800cc version of the same engine bolted into it. Using the 'de-stroked 1,000' as this year's race bike meant

that anything tested on the 1,000 can theoretically be used on the '11.1' 800, making a bit of a mockery of the MSMA 'gentlemen's agreement' on testing limits. However, for the good of the sport it was necessary for the Ducati to get quicker, and very quickly.

It seems that Rossi's engine number six, which he used at the Misano GP, was made with its old 'steel tube' frame mounts fully operational. The older engines in Valentino's allocation didn't have the front engine mounts that were needed to work with this interim chassis, so the second bike built up at Aragon had a seventh engine in it. That wasn't used on the Saturday, because to use it would have meant starting from pit lane; had Rossi qualified well he would have kept that engine unused in order to retain a good grid position. As it turned out he didn't qualify well and so the seventh engine was used, with the Ducati starting from pit lane. This meant he had the use of two identical bikes in practice for the ensuing GPs, something that allowed him to keep swapping between machines, leaving the bike in the garage to be adjusted while he was on track, speeding up chassis experimentation dramatically.

In use it hasn't been as big an improvement as had been hoped. The geometry change seems to be one of the most pressing needs, and a new frame with the current fork position taken as the new central point seems the most likely outcome.

At Aragon the lack of front-wheel grip cost Rossi dearly, while at Motegi a slightly improved front weight setting combined with a circuit that focuses bike set-up on braking and acceleration meant Valentino was as happy with the bike as he'd been since the start of the year. Unfortunately, an early crash in the race prevented anyone finding out just how good the bike had become. The problems were back at Phillip Island where a front-end crash cost Rossi a decent placing.

THE FUTURE

In addition to the aluminium frame that was seen at the Mugello test and the Aragon and Motegi GPs, there was also another frame, a 'twin beam' design, under development and testing. Pictures were taken at Misano of a senior design engineer showing the team CAD drawings of a 'full beam' frame and sub-frame design. That design requires completely new rear engine mountings to be cast on to the engine. It's known that Rossi tested something new at Jerez, the week before Motegi, but he wasn't saying anything. However, it was also common knowledge that Ducati's test riders were currently setting personal best lap times. The 'fly-away' nature of three of the last four races meant it was only likely to be seen as a 1,000 at the first test after Valencia.

The twin aluminium beams of a conventional GP bike allow the steering head to deflect – not much, but just enough to allow the front tyre to move over bumps when the bike is right over at maximum lean, more than 60 degrees, and the conventional forks aren't working very well. Length is what is needed: the current Yamaha, for instance, has its rear engine mount right at the back of the gearbox and the front engine mounts right at the bottom of the front crankcases. The right material is also vital, and each factory guards very tightly the specification of the aluminium they use.

Between the two, however, there can be a swingarm and mainframe that deflect slightly at high cornering lean angles and that use aluminium's other property, a high level of internal damping, to make those movements soft and almost free of rebound. All that's required to know then is the right balance of lateral and torsional rigidity, just how much sideways the frame should deflect, and how much it must be allowed to twist at the same time in order to get the 'feel' Rossi can use.

That is what Ducati are learning now. It's the start of a long road to get the right mix of weight distribution and movement, but at least they are on their way. Perhaps, once they have the aluminium working well, they can try to duplicate the 'feel' flex and damping characteristics in a carbon-fibre design, but that's possibly a while away yet.

Right now, the prize is a group of Ducati works and customer bikes that can go a second a lap quicker and be easier to ride – and that will make a massive difference to the races we love to watch!

Above A glimpse of the future. A senior designer from Ducati Corse shows the team a CAD drawing of the aluminium beam frame that will feature on Rossi's 2012 GP 12 1000

ALUMINIUM FRAMES

This isn't the first aluminium Ducati frame. A cast aluminium box was made when the carbon airbox chassis were initially being built. Guareschi tested at Jerez to prove that the concept worked. It seems, though, that the 'box' was conducting heat in from the engine and this was heating all the air going into the engine, and that would reduce power significantly.

ORIGINAL EQUIPMENT
brembo

HIGH PERFORMANCE

RACING
brembo

brembo
Racing
brembo
mode
performance
SOLE UK IMPORTER & DISTRIBUTOR

THE BIKES
2011 MotoGP MACHINERY

HONDA
RC212V 2011

1. Getting exactly the right diameter exhaust pipes into exactly the right bends needs some gorgeous welding
2. Honda keeps its tiny ECU hidden under the front cowling
3. The pit lane speed limiter switch gets a guard to prevent accidental use
4. Honda's 'Torducter', situated on the end of the output shaft, was critical to the smooth operation of the 'seamless shift' gearbox

From the start of the 800cc MotoGP era the Honda simply hasn't impressed – until now. In 2010 Honda began really sorting out their bike. Starting with an evil-handling 'too loose' frame, the bike was progressively stiffened in the first half of the year to the point where it finally had the level of handling needed. This entailed many different chassis, regular new aluminium frames, then carbon fibre bonded on in different places for selective stiffening, taking the number of variations in stiffness tested during racing to over 20. Under Shuhei Nakamoto's guidance, Honda solved their lack of development direction by taking a big step, and then focusing their riders on fixing the problem. It was a massive gamble, but one that has paid off handsomely in 2011.

Honda have invested elsewhere too. They have a new gearbox, a so-called 'seamless shift' transmission which means that no time is lost during gearchanges, improving both acceleration and fuel consumption at the same time. This sophisticated gearbox needs careful control of the throttles to stop each shift being accompanied by a big jerk – and that is where the 'Torducter' fitted to the output shaft makes a difference, by allowing very precise measurement of the bike's torque output. In addition, Honda have worked with Ohlins to develop better suspension front and rear.

The resulting bike makes more usable power than anyone else's machine. It also extracts better fuel consumption and handles well enough to allow the top riders to lap right at the front. It is now an impressive piece of kit.

YAMAHA
M-1 800 2011

1 A wider front cowl helped aerodynamics, and was used in two colour schemes

2 Yamaha's 2011 frame seat support showing the very small difference in the lower seat unit mount, and therefore the section of the swingarm support area

3 Tech 3 had the better 2010 main frames all year – the very long front engine mounts and the unused centre beam bolthole can be seen

4 The 2010 frame was identifiable by the simple lower seat unit mount

MotoGP World Championship winners in 2010, Yamaha have the most finely developed bike in the class. The Yamaha M-1 has a simple but extremely well developed twin-spar aluminium frame with an 'upside-down' swingarm and an engine with a reverse rotating cross-plane crank, pneumatic valve springs and the best electronic control system in motorcycling. The bike is obviously optimised for agility and corner speed. It's not a bad spec, and has won three 'triple crowns' to date.

The 2011 machine was very similar to the bikes used in the previous three years of competition, but two slightly different frames were tried in the early part of the season, and a heavier crankshaft too. None of them really made the bike go any quicker, and by Assen the new frames had gone and both the factory riders, Jorge Lorenzo and Ben Spies, had reverted to the 2010 frame design.

Different exhaust pipes and intake lengths were occasionally used to enhance mid-range or top-end power as required. Engine-wise, the bike always seemed to be slow, but the chosen crankshaft weight did seem to help corner entry and exit. Yamaha also brought along a few electronics improvements to help out, but in the end the bikes being ridden by Jorge and Ben were last year's machines with just a few small changes for better power and ease of operation.

Yamaha grabbed a massive development lead three years ago, but now Honda, at least, have caught up.

DUCATI
DESMOSEDICI D16-11

1 Nicky Hayden got a GP11.1 but had to persevere with the carbon box frame version; he used completely different settings to good effect

2 A series of new bikes didn't stop Ducati coming out with the cool stuff, Nicky's toe protectors being a good example

3 An aluminium beam peeks out from under the fuel tank – Rossi's interim frame

4 The rear of the aluminium frame attached on to the outside of the existing rear sub-frame mounts, making the frame as long as possible within the constraints of the existing parts

2

3

4

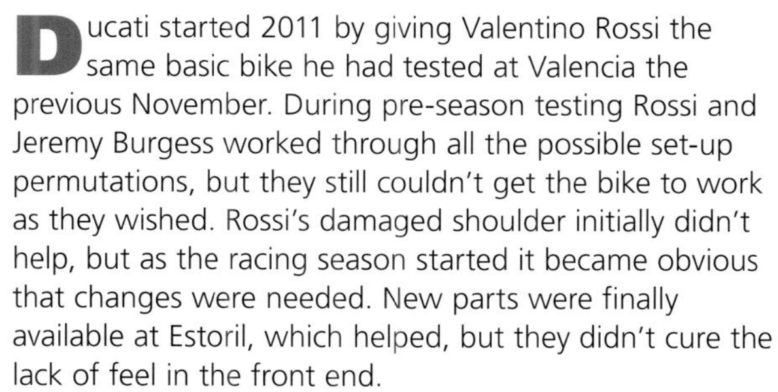

Ducati started 2011 by giving Valentino Rossi the same basic bike he had tested at Valencia the previous November. During pre-season testing Rossi and Jeremy Burgess worked through all the possible set-up permutations, but they still couldn't get the bike to work as they wished. Rossi's damaged shoulder initially didn't help, but as the racing season started it became obvious that changes were needed. New parts were finally available at Estoril, which helped, but they didn't cure the lack of feel in the front end.

Rossi tested the 2012 1,000cc bike in mid-June and decided that it was a better machine on which to base any further development, as it gave him access to superior rear grip and a seamless-shift gearbox. When converted to an 800, however, with longer rods and a short-stroke crankshaft, some of the handling improvements disappeared.

The improved rear grip made the front push on any long corner, with Sachsenring by far the worst for that behaviour, but the simple fact that the engine was now an 800, with a lighter, higher-revving crankshaft, made its behaviour in corners very different. The 800s required much more time at full lean in the corners for the best lap times, and that just meant the bike felt a lot worse as an 800 than it did as a 1,000.

By Aragon a new aluminium 'stop-gap' frame had been built. This used the seat sub-frame mounts on the back of the rear head and resurrected front engine mounts from the old steel chassis days; the structure was like a four-legged starfish and could theoretically flex a lot more. Unfortunately, the range of chassis adjustment available with this stop-gap item was no bigger than with the original carbon airbox piece, so real progress was stalled.

A full twin-beam aluminium chassis was also being tested, but that would not be seen until 2012.

SUZUKI
GSV-R 800 2011

1 Le Mans saw the first race use of the new frame

2 The bike went better with some new ratios at Aragon

3 A new, shorter, almost organic swingarm really made a difference towards the end of the year

4 The new mainframe came with longer front engine mounts and improved flex

Towards the end of 2010 Suzuki swapped their chassis construction over to CNC-machined aluminium, a technology that allows for much closer tolerances and makes adjusting the thickness of beams to manage their flexibility much easier. A new chassis was brought to the post-Estoril test, the first actually to look different for several years, and it was soon clear that it was an improvement. Bautista, Suzuki's sole rider in 2011, took some time to get back to full fitness from the broken leg he suffered in his Qatar practice crash.

The new frame, however, didn't help Suzuki's long-term *bête noire* – their bike's cold-weather behaviour. Assen was particularly chilly and, in order to make the bike work, a really short and high set-up was used. It didn't fully cure the problem, but it definitely helped. Since then the Suzuki has gone better. The bike was lowered again, but it has stayed short, and now turns with the best of them. New swingarms were available for Misano, shorter still to allow more set-up choice and to keep the required flexibility as the designed-in set-up became shorter.

Suzuki is still the third Japanese player and, considering their limited resources, they have taken a big step forward this year. We can only hope for a new 1,000 machine, and a return to a two-rider team for 2012.

THE RIDERS
2011
Red Bull

THE SEASON IN FOCUS

Every MotoGP rider's season analysed, from the World Champion to the wild-card entry whose race lasted less than a lap

1	Casey Stoner	350
2	Jorge Lorenzo	260
3	Andrea Dovizioso	228
4	Dani Pedrosa	219
5	Ben Spies	176
6	Marco Simoncelli	139
7	Valentino Rossi	139
8	Nicky Hayden	132
9	Colin Edwards	109
10	Hiroshi Aoyama	98
11	Hector Barbera	82
12	Cal Crutchlow	70
13	Alvaro Bautista	67
14	Karel Abraham	64
15	Toni Elias	61
16	Randy de Puniet	49
17	Loris Capirossi	43
18	Katsuyuki Nagasuga	10
19	Josh Hayes	9
20	Kousuke Akiyoshi	7
21	John Hopkins	6
22	Shinichi Ito	3
	Sylvain Guintoli	0
	Ben Bostrom	0
	Damian Cudlin	0

1 CASEY STONER
REPSOL HONDA TEAM

NATIONALITY Australian
DATE OF BIRTH 16 October 1985
2011 SEASON 10 wins, 16 rostrums, 12 pole positions, 7 fastest laps
TOTAL POINTS 350

For once the label 'awesome' is entirely appropriate. Casey Stoner didn't just win – he became only the fifth man in history to be champion of the premier class on two different makes of motorcycle.

This victory, on a Honda, also put his 2007 title with Ducati into sharp focus. The Honda was the best motorcycle of the year but the Ducati certainly wasn't – yet he won races on both. While it would be wrong to suggest Casey has become comfortable with fame, he certainly seemed more at ease with his status, although that didn't seem to mellow him.

He was as vociferous as ever in his criticisms of tracks and riders and, just to show he wasn't biased, his volley at the Indy Motor Speedway was counterbalanced by similar criticism of Phillip Island.

On track, he was unanswerable. He finished on the rostrum in every race except Jerez, where he was knocked off by Valentino Rossi, and he only failed to start from the front row once. At the beginning of the year he couldn't resist a few sly digs at his ex-employers, Ducati, but as they spiralled into the depths of despair Casey kept his counsel.

Search out the 1,000 frames-per-second film clip of him at Catalunya as a reminder of just how much he could do with the bike: rear spinning, elbow brushing the kerb and carrying so much corner speed. He rode like that everywhere and, unlike previous years, he gave every impression he was enjoying it.

Casey isn't just the stand-out rider of the 800cc era, then. He's knocking on the door of greatness.

2 JORGE LORENZO
FIAT YAMAHA TEAM

NATIONALITY Spanish
DATE OF BIRTH 4 May 1987
2011 SEASON 3 wins, 10 rostrums, 2 pole positions, 2 fastest laps
TOTAL POINTS 260

If it weren't for Stoner, Jorge Lorenzo would have retained his title on a motorbike that has changed little in the face of an armada of much-improved Hondas. There hasn't been a better rearguard action in defence of a crown since the days of Wayne Rainey. Jorge said after the first race of the year, where he finished second, that if he had to ride like that all season he would fall off.

It's a measure of how well he did ride that his only race crash was in monsoon conditions at Silverstone, the sixth round of the year. It also, however, cost him the championship lead. Next time out, at Assen, he had to come back from a first-lap crash instigated by Marco Simoncelli. After that sixth place he was relying on Stoner having problems. Nevertheless, he won the next race, Mugello, with two of the best overtakes of the year.

Jorge didn't just push hard in the races. The crash that terminated his season came at Phillip Island in Sunday morning warm-up as he strove to postpone the inevitable coronation of Casey. Unlike the previous season, where he would often be fastest in every session, Jorge spent a good few weekends working his way up to the front row after being blitzed by the Hondas in free practice. There was even the odd flash of the petulant young Lorenzo along the way. The Yamaha still had the best corner entry and Jorge's corner speed was amazing to behold.

Second overall despite one fall and two races missed through injury is some achievement. He never gave up.

3 ANDREA DOVIZIOSO

REPSOL HONDA TEAM

NATIONALITY Italian
DATE OF BIRTH 23 March 1986
2011 SEASON 7 rostrums, 1 fastest lap
TOTAL POINTS 228

Honda wanted Andrea Dovizioso to move to a satellite team for the 2011 season, but his management insisted on enforcing a performance clause in his contract, so Dovi became the third man in the Repsol Honda team. This was not necessarily a good idea with team-mates like Casey Stoner and Dani Pedrosa. Dovi had his most consistent and impressive season so far in MotoGP, although it ended with him leaving for Yamaha's satellite team after spending all of his ten years in Grands Prix with Honda.

Dovi moved up to MotoGP in 2008 and went to the factory team the following year, but he has only amassed one win, one pole and one fastest lap. He was clearly in competition with Marco Simoncelli for the factory's favour this year and it took until Misano for Marco to finish a race in front of Andrea. However, HRC took the view that Marco's career was still on the up while Andrea's appeared to have reached a plateau, hence the move to Tech 3 Monster Yamaha for the 2012 season.

Andrea's best race of the year was Mugello, where he shoved Casey Stoner out of the way on the last lap to take second place. Unfortunately, after the summer break, he only made it on to the rostrum three times and had three fifth-place finishes. He clinched third overall in a head-to-head with Dani Pedrosa at the final round. Dovi said mid-season that the media shouldn't ignore him because he was an ordinary family man who didn't go in for bouts of flamboyant self-promotion. He had a point. At times he rode superbly this season, but his real problem was his choice of team-mates.

4 DANI PEDROSA

REPSOL HONDA TEAM

NATIONALITY Spanish
DATE OF BIRTH 29 September 1985
2011 SEASON 3 wins, 9 rostrums, 2 pole positions, 4 fastest laps
TOTAL POINTS 219

Yet again Dani Pedrosa started the season injured; it's just that he didn't know it. He found out during the first race of the year that the damage associated with the collarbone he'd broken in Motegi at the 2010 Japanese GP meant he lost power in his arm and feeling in his hand. On the Qatar rostrum he looked like a man facing the end of his career, not just the loss of a race win.

Thankfully, the problem turned out to be vascular obstruction rather than nerve damage and further surgery fixed it, but then came the coming-together with Marco Simoncelli at Le Mans that broke his other collarbone. He missed three races, then won his second race back. Dani also seemed to have become a different character. He has always been quiet and distrustful of the media, especially the Spanish variety, but he was now speaking his mind, principally about Marco.

The end of the season turned into a fight with Andrea Dovizioso for third in the championship, a fight given added spice by the Italian's imminent departure from Honda. Just how well did Dani ride? All season long he was only off the rostrum three times in races he finished, including his comeback race from surgery. That's proof enough that he's still one of the best out there.

It was a remarkable return both on and off the track. The questions for 2012 are whether he'll be as fast on the new 1,000s as on the 800s which most people thought would be his best chance of the championship – and what the ascent of Marc Marquez will do to Dani's standing with the team's sponsor.

5 BEN SPIES

FIAT YAMAHA TEAM

Although his second year in MotoGP, and his first with the factory team, wasn't trouble-free, Ben Spies did become the first and only man outside the four 'aliens' to win a race in the 800cc era. The win came at Assen, and he also took his first fastest lap. Victory came despite a massive crash at Silverstone the previous week while in a rostrum position.

On the face of it, then, 2011 wasn't much of an improvement on his first season, in which he scored two rostrum finishes and a pole position for sixth in the championship. It certainly started slowly, with two sixth places and two crashes. One was from a rostrum position in Spain, the other due to an error by his crew. That put him 12th in the championship going into Catalunya, where he promptly got on the rostrum. 'Nothing really went right, it's just that nothing went wrong,' was his laconic analysis. Just to confuse the issue even further, he crashed again next time out at Silverstone, again while in a rostrum position, then won at Assen.

In the second half of the year Ben was strangely anonymous, with just that third place in Indy, and it looked like injury in Australia had ruined the end of his year. Then he reminded us of his true form by failing to win Valencia by just fifteen thousandths of a second. He had appeared to revert to his old habit of taking time to put his trust in the tyres, but his pace in the middle and at the end of a race was usually right up there with the leaders. The fact Ben didn't claim 'alien' status is more than outweighed by that win at Assen; and it's expected that he'll be more at home on one of the 1,000s than on an 800.

NATIONALITY American
DATE OF BIRTH 11 July 1984
2011 SEASON 4 rostrums, 1 fastest lap
TOTAL POINTS 176

6 MARCO SIMONCELLI

SAN CARLO HONDA GRESINI

The tragedy of any young life cut short is what might have been. We certainly hadn't seen the best of Marco before his fatal accident in Sepang, just a week after he had achieved the best result of his MotoGP career with second behind Casey Stoner. The champ remarked how much Marco had enjoyed that experience compared with his first rostrum at Brno, where the overriding emotion appeared to have been relief.

There is no escaping the fact that the start of Marco's season was a crash fest. He hit the deck in three of the first six races and more frequently in practice. Then came the most controversial event of the year – his coming-together with Dani Pedrosa at Le Mans. The 'polemic', as he so charmingly put it, that followed obviously affected him. Two pole positions were wasted and it wasn't until after the summer break that he looked properly competitive again.

The rostrum in the Czech Republic changed everything. Suddenly Marco was beating Dovizioso and Spies. The run of three fourth places from Misano to Motegi would, earlier in his caeeer or even in this season, have been the prelude to another crash born of frustration. Not this time. Phillip Island wasn't just Marco's career-best finish, it was his best race.

He undoubtedly would have won a race in the very near future. Would he have won the championship? We'll never know.

NATIONALITY Italian
DATE OF BIRTH 20 January 1987
2011 SEASON 2 rostrums, 2 pole position
TOTAL POINTS 139

7 VALENTINO ROSSI
DUCATI TEAM

NATIONALITY
Italian

DATE OF BIRTH
16 February 1979

2011 SEASON
1 rostrum, 1 fastest lap

TOTAL POINTS
139

What should have been the Italian dream team, Valentino and Ducati, endured a horrible year. Rossi couldn't get the feel he needs from the front end of the bike. Whatever the team did, it made no difference. To rub salt into the wounds, Valentino found himself repeating the complaints Casey had about the bike the previous year. The difference being, of course, that Casey won on it. Changes are on the way. Valentino and Ducati cannot have such an awful season in 2012 – the Italian public would not tolerate such disappointment again.

8 NICKY HAYDEN
DUCATI TEAM

NATIONALITY
American

DATE OF BIRTH
30 July 1981

2011 SEASON
1 rostrum, 1 fastest lap

TOTAL POINTS
132

Once again Nicky played the role of loyal, uncomplaining team man. The only time he looked like losing his temper with the fickle Ducati was during practice at Indianapolis. Struggling for sixth place is one thing, doing it in front of your home crowd and friends is quite another. At least Nicky had the satisfaction of taking the Ducati team's first rostrum of the year, even though, as he admitted, it wasn't his strongest race. Like his team-mate, Nicky was only able to ride the bike as he wanted when the track was wet. His rostrum came on a drying track in Jerez, his fastest lap in the monsoon conditions of Silverstone.

9 COLIN EDWARDS
MONSTER YAMANA TECH 3

NATIONALITY
American

DATE OF BIRTH
27 February 1974

2011 SEASON
1 rostrum

TOTAL POINTS
109

After a terrible 2010, Colin reclaimed his rightful position as top non-factory rider. He was the only satellite team rider to get on the rostrum all year and he did it in terrible conditions at the British GP just a week after breaking his collarbone at Catalunya. Yamaha have decided that they do not require his services for 2012, so Colin will be a pioneer on the new Claiming Rule Team machinery. He will ride a Suter-framed BMW for the Italian Forward Racing team. Colin's development skills will be needed if the new class of bike is to be competitive.

10 HIROSHI AOYAMA
SAN CARLO HONDA GRESINI

NATIONALITY
Japanese

DATE OF BIRTH
25 October 1981

TOTAL POINTS
98

Another tough year for Hiro. He started the season still not fully recovered from the back injury he suffered at Silverstone in 2010, and then, like all Japanese riders and staff in the paddock, was seriously affected by the double disaster of the earthquake and tsunami that devastated the north-east of Japan. He never gained confidence in the bike or found a set-up he trusted. Another big crash, this time at Assen while standing in for Pedrosa on the factory bike, took a long time to get over. For 2012, Hiro moves to the Castrol Honda team in the World Superbike Championship.

11 HECTOR BARBERA
MAPFRE ASPAR TEAM MotoGP

NATIONALITY
Spanish

DATE OF BIRTH
2 November 1986

TOTAL POINTS
82

Hector's best result, sixth, came early in the year at Jerez and although he occassionally showed better form he often struggled with the set-up of the satellite Ducati Desmosedici. He wasn't alone in that. He looked to be recovering from a mid-season loss of form and confidence when he had a big accident at Motegi, a track that has never been kind to him. The collarbone injury he suffered ruined the end of his year. As Aspar's team will be running CRT-spec bikes in 2012, Hector has moved to the Pramac Ducati squad where he will continue to race a satellite Desmosedici.

12 CAL CRUTCHLOW
MONSTER YAMANA TECH 3

NATIONALITY
British

DATE OF BIRTH
29 October 1985

TOTAL POINTS
70

Cal clinched the Rookie of the Year title at the last round after a spirited season-long fight with Karel Abraham. He started the season impressively but struggled to regain his form after breaking his collarbone at Silverstone – although he'd point to Assen where he was riding well before his front tyre gave up. After crashes either side of the summer break it was a matter of rebuilding his confidence. He only crashed once more, at Phillip Island, and that wasn't his fault. The fighting fourth place with which he ended the season was the best result by a British rider in the MotoGP era and just the springboard he needs for that crucial second year in the class.

13 ALVARO BAUTISTA
RIZLA SUZUKI MotoGP

NATIONALITY
Spanish

DATE OF BIRTH
21 November 1984

TOTAL POINTS
67

Suzuki's lone rider and the team improved the factory's situation beyond measure. Alvaro was able to fight with, and beat, the factory Ducatis regularly: the sight of a Suzuki on the front row at Phillip Island was astonishing as the cold tarmac and long corners were exactly what the bike hated. It is also worth recalling that this is only Alvaro's second year in MotoGP and it started with a broken femur. As in his rookie year, he spent much of the time recovering from injury, which puts an even better light on his results. It is to be hoped that his and the team's efforts persuade Suzuki to stay in MotoGP.

14 KAREL ABRAHAM
CARDION AB MOTORACING

NATIONALITY
Czech

DATE OF BIRTH
2 January 1990

TOTAL POINTS
64

When it was announced that the Cardion team was coming to MotoGP there was a lot of sniping about Karel's lack of credentials for the top class. That soon stopped. He was seventh in the second race of the year, Spain, despite crashing and remounting, and clearly was able to race with the other satellite bikes. A flurry of crashes later in the year didn't help his final championship position, and he hasn't yet got over his tendency to get very wound up by the attention at his home event. Karel and his team stay with a leased Ducati for 2012.

15 TONI ELIAS
LCR HONDA MotoGP

NATIONALITY
Spanish

DATE OF BIRTH
26 March 1983

TOTAL POINTS
61

The first Moto2 World Champion returned to MotoGP with a satellite Honda. Unfortunately, while this decision may have been a good way of validating the new intermediate class of racing, it didn't take account of Toni's riding style and quite extreme set-up preferences. They were never going to gel with the requirements of the Bridgestone control tyres. And so it was: Toni couldn't get any confidence in or feeling from the bike, and the team couldn't do anything about it. A sad year for a man who has won races in 125, 250, Moto2 and MotoGP.

16 RANDY DE PUNIET
PRAMAC RACING TEAM

NATIONALITY
French

DATE OF BIRTH
14 February 1981

TOTAL POINTS
49

Randy didn't find the change to a satellite Ducati easy; mind you, nor has anyone else. He crashed out of five of the first seven races but found some consistency, and the ability to stay on his bike, after the summer break. His best result of the year came at the penultimate race, his best qualifying at the last one. Just to show that when your luck's out, it's really out, his only second-row start of the year was at Valencia, the final round, where he was an innocent victim of the first-corner crash. Things haven't gone well for Randy since he broke his leg in Germany in 2010, but he will be back in 2012 and with a more competitive motorcycle.

17 LORIS CAPIROSSI
PRAMAC RACING TEAM

NATIONALITY
Italian

DATE OF BIRTH
4 April 1973

TOTAL POINTS
43

After a world championship career spanning 22 years and three titles, Loris retired from racing. Valencia was his 328th GP, which means he's taken part in over 41 per cent of all the Grand Prix events ever staged. His first world title, the 125s in 1990, his rookie year, saw him become the youngest ever World Champion at 17 years and 165 days, a record he still holds. Along the way he became Ducati's first ever winner in the top class, and his final win – at Japan in 2007 – came 16 years and 15 days after his first, another record. That, rather than the last two years, is what he will be remembered for.

18 KATSUYUKI NAKASUGA
YAMAHA FACTORY RACING

REPLACEMENT RIDER

NATIONALITY
Japanese

DATE OF BIRTH
9 August 1981

TOTAL POINTS
10

Yamaha made a policy decision at the start of the season: any replacement rides in the factory team would go to factory testers rather than racers from other classes or formulae. So when Jorge Lorenzo suffered that nasty injury to his left ring finger at Phillip Island, Nakasuga-san, who has some experience of GPs as a 250 wild card, was drafted in for the last two races of the season. After the Malaysian race was abandoned, that left only Valencia where he finished a creditable sixth.

19 JOSH HAYES
MONSTER YAMAHA TECH 3

REPLACEMENT RIDER

NATIONALITY
American

TOTAL POINTS
9

The AMA Superbike Champion was due at the post-Valencia test and instead found himself replacing Colin Edwards. He ran a mistake-free meeting despite conditions.

20 KOUSUKE AKIYOSHI
SAN CARLO HONDA GRESINI

REPLACEMENT RIDER

NATIONALITY
Japanese

TOTAL POINTS
7

The Japanese Superbike Champion rode two GPs: Assen for Gresini (as their regular rider, Aoyama, moved up to replace Pedrosa) and Motegi (as a wild card for LCR Honda).

21 JOHN HOPKINS
RIZLA SUZUKI MotoGP

REPLACEMENT RIDER

NATIONALITY
American

TOTAL POINTS
6

Replaced the injured Bautista at Jerez and was due to do Brno and Motegi as a wild card. Unfortunately a badly broken finger at the first venue effectively ended those plans.

22 SHINICHI ITO
HONDA RACING TEAM

WILD CARD

NATIONALITY
Japanese

TOTAL POINTS
3

The veteran was a wild card at Motegi on an RCV in RC30 colours. He was there because he is from Miyagi, the area amost affected by the tsunami, as Honda's symbol of hope.

DAMIAN CUDLIN
PRAMAC RACING TEAM

REPLACEMENT RIDER

NATIONALITY
Australian

In among his regular commitment to ride for BMW in the World Endurance Championship, Damian rode as a replacement for Pramac and then Aspar Ducati.

SYLVAIN GUINTOLI
PRAMAC RACING TEAM

REPLACEMENT RIDER

NATIONALITY
French

When Loris Caprossi got hurt at Assen, the Pramac team had to find a replacement for the Sachsenring. Three years after he last rode a MotoGP bike, Sylvain Guintoli got the job.

BEN BOSTROM
LCR HONDA MotoGP

WILD CARD

NATIONALITY
American

He's been around for a long time, but Ben finally got to ride a MotoGP bike at Laguna Seca as a second Honda LCR entrant. He was faster in the race than the regular team man.

RIDER'S RIDER OF THE YEAR

Regular readers will have expected to see the results of our annual Riders' Rider of the Year poll on these pages. Every one of the first seven editions of the *Official MotoGP Season Review* has carried the results of our survey in which every rider who has taken part in more than one race, without exception, voted. The vote for this, the eighth edition of the season review, had just started at Sepang when we lost Marco Simoncelli. Under the circumstances, it was deemed inappropriate to continue with the contest.

You will find an obituary of Marco where the Riders' Rider of the Year usually appears. It will be back for the ninth edition of the *Official MotoGP Season Review.*

AirAsia.com
FIM
motoGP
SILVERSTONE

THE RACES
MotoGP 2011

QATARI GP

LOSAIL INTERNATIONAL CIRCUIT

ROUND 1

March 20

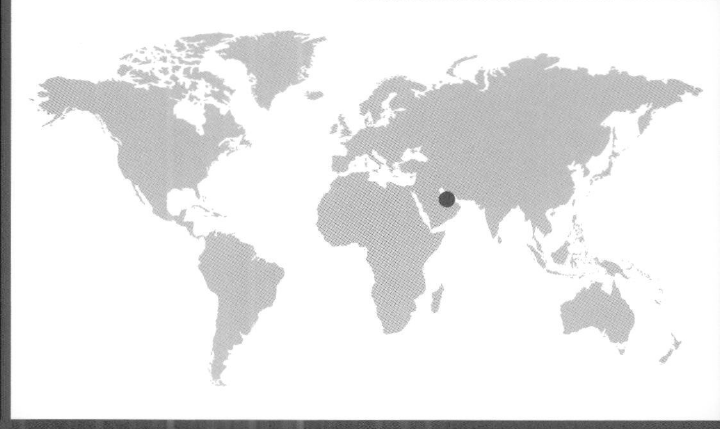

WARNING SHOT

Casey Stoner lived up to the pre-season hype as four Hondas finished in the top five

Looking at *parc fermé* it was difficult to tell who had won. It obviously wasn't Dani Pedrosa. Jorge Lorenzo, who came second, was celebrating as if he'd already retained his title, while Casey Stoner, the convincing victor, merely looked quietly satisfied. He had just proved several points.

Casey was a very short-odds favourite for the title before the season began, but after stalking Pedrosa for half the race, then pulling away with consummate ease, he was now an odds-on bet. The contrast with the hectic riding style he'd had to adopt to force the Ducati to bend to his will was astonishing. Top sportsmen always talk about being 'in the zone', a seemingly counter-intuitive amalgam of total concentration and complete relaxation. In Qatar, Stoner was the perfect example. He didn't put a wheel wrong, setting pole and the fastest lap on his way to the win. And he looked ridiculously relaxed on the bike. If he did make a mistake at any time during the weekend, nobody noticed. He was fulsome in his praise of the Honda, describing it as 'flowing' round the track. He also took a small dig at his ex-employers when he mentioned that he hadn't found the limits of the Honda yet – or lost the front all weekend. In his Ducati days, he talked about losing it all the time.

Over at the Ducati garage, new recruit Valentino Rossi could only recycle Casey's complaints. The word 'understeer' was heard a lot, along with the insistence that it couldn't be cured by set-up tweaks. No quick fix, then, but rumours of some radical modifications to come for the test after the Portuguese GP six weeks later. He might not have been in contention for a rostrum finish, but Valentino's bike was the first Ducati

Above Valentino Rossi's first race on a Ducati only hinted at the problems to come home and, along the way, he made one amazing save while trying to prevent Ben Spies from passing him. So no repeat of the miracles of South Africa in 2004, and the admission that Valentino's lingering shoulder problem and the Desmosedici's imperfections meant that a title challenge was out of the question.

The same could be said of Dani Pedrosa. He looked shattered and devastated after the race, not because he had been beaten by his new team-mate and by his old foe Lorenzo, but because his shoulder problem had recurred. When he came back from his Motegi crash at the end of 2010 he'd experienced numbness in his left hand and arm. Now, instead of giving team-mate Stoner a race, Dani had had what he described as one of the toughest rides of his career, which he finished with his arm numb and no feeling in his fingers. If this was down to the nerve damage diagnosed after the collarbone-breaking crash, the implications were clear. Only time, lots of it, cures that sort of problem. It also emerged that he hadn't covered race distance in any pre-season testing.

The contrast with Jorge Lorenzo could not have been more extreme. After an awful final test and troubles in practice, there were signs of the old petulance returning, but the result exceeded his, or anyone else's, expectations. Second was the reward for a race of stunning consistency and daring in which he rode closer to the edge for longer than he'd ever done; he was combative off the start, ferocious in his fight with Pedrosa and less than 3.5s behind Stoner at the flag. 'I can't race like that at every track,' he reported. Well, not if he wanted to finish some races.

'EVERYTHING KEPT GETTING BETTER AND BETTER FOR US'
CASEY STONER

Above Cal Crutchlow's first MotoGP race showed the British rookie wasn't overawed by the competition

Below Pedrosa and Lorenzo fighting for second place

Above Valentino Rossi saved this big front-end moment as he tried to fend off Ben Spies

Opposite The paddock was deeply affected by the Japanese earthquake and tsunami

Below Marco Simoncelli's race was better than his fifth-place finish would suggest

Jorge identified several areas in which the Hondas were noticeably superior to his Yamaha. As usual, the Hondas had better top speed, but this was now coupled with better drive out of corners. The M1 was still more stable under braking, though, an opinion echoed by the Honda riders.

There were mixed fortunes for the other Yamahas. Ben Spies, newly promoted to the factory squad, rediscovered his old distrust of the tyres at the start of the race, then took six laps to push his way past Rossi. The satellite Tech 3 riders had a better time, with Colin Edwards rediscovering his form and rookie Cal Crutchlow impressing. However, the fight behind the rostrum men was between two more Hondas, the factory bikes of Dovizioso and Simoncelli. Despite losing out in the closing stages Marco was the happier of the two. He felt that he had proved for the first time that he could run with the top men for race distance and that only his old problem of using up his tyres lost him fourth. Andrea thought he should have been fighting for a rostrum position too, and was mildly critical of one of Simoncelli's overtaking moves.

The only unhappy Honda rider was Toni Elias, whose particular set-up requirements seem to be incompatible with making the Bridgestones work. Only Suzuki had a worse weekend after their lone rider, Alvaro Bautista, broke his left femur on Saturday. John Hopkins had been in Qatar on Monday for PR filming work but had gone home to California. The earliest he could have got back to Losail was half an hour before qualifying, so that plan was abandoned and Suzuki management talked to the obvious candidates in the Moto2 field. Ant West was their first choice, but his MZ team put so many conditions on the deal that talks soon broke down, so there wasn't a Suzuki on the grid for the premier Grand Prix class for the first time since the boycotted German GP of 1974.

For once the trends flagged up by pre-season testing seemed to carry over to the season itself. The Hondas were as fast in racing as they were testing and were now clearly the best bikes. Yamaha's all-round useability was still there, but the M1's lack of punch now looked too much of a handicap. As for Ducati, the post-Stoner era was obviously going to be difficult. Even Valentino Rossi couldn't perform another miracle on the Desmosedici. So what was to be done? Jerry Burgess's comments vividly illustrated the scale of the problem: 'Well, I wouldn't start from here.'

COG SWAPPING

A certain amount of hysteria surrounded the gearboxes of the factory Hondas at Losail.

During pre-season testing it had been suggested that the RCV was using a dual-clutch system, something specifically forbidden by the regulations. This was obviously nonsense, but the upchanges sounded very slick and the riders reported an advantage powering out of corners as the bike wasn't getting unsettled during shifts. Some extravagant claims were being made about the new transmission's contribution to lap-time improvements, but it's doubtful if saving a few milliseconds on each change added up to even a tenth of a second a lap, especially as riders reported that what they were gaining in stability on upshifts they were losing on the more difficult downshifts

Which leaves two questions: what technology is being used, and why?

Formula 1 has been experimenting with 'seamless shift' transmission for years. The principle is that two gears are engaged simultaneously for a very short period of time during changes and effectively transmission of power to the rear wheel is never interrupted. The best-known independent company in the field is the British firm Zeroshift, which uses 'bullets' carried by a hub on the gearbox shaft to engage and disengage gears. One set of bullets transmits drive, the other overrun, and the hub is moved by conventional-looking forks controlled by an equally conventional-looking selector drum.

However, the new Honda system appeared to be different again. Patent drawings showed a total absence of selector forks; the mechanism that engages and disengages gears is carried inside the gearbox shafts. This book's technical correspondent, Neil Spalding, likens it to the mechanism of a fine watch. As there is no restriction on the number of gearboxes that can be used in a season, service life is not an issue. Price could be, though, as Nakamoto-san of HRC said one cost 'more than my house' at £700,000.

But back to the fundamental question: why bother with this technology for a few tenths of a second over a race? The answer is, of course, fuel economy. Smoothing out those gearchanges means fuel that would otherwise be blown unburnt out of the exhaust is used to make power.

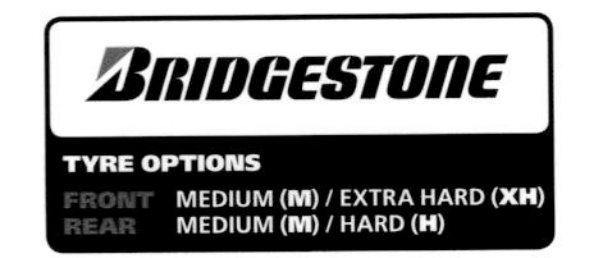

QATARI GP

LOSAIL INTERNATIONAL CIRCUIT

ROUND 1

March 20

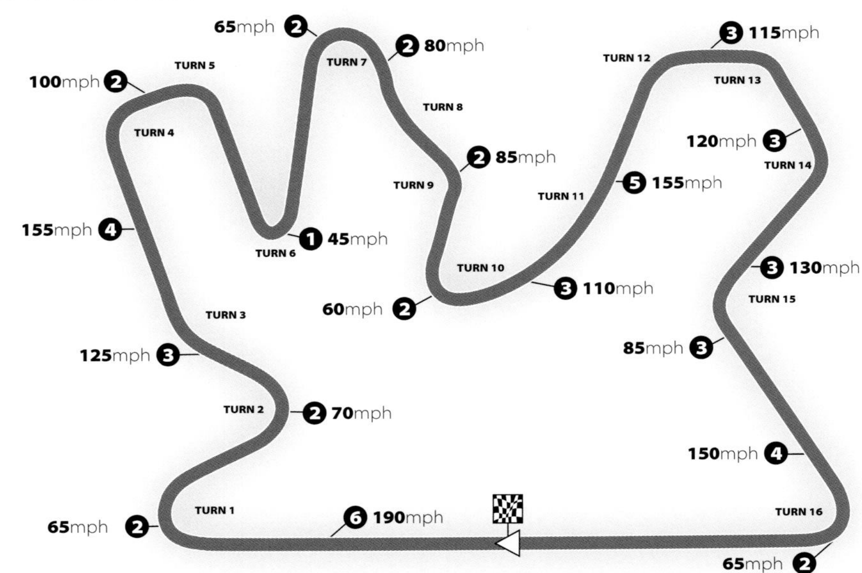

RACE RESULTS

CIRCUIT LENGTH 3.343 miles
NO. OF LAPS 22
RACE DISTANCE 73.546 miles
WEATHER Dry, 19°C
TRACK TEMPERATURE 20°C
WINNER Casey Stoner
FASTEST LAP 1m 55.366s, 104.328mph, Casey Stoner
LAP RECORD 1m 55.153s, 104.510mph, Casey Stoner, 2008

QUALIFYING

	Rider	Nationality	Team	Qualifying	Pole +	Gap
1	Stoner	AUS	Repsol Honda Team	1m 54.137s		
2	Pedrosa	SPA	Repsol Honda Team	1m 54.342s	0.205s	0.205s
3	Lorenzo	SPA	Yamaha Factory Racing	1m 54.947s	0.810s	0.605s
4	Simoncelli	ITA	San Carlo Honda Gresini	1m 54.988s	0.851s	0.041s
5	Spies	USA	Yamaha Factory Racing	1m 55.095s	0.958s	0.107s
6	Barbera	SPA	Mapfre Aspar Team	1m 55.223s	0.086s	0.128s
7	Dovizioso	ITA	Repsol Honda Team	1m 55.229s	1.092s	0.006s
8	Crutchlow	GBR	Monster Yamaha Tech 3	1m 55.578s	1.441s	0.349s
9	Rossi	ITA	Ducati Team	1m 55.637s	1.500s	0.059s
10	Edwards	USA	Monster Yamaha Tech 3	1m 55.647s	1.510s	0.010s
11	De Puniet	FRA	Pramac Racing Team	1m 55.656s	1.519s	0.009s
12	Aoyama	JPN	San Carlo Honda Gresini	1m 55.724s	1.587s	0.068s
13	Hayden	USA	Ducati Team	1m 55.881s	1.744s	0.157s
14	Capirossi	ITA	Pramac Racing Team	1m 56.323s	2.186s	0.442s
15	Abraham	CZE	Cardion AB Motoracing	1m 56.665s	2.528s	0.342s
16	Elias	SPA	LCR Honda MotoGP	1m 57.992s	3.855s	1.327s
*	Bautista	SPA	Rizla Suzuki MotoGP			

FINISHERS

1 CASEY STONER Victory on his factory Honda debut made him the first rider to win on two different makes under the 800cc formula. Fastest in every session except warm-up, he shadowed Pedrosa to half-distance, then made his move and pulled away with sufficient ease to frighten the competition.

2 JORGE LORENZO Improved massively from the final pre-season test to put the M1 on the front row for the fourth year running, then maintained his 100% record of podium finishes at Losail. Had to ride close to the edge for the entire race and celebrated second place like he'd won another title.

3 DANI PEDROSA Led the race and his new team-mate Stoner for 12 of the 22 laps, then diced with Lorenzo before his shoulder injury from Motegi the previous season made itself felt. Looked devastated on the rostrum and in post-race interviews.

4 ANDREA DOVIZIOSO Improved on his distinctly average qualifying thanks mainly to a great start. Spent the middle part of the race tangled up with Simoncelli, which cost both men the chance of overhauling Pedrosa in the final laps. Not happy with one of Marco's passes, which he described as 'on the limit'.

5 MARCO SIMONCELLI Not his best race in terms of final position but definitely best for consistency and distance to the winner. Thought he had a chance of catching Pedrosa after he passed Dovizioso but a small mistake, and fuel consumption issues, saw him drop back. Still having trouble when the tyres are seriously worn.

6 BEN SPIES A strangely low-key race after good qualifying. Got pushed out at Turn 2, took a long time to get past Barbera and Rossi, and then set the fourth-fastest lap of the race.

7 VALENTINO ROSSI Unable to push hard in qualifying because of his shoulder so started off the third row. Took time to get past Barbera and Hayden before his shoulder again made itself felt. Couldn't hold off Spies, but made one incredible save as he tried to defend against Ben's inside pass. Still top Ducati finisher.

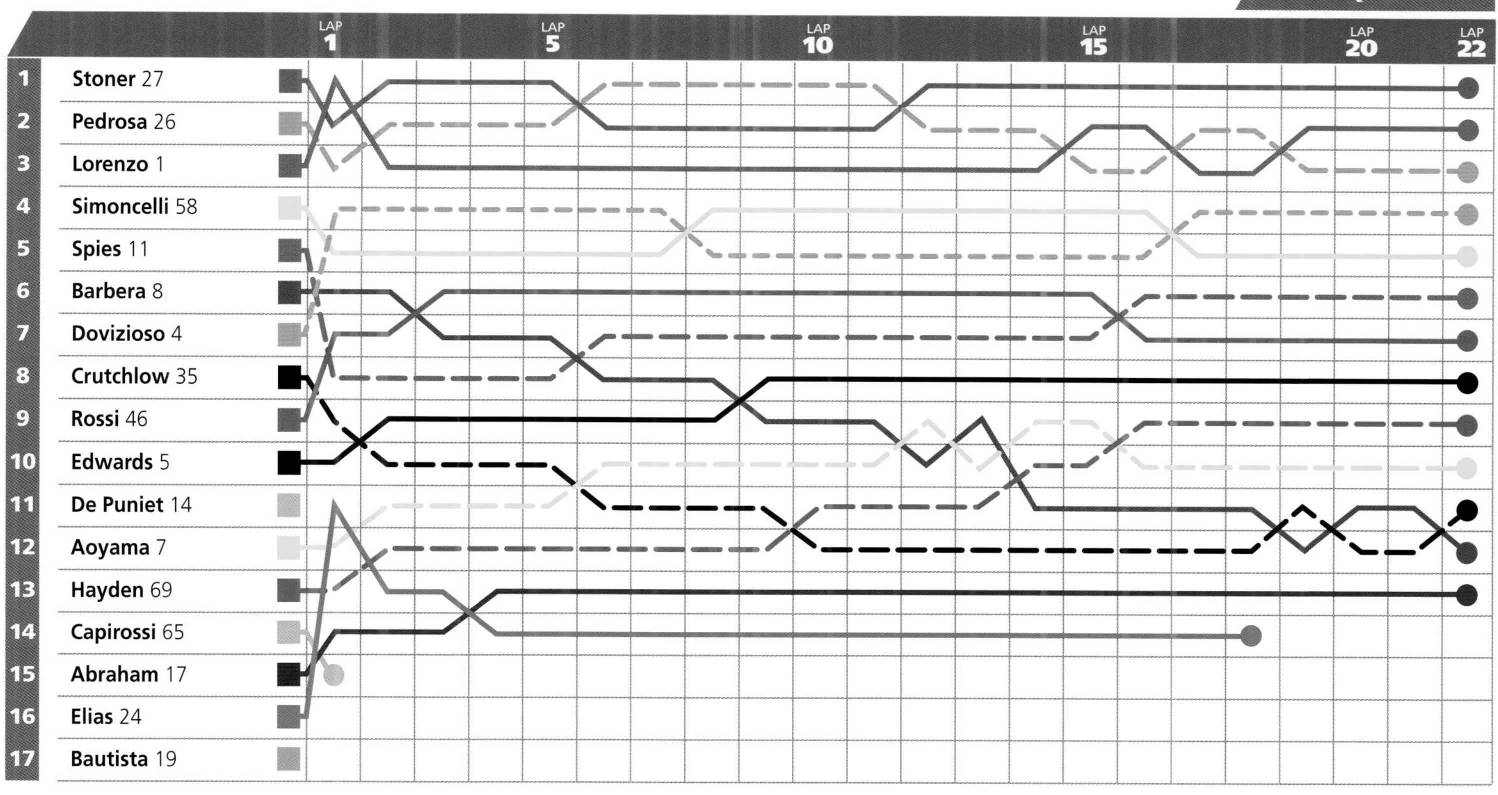

RACE

	Rider	Motorcycle	Race Time	Time +	Fastest Lap	Av Speed	
1	Stoner	Honda	42m 38.569s		1m 55.366s	103.484mph	XH/H
2	Lorenzo	Yamaha	42m 42.009s	3.440s	1m 55.730s	103.345mph	XH/H
3	Pedrosa	Honda	42m 43.620s	5.051s	1m 55.392s	103.280mph	XH/H
4	Dovizioso	Honda	42m 44.511s	5.942s	1m 55.837s	103.243mph	XH/H
5	Simoncelli	Honda	42m 45.927s	7.358s	1m 55.871s	103.188mph	XH/H
6	Spies	Yamaha	42m 49.037s	10.468s	1m 55.812s	103.062mph	XH/H
7	Rossi	Ducati	42m 55.000s	16.431s	1m 56.053s	102.823mph	XH/H
8	Edwards	Yamaha	43m 04.842s	26.293s	1m 56.615s	102.430mph	XH/H
9	Hayden	Ducati	43m 05.985s	27.416s	1m 56.600s	102.387mph	XH/H
10	Aoyama	Honda	43m 07.489s	28.920s	1m 56.493s	102.327mph	XH/H
11	Crutchlow	Yamaha	43m 13.108s	34.539s	1m 56.828s	102.105mph	XH/H
12	Barbera	Ducati	43m 13.398s	34.829s	1m 56.663s	102.094mph	XH/H
13	Abraham	Ducati	43m 16.526s	37.957s	1m 56.680s	101.971mph	XH/H
NF	Elias	Honda	35m 41.564s	4 laps	1m 57.957s	101.152mph	XH/H
NF	Capirossi	Ducati	2m 16.031s	21 laps	2m 16.031s	88.470mph	XH/H
NF	De Puniet	Ducati					XH/H
NS	Bautista	Suzuki					

CHAMPIONSHIP

	Rider	Team	Points
1	Stoner	Repsol Honda Team	25
2	Lorenzo	Yamaha Factory Racing	20
3	Pedrosa	Repsol Honda Team	16
4	Dovizioso	Repsol Honda Team	13
5	Simoncelli	San Carlo Honda Gresini	11
6	Spies	Yamaha Factory Racing	10
7	Rossi	Dulcati Team	9
8	Edwards	Monster Yamaha Tech 3	8
9	Hayden	Dulcati Team	7
10	Aoyama	San Carlo Honda Gresini	6
11	Crutchlow	Monster Yamaha Tech 3	5
12	Barbera	Mapfre Aspar Team MotoGP	4
13	Abraham	Cardion AB Motoracing	3

8 COLIN EDWARDS Took a few risks after a good start and looked set to fight with Spies and Rossi, but a couple of near-misses saw him end up a lonely eighth. Not happy with the position but delighted to be the top satellite team finisher.

9 NICKY HAYDEN Out of touch in qualifying, then severely hampered by the two Pramac Ducatis coming together. Came to a stop, avoiding de Puniet, and got going in last place. Fought his way back up and nearly got to Edwards, but typically self-critical of his riding after the race.

10 HIROSHI AOYAMA Profoundly moved by the minute's silence before the race for the victims of the earthquake and tsunami back in Japan. Baulked, like Hayden, by the de Puniet/Capirossi crash and then shadowed the American's climb back to a top-ten finish.

11 CAL CRUTCHLOW An aggressive start to his MotoGP career despite his recovering shoulder and a painful injury to the little finger of his left hand. Qualified a superb eighth, then raced with Hayden and Aoyama before getting stuck behind Barbera's Ducati. When he finally got past, it was too late to make up more places.

12 HECTOR BARBERA Top Ducati in qualifying and most of practice. Sixth early on, keeping Rossi behind him for a few laps, then lost places as the bike behaved differently both under acceleration and braking. Disappointed, but his sixth-place qualifying was the first time the fastest Ducati on the grid was a satellite bike.

13 KAREL ABRAHAM A solid start to his MotoGP career – got to the flag, wasn't lapped and was as fast as the midfield men in the closing stages. Beat Elias in qualifying and was in front of him when Toni crashed.

NON-FINISHERS

TONI ELIAS A horrible return to MotoGP. Qualified last and was running in last place when he crashed out four laps from home. His set-up requirements just didn't seem to work with the Bridgestone tyres.

LORIS CAPIROSSI De Puniet's crashing Ducati clipped Loris's clutch lever, bending his fingers back painfully. Unable to control the bike properly, he was forced to pull out.

RANDY DE PUNIET Lost the rear early on lap two and, to make matters worse, clipped his team-mate, who was later forced to retire. Nevertheless, Randy's style looked to suit the Ducati.

NON-STARTERS

ALVARO BAUTISTA Broke his thigh when he crashed in the third free practice session. He was out on a new tyre and tried to follow Pedrosa, only to become another victim of the cold-tyre highside.

SPANISH GP

CIRCUITO DE JEREZ

ROUND 2

April 3

WET, WET AND WET

Jorge Lorenzo won the first wet race of his career as Rossi and Stoner crashed in front of him

In the first ten laps it looked as if no-one wanted to win this race. In the last five laps it looked as if no-one wanted to come second. The drama was produced by a track that started wet and dried out, resulting in the soft Bridgestone tyres, both front and rear, impersonating slicks by the end of the race.

Casey Stoner understood this, as did Dani Pedrosa, and both started with the intention of setting a pace that would leave them with some tread 27 laps later. Stoner led but was content to let Simoncelli and Lorenzo go past; he would have been happy to let them open up a three- or four-second gap. He would also have been happy to let Rossi push past, but he wasn't that lucky. Pedrosa finished the first lap in ninth place, causing instant panic about the state of his shoulder. The man himself looked at his lap times, saw he was faster than he'd been in morning warm-up, and refused to panic.

Most eyes were on Valentino Rossi, who was looking more like his old self. From 12th on the grid, he took just three laps to work his way up to the leading group, setting the fastest lap of the race on the way. For the first time in a year he was able to ride a bike exactly as he wanted, which turned out to be too much even for Rossi. He didn't intend to pass anyone on the brakes but on lap eight he got into Turn 1 too fast, passing Stoner on the way, then lost the front and took the Australian down with him. Casey knew Valentino was there and wasn't interested in defending the corner. It was an astonishing mistake, the effect of which was compounded by Rossi being able to restart because his motor hadn't stopped while Casey's had. The

YAMAHA
PRAMAC
PRAMAC
GENERALI
HONDA

marshals did try to push-start the Honda but, not surprisingly, didn't fancy spending too much time on the racing line. Stoner detected favouritism and added another item to his collection of grudges against Valentino.

As Rossi started his climb back through the field, Lorenzo found himself second, two seconds behind Simoncelli. Four laps later he found himself leading by over 2.5s after the Gresini Honda rider highsided out of the race. From then on it was a matter of concentration and tyre conservation – Jorge's inch-perfect race belied the state of his tyres in *parc fermé*. Amazingly, it was his first wet-weather victory at any level, from the Balearic championships upwards.

Pedrosa illustrated just how difficult the conditions were. Now up into second, his lap times went up by nearly five seconds in the last ten laps. Like the rest he was short-shifting everywhere, and struggling for grip even on the straight. Ben Spies came past, pulled away easily, slowed down, and then lost the front. That left Pedrosa in a safe second but Nicky Hayden, whose Ducati had chewed up its tyres more quickly than the rest,

Above John Hopkins returned to MotoGP a changed man after a two-year absence

Left The whole field started on wet tyres but the drying track caught out many in the closing stages

'THIS IS THE FIRST TIME I HAVE WON IN WET CONDITIONS, THE FIRST TIME EVER!'
JORGE LORENZO

was struggling in third. Colin Edwards passed him with ease and looked set to put a satellite team on the rostrum, only to coast to a halt at the start of the last lap with fuel-pump failure. So Hayden got Ducati's first rostrum of the year, not his strongest race, as he readily admitted, but no way was the grinning Kentuckian apologising for it.

The man who did have some apologising to do was Rossi. Expecting a volley of four-letter words, he went to the Repsol Honda pit only to be greeted by some mild sarcasm. In response to the apology offered from under Rossi's crash helmet, Stoner enquired if Valentino had had a problem with his shoulder. If you can look confused while wearing an AGV, Rossi managed it. Casey followed up with his best line: 'Obviously your ambition outweighed your talent.' Which confused Valentino even more. The Italian was left to rue throwing away what had looked like a realistic chance of a rostrum place, at least. Several other riders felt the same way. Hiro Aoyama ended up a close fourth and regretted his ultra-cautious opening laps. Impressive rookies Cal Crutchlow and Karel Abraham both fell and remounted to finish in the top ten although, typically, Cal refused to apologise for continuing to press hard within sight of a rostrum finish.

Above Randy de Puniet was one of eight crashers, but not one of the three who managed to get going again

Below Nicky Hayden took Ducati's first podium of the year after Colin Edwards' Yamaha stopped on the last lap

Opposite Jorge Lorenzo celebrates his win

One finisher was greeted with universal applause. John Hopkins was back in MotoGP after two years in the sporting and personal wilderness. Looking lean and not having had a drink for 17 months (his precise figure), Hopper looked like a man who knew that second chances rarely happen at this level and was completely realistic about his targets for the weekend. On race-day morning he told team manager Paul Denning that a top-ten finish would be 'a dream'. It was nearly even better. Hopkins easily kept with the midfield group until his complete lack of experience with the Bridgestone wets showed, while imperfect electronics settings chewed up the Suzuki's rear tyre more quickly than the opposition's. The team looked like they'd won the race, probably because they'd achieved the unstated ambition of beating Loris Capirossi. With Bautista on course for his comeback at the next race and Hopkins' British Superbike Championship commitments clashing with the next two races, it looked as if it would take a wild-card entry from Suzuki to get Hopkins on to a MotoGP grid again in 2011.

Jerez 2011 was one of the craziest races seen in years. It will be remembered for all sorts of weird goings-on, such as three top-ten finishers crashing and remounting, rather than for Jorge Lorenzo's masterful, controlled ride. Prime among the dramas, of course, was the Rossi/Stoner incident. It didn't just hand Lorenzo a win and a championship lead he wasn't expecting, it also brought to the surface the latent hostility between Valentino and Casey. War had been declared.

BURNING RUBBER

Given the number of crashes and the state of the tyres on the bikes that finished the race, one might have expected Bridgestone to come in for some criticism. Tyre regulations stipulate that only one compound of wets is brought to each GP – the riders have no choice. Bridgestone's choice this time was their soft option. Several factors then conspired to give the tyres the most difficult time imaginable. Though the race started in rainy conditions, the Jerez track drains very efficiently and there was no standing water. Then the rain stopped and the abrasive tarmac combined with surprisingly high track temperature to wear the tyres extremely rapidly. Dani Pedrosa, waiting behind the podium, mimed sitting on his bike, twisting the throttle and going nowhere to a nodding Nicky Hayden. But neither of those two, or any other rider, thought the choice of the soft tyre was a mistake.

Given the option, they said, it was a much better choice than a hard tyre. With a hard tyre, the danger would have been transferred from the end of the race to the opening laps. Given the conditions, said Hirohide Hamashima, Director of Bridgestone Motorsport Tyre Development, a harder option would have lasted only a couple of laps longer than the softs. And, he added, 'Although grip dropped off considerably in the race, it did so consistently, which made it a little easier for the riders to manage.'

One interesting suggestion came from factory Yamaha team manager Wilco Zeelenberg, who pointed out that the race took about five minutes longer than in 2010. Maybe the solution was to shorten wet races by a lap or two and minimise any chance of problems with soft tyres.

SPANISH GP

CIRCUITO DE JEREZ

ROUND 2
April 3

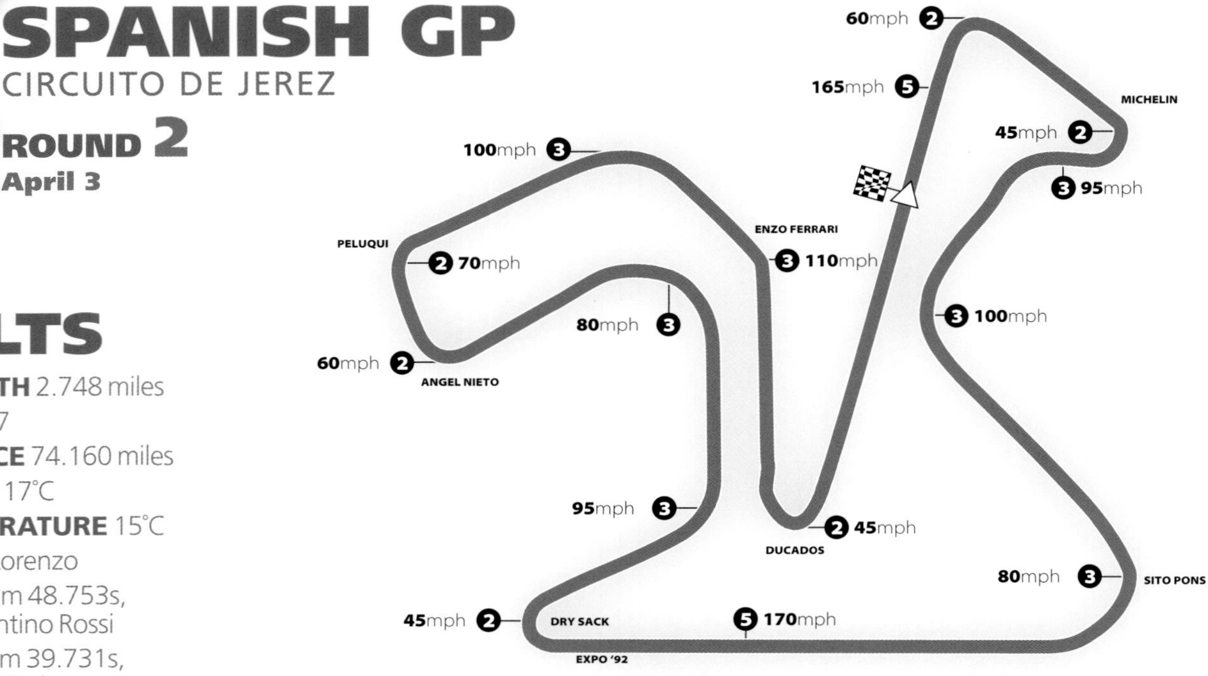

RACE RESULTS

CIRCUIT LENGTH 2.748 miles
NO. OF LAPS 27
RACE DISTANCE 74.160 miles
WEATHER Wet, 17°C
TRACK TEMPERATURE 15°C
WINNER Jorge Lorenzo
FASTEST LAP 1m 48.753s, 90.969mph, Valentino Rossi
LAP RECORD 1m 39.731s, 98.285mph, Dani Pedrosa

QUALIFYING

	Rider	Nationality	Team	Qualifying	Pole +	Gap
1	Stoner	AUS	Repsol Honda Team	1m 38.757s		
2	Pedrosa	SPA	Repsol Honda Team	1m 38.915s	0.158s	0.158s
3	Lorenzo	SPA	Yamaha Factory Racing	1m 38.918s	0.161s	0.003s
4	Spies	USA	Yamaha Factory Racing	1m 39.390s	0.633s	0.472s
5	Simoncelli	ITA	San Carlo Honda Gresini	1m 39.486s	0.729s	0.096s
6	Dovizioso	ITA	Repsol Honda Team	1m 39.709s	0.952s	0.223s
7	De Puniet	FRA	Pramac Racing Team	1m 39.892s	1.135s	0.183s
8	Edwards	USA	Monster Yamaha Tech 3	1m 39.895s	1.138s	0.003s
9	Crutchlow	GBR	Monster Yamaha Tech 3	1m 40.019s	1.262s	0.124s
10	Aoyama	JPN	San Carlo Honda Gresini	1m 40.168s	1.411s	0.149s
11	Hayden	USA	Ducati Team	1m 40.175s	1.418s	0.007s
12	Rossi	ITA	Ducati Team	1m 40.185s	1.428s	0.010s
13	Barbera	SPA	Mapfre Aspar Team	1m 40.217s	1.460s	0.032s
14	Hopkins	USA	Rizla Suzuki MotoGP	1m 40.310s	1.553s	0.093s
15	Capirossi	ITA	Pramac Racing Team	1m 40.523s	1.766s	0.213s
16	Abraham	CZE	Cardion AB Motoracing	1m 40.601s	1.844s	0.078s
17	Elias	SPA	LCR Honda MotoGP	1m 41.114s	2.357s	0.513s

FINISHERS

1 JORGE LORENZO A triumph of patience brought his first-ever win at any level in wet conditions and took him to the top of the points standings. Kept his head as he saw three men crash out ahead of him and nursed the tyres – although you couldn't tell by the look of his rear Bridgestone after the race.

2 DANI PEDROSA Contemplated pulling out because of his shoulder problem after Friday's dry sessions but on race day the wet conditions made life easier, although he still suffered numbness. Kept calm despite a bad start and, like Lorenzo, babied the tyres, but despite this he had no grip, even on the straight, for the last ten laps.

3 NICKY HAYDEN At last some luck for Nicky, although it was at the expense of fellow Americans Spies and Edwards. Was more worried about holding off Aoyama than attacking the men in front of him when the two Texans went out in the closing stages. 'You take 'em any way you can get 'em, and don't apologise.'

4 HIROSHI AOYAMA The definition of steady. Very tentative in the opening laps and left wondering afterwards if a little bit more aggression at the start might have put him on the rostrum.

5 VALENTINO ROSSI Could ride as he wanted for the first time in a year, and looked like his old self as he cut through the field from 12th on the grid before he got into Turn 1 too hot and took down Stoner. He was able to restart but was left contemplating what looked like a victory thrown away.

6 HECTOR BARBERA His best MotoGP result – and from 13th on the grid. Said the bike couldn't have moved about more if he'd tried from the start so, like Aoyama, he took it as gently as possible. Didn't know what to make of what he described as the 'weirdest race' of his life.

7 KAREL ABRAHAM Another calm display. Crashed while dicing with Aoyama but remounted for the best result by a rookie rider on a satellite Ducati. Without that incident, he could have been fifth.

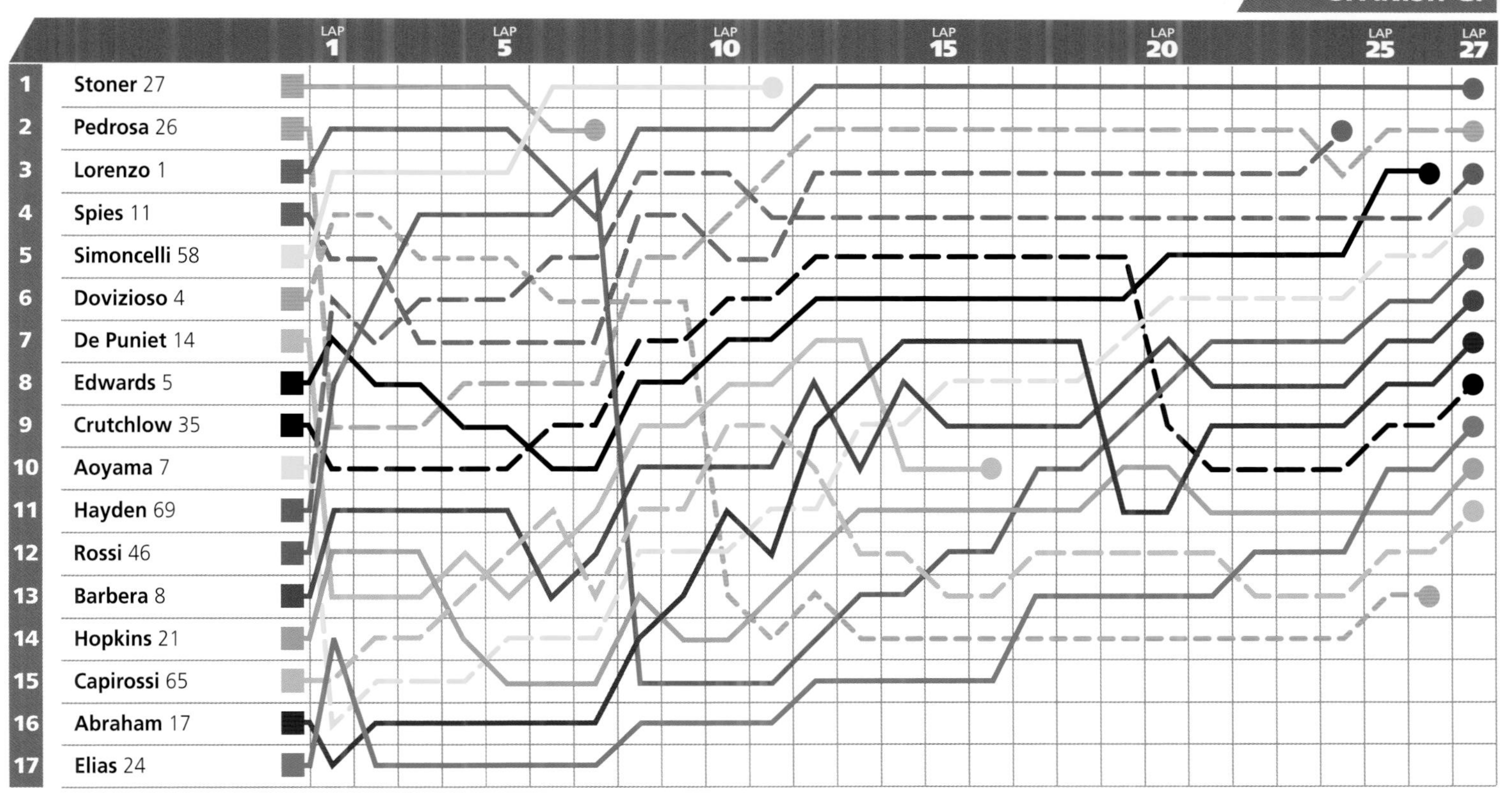

RACE

	Rider	Motorcycle	Race Time	Time +	Fastest Lap	Av Speed	B
1	Lorenzo	Yamaha	50m 49.046s		1m 48.871s	87.616mph	ws/ws
2	Pedrosa	Honda	51m 08.385s	19.339s	1m 49.177s	87.063mph	ws/ws
3	Hayden	Ducati	51m 18.131s	29.085s	1m 49.434s	86.788mph	ws/ws
4	Aoyama	Honda	51m 18.597s	29.551s	1m 50.812s	86.774mph	ws/ws
5	Rossi	Ducati	51m 51.273s	1m 2.227s	1m 48.753s	85.863mph	ws/ws
6	Barbera	Ducati	51m 57.486s	1m 8.440s	1m 50.581s	85.692mph	ws/ws
7	Abraham	Yamaha	52m 03.166s	1m 14.120s	1m 51.065s	85.536mph	ws/ws
8	Crutchlow	Yamaha	52m 08.156s	1m 19.110s	1m 49.581s	85.400mph	ws/ws
9	Elias	Honda	52m 31.952s	1m 42.906s	1m 52.897s	84.755mph	ws/ws
10	Hopkins	Suzuki	52m 37.441s	1m 48.395s	1m 50.540s	84.608mph	ws/ws
11	Capirossi	Ducati	52m 40.922s	1m 51.876s	1m 50.652s	84.514mph	ws/ws
12	Dovizioso	Honda	51m 39.633s	1 lap	1m 49.619s	82.993mph	ws/ws
NF	Edwards	Yamaha	49m 17.289s	1 lap	1m 49.959s	86.988mph	ws/ws
NF	Spies	Yamaha	45m 04.399s	3 laps	1m 49.864s	87.805mph	ws/ws
NF	De Puniet	Ducati	30m 15.977s	11 laps	1m 50.553s	87.175mph	ws/ws
NF	Simoncelli	Honda	20m 17.285s	16 laps	1m 48.780s	89.409mph	ws/ws
NF	Stoner	Honda	12m 53.841s	20 laps	1m 49.010s	70.859mph	ws/ws

CHAMPIONSHIP

	Rider	Team	Points
1	Lorenzo	Yamaha Factory Racing	45
2	Pedrosa	Repsol Honda Team	36
3	Stoner	Repsol Honda Team	25
4	Hayden	Ducati Team	23
5	Rossi	Ducati Team	20
6	Aoyama	San Carlo Honda Gresini	19
7	Dovizioso	Repsol Honda Team	17
8	Barbera	Mapfre Aspar Team MotoGP	14
9	Crutchlow	Monster Yamaha Tech 3	13
10	Abraham	Cardion AB Motoracing	12
11	Simoncelli	San Carlo Honda Gresini	11
12	Spies	Yamaha Factory Racing	10
13	Edwards	Monster Yamaha Tech 3	8
14	Elias	LCR Honda MotoGP	7
15	Hopkins	Rizla Suzuki MotoGP	6
16	Capirossi	Pramac Racing Team	5

8 CAL CRUTCHLOW Another rider who crashed and remounted. Cal was in fifth when he went down while chasing Hayden. Made no apology for pushing hard when there was the possibility of a rostrum finish.

9 TONI ELIAS Another horrible weekend redeemed at least partially by a top-ten finish. Just as in Qatar, Toni qualified last and was unhappy with his dry set-up. Used his experience to get it home but was beaten by three men who remounted after crashing.

10 JOHN HOPKINS Replaced the injured Bautista and did an admirable job. Involved in the six-man battle for eighth until his tyres dropped off in an even more extreme fashion than those on the bikes around him. Delighted to get the top-ten finish he wanted.

11 LORIS CAPIROSSI Troubled by a sore shoulder, which Loris was scheduled to have examined by a specialist, and then by a misfire that was traced to a broken spark plug, but the team signalled him to stay out and collect some points.

12 ANDREA DOVIZIOSO Spun the tyre so much that he had to come in for a new set of Bridgestones with ten laps to go. Much too little traction control seemed to be the culprit.

NON-FINISHERS

COLIN EDWARDS A controlled and clever race saw Colin conserve his tyres so well that he was able to breeze past Hayden and into third with three laps to go, only to coast to a halt at the start of the final lap. The fuel pump had failed.

BEN SPIES Looked set to make it a one-two finish for the factory Yamaha team when he slipped off two laps from the flag. Had slowed down when he passed Pedrosa but was still caught out by the worn tyres.

RANDY DE PUNIET Fought his way up to the group dice after a bad start but was always in trouble with the front of the bike. Crashed out on lap 17 and was unable to get the bike going.

MARCO SIMONCELLI Pressed as hard as usual to open up a significant lead but highsided out of the race at the first corner of lap 12.

CASEY STONER Looked as comfortable as in Qatar until taken out by Rossi's sliding Ducati. His bike was undamaged, but unable to push-start it on his own. Unhappy with the marshals and – obviously – with Rossi, sarcastically applauding him from trackside, then greeting the proffered apology with a couple of well-chosen one-liners.

NON-STARTERS

ALVARO BAUTISTA Recovering from the broken thigh he suffered in Qatar; replaced by John Hopkins.

PORTUGUESE GP
ESTORIL
ROUND 3
May 1
REPSOL
HONDA
Red Bull
Arai

WORDS AND DEEDS

Dani Pedrosa rose above the paddock bitching and proved that, fit again, he is a championship contender

At the first race of the year Dani Pedrosa finished on the rostrum but acted as though his season was over. The reason? A recurrence of the serious shoulder problems that had threatened not just his season but potentially his career as well. At the end of the Portuguese GP Dani's shoulder was hurting like hell, but the man himself was grinning; he knew he was back. Not only had he won his first race since Misano at the start of September 2010, he had won for the first time at Estoril and, in the process, he'd ended Jorge Lorenzo's unbeaten record at the track.

It was a near-perfect race, made doubly significant by the doubts over his ability to last the distance. Once the dust had settled from the rash of early crashes, Dani shadowed Jorge until just four laps were left. He then breezed past, immediately opening up a gap and setting fastest lap of the day on the 26th and 27th laps. Lorenzo, exhausted by leading for 24 laps on a bike he wasn't quite happy with, couldn't respond. The contrast with Qatar could not have been more pronounced. Dani was animated, visibly delighted and chatty. His most upbeat comments were about the injury; after six months of doubt he now knew that he could be competitive again, not just for wins but also for the title.

Dani's team-mate, Casey Stoner, had a strangely low-key weekend and had to be content with third. He too had an issue with an old injury. His on-board camera showed Casey feeling the small of his back, and he later reported that it 'completely locked up' for a few corners and he'd seriously contemplated pulling in. The problem dated back to a big crash at Catalunya in 2003. However, the Aussie never got his Honda

Above Colin Edwards was yet again the best non-factory rider

working properly either, and then didn't have confidence in the rear tyre's left side in the race's opening stages, so he ended up pretty happy with third.

MotoGP's other high-profile shoulder, belonging to Valentino Rossi, had also shown significant improvement over the month since the previous GP. However, that didn't prevent Andrea Dovizioso mugging him for fourth place out of the last corner. Dovi had to wait and gamble on the drag race out of that corner to avoid being re-passed instantly on the brakes. Stability on the brakes is one area where the Ducati doesn't have a problem. The major problems – front-end feel and the low-inertia crankshaft – were addressed at the test on the Monday after the race. There were suspicions that Rossi raced with a new, softer chassis, but all Ducati would admit to was a major revision of the engine-management electronics. It was a measure of this first Rossi/Burgess-inspired update that Valentino's mood improved dramatically after Friday practice.

Below Crutchlow leads Hayden, Aoyama and Spies in the fight that enlivened the second half of the race

At the Thursday press conference he'd looked like he would rather be anywhere else, a figure on the fringes having to listen to Casey repeat that he'd been knocked off by 'somebody' at Jerez and had some conditions if he were to crash again: 'If I end up in the gravel trap, I hope it's from my own fault, not somebody else's.' At this point Rossi was looking down, so all you could see was the peak of his cap. He was also massaging his injured shoulder... Valentino was then asked if he'd talked to Casey since that encounter in the Repsol garage. He hadn't. Casey assumed a faint smile that was trying very hard not to grow into a smirk.

Twenty-four hours later Rossi went on the attack, emboldened by improvements in the bike and his own condition. It was the first time this season that he'd bettered his lap time from session one to session two and reduced the gap to the leaders. Admitting that, like Pedrosa, he had been scared that the damage might never heal completely, Vale was nevertheless upbeat: 'We are on the way; I enjoy a lot now.' And he promptly launched an attack on Stoner for saying

Below Ben Spies's race was compromised by a clamp that wasn't removed from the fuel tank breather before the race started

Above The story of the race: Dani Pedrosa stalked Jorge Lorenzo for 24 of the 28 laps

Below Rossi was happy with everything except Dovizioso passing him out of the last corner of the final lap

Opposite Shoulder problem! What shoulder problem? Pedrosa celebrates more than just a win

'a lot of bad things about me and my team'. Subjects included Rossi's reasons for leaving Yamaha, his riding style and his shoulder. All areas, said Valentino, about which the Aussie knew nothing. Rossi also identified the root cause of the antagonism as Casey being unable to accept that he had been beaten in that epic race at Laguna Seca in 2008. Had he seen Stoner patting his Honda's seat hump when Rossi was behind him in practice, the gesture implying that Rossi was looking for a tow? 'I see and I expect.'

Casey merely professed himself amused that he was getting this sort of reaction out of the psychological warfare expert.

At the front-row press conference Marco Simoncelli was asked about Jorge Lorenzo's reported criticism of his riding, a question made even more inflammatory as the two were sitting beside each other at the time. Had Marco read what Jorge had been saying about him? He had. And he didn't agree. 'He say some wrong things.' At this point Jorge started looking tense. Naturally, the coming-together in Valencia last year was referred to. 'Your example was wrong,' said Marco, before claiming he'd been in front and had actually been the victim of a risky re-overtake. Jorge was now looking ready to explode and pointed out that he was not alone in his opinion.

'What other riders?' demanded Marco.

'Dovizioso,' came the answer, 'Aoyama…'. At which point, with the pair making eye contact, Jorge said that if nothing happened in the future then there wouldn't be a problem. 'But if something does happen with you in the future it will be a problem.'

STAKING A CLAIM

This year saw the last season of the 800cc formula in MotoGP. In 2012 the capacity limit increases to 1,000cc and a new category of Claiming Rule Team (CRT) will be introduced.

The basic rules for both classes were announced in 2010. The bikes can be up to 1,000cc, with up to four cylinders with a maximum bore of 81mm. Fuel and engine numbers remain the same as current regulations for factory bikes only, while the new CRTs are allowed an extra three litres of fuel (making 24 litres for the race) and double the number of engines for the season, i.e. 12. The crucial new word in the regulation is 'production', for CRTs will be allowed to use bikes based on production engines, something previously expressly forbidden.

Back in 2003, the WCM team was not allowed to race their four-stroke until it used major engine castings of their own design and manufacture rather than modified Yamaha R1 parts. Today, that bike looks like a model for any aspiring MotoGP team without the increasingly enormous budget needed to lease a bike from Honda or Ducati.

A new announcement shortly after the race fleshed out some of the detail. There was no strict definition of what will constitute a Claiming Rule Team – it is whatever the Grand Prix Commission deems not to be a factory effort. Only members of the MSMA, i.e. the factories, will be able to claim an engine from one of the new teams for €15,000, or €20,000 including the transmission. A maximum of four engine claims can be made against one CRT in any one racing season, and an MSMA manufacturer may not claim more than one engine per year from the same CRT.

The question is whether anyone can envisage a Japanese factory actually claiming a privateer's motor. Surely the loss of face would be unthinkable? Or is it a warning to factories like Aprilia and BMW not to try to enter MotoGP camouflaged as a private team?

Above The Suter BMW at a test session; the rider, Mika Kallio, is sat behind the bike

'Then I will be arrested,' said Marco. He also reminded Jorge that he, Jorge Lorenzo, was the one who'd been banned for dangerous riding.

At this point, Jorge went into lecture mode and told everyone that this was a dangerous sport and that, yes, he did once cause Alex de Angelis to crash and since than had taken great pains to make sure it didn't happen again. Jorge's wound-up, serious attitude – a World Champion must set an example – contrasted wonderfully with Marco leaning back in his chair, looking hairier than ever (in every sense) and unleashing the one-liners. And of course Marco, who had already been on the floor twice, did his best to prove Jorge right by crashing spectacularly on the first lap of the race.

The other rider at that conference was Dani Pedrosa. He just sat there smiling.

'I WAS WAITING FOR THE NUMBNESS TO COME TOGETHER WITH THE LOSS OF POWER, BUT IT DIDN'T COME!'
DANI PEDROSA

PORTUGUESE GP

ESTORIL

ROUND 3

May 1

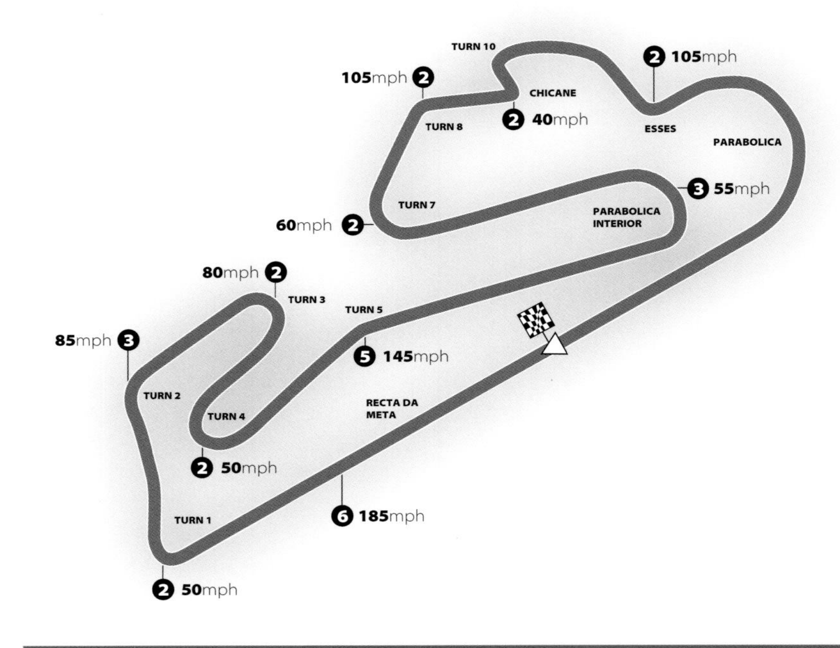

RACE RESULTS

CIRCUIT LENGTH 2.599 miles
NO. OF LAPS 28
RACE DISTANCE 72.772 miles
WEATHER Dry, 20°C
TRACK TEMPERATURE 38°C
WINNER Dani Pedrosa
FASTEST LAP 1m 37.629s, 95.815mph, Dani Pedrosa
LAP RECORD 1m 36.937s, 96.505mph, Dani Pedrosa

QUALIFYING

	Rider	Nationality	Team	Qualifying	Pole +	Gap
1	Lorenzo	SPA	Yamaha Factory Racing	1m 37.161s		
2	Simoncelli	ITA	San Carlo Honda Gresini	1m 37.294s	0.133s	0.133s
3	Pedrosa	SPA	Repsol Honda Team	1m 37.324s	0.163s	0.030s
4	Stoner	AUS	Repsol Honda Team	1m 37.384s	0.223s	0.060s
5	Spies	USA	Yamaha Factory Racing	1m 37.866s	0.705s	0.482s
6	Dovizioso	ITA	Repsol Honda Team	1m 38.073s	0.912s	0.207s
7	Edwards	USA	Monster Yamaha Tech 3	1m 38.080s	0.919s	0.007s
8	Crutchlow	GBR	Monster Yamaha Tech 3	1m 38.189s	1.028s	0.109s
9	Rossi	ITA	Ducati Team	1m 38.271s	1.110s	0.082s
10	Barbera	SPA	Mapfre Aspar Team	1m 38.363s	1.202s	0.092s
11	Aoyama	JPN	San Carlo Honda Gresini	1m 38.497s	1.336s	0.134s
12	Abraham	CZE	Cardion AB Motoracing	1m 38.786s	1.625s	0.289s
13	Hayden	USA	Ducati Team	1m 38.922s	1.761s	0.136s
14	Capirossi	ITA	Pramac Racing Team	1m 38.934s	1.773s	0.012s
15	Bautista	SPA	Rizla Suzuki MotoGP	1m 39.172s	2.011s	0.238s
16	De Puniet	FRA	Pramac Racing Team	1m 39.378s	2.217s	0.206s
17	Elias	SPA	LCR Honda MotoGP	1m 39.894s	2.733s	0.516s

FINISHERS

1 DANI PEDROSA The most significant win of his career executed with, given the circumstances, amazing coolness. Stalked Lorenzo for most of the race, blew by four laps from home and opened up a gap instantly. It was Dani's first win ever at the Portuguese GP.

2 JORGE LORENZO Started from pole for the first time this season, but for the third year in a row at Estoril. Led for 24 laps before Pedrosa finally showed his hand, and a tired Lorenzo had no answer. Not as happy with his bike here as in previous years, but had no excuses and gave Dani the credit he deserved.

3 CASEY STONER A strange race and the first sign of any weakness in his season. Subdued qualifying, nervous about his tyre's left side and unhappy with Simoncelli's first-lap move. An old back injury made itself felt and he thought about pulling in, then had difficulty climbing the rostrum. A good result under the circumstances.

4 ANDREA DOVIZIOSO A very similar race to his team-mate, only Andrea left it even later. Spent the bulk of it shadowing Rossi and was confident and clever enough to make his move when Vale couldn't strike back, out of the very last corner. Happy with the move but not with the gap to the front men, in the race or in qualifying.

5 VALENTINO ROSSI Happy with everything except Dovizioso. Pleased that his shoulder was only 15% from full fitness, that his lap times were very consistent and right on his qualifying time, that he got everything out of the bike – and that there was an important test on the Monday after the race.

6 COLIN EDWARDS Leading satellite team rider again. Stuck with Rossi and Dovizioso in the early laps but hit a problem with side grip. The wheelspin which that generated dropped him off the dice, then had a lonely ride to the flag – but his best result of the season so far.

7 HIROSHI AOYAMA Just held off Crutchlow in an entertaining fight that

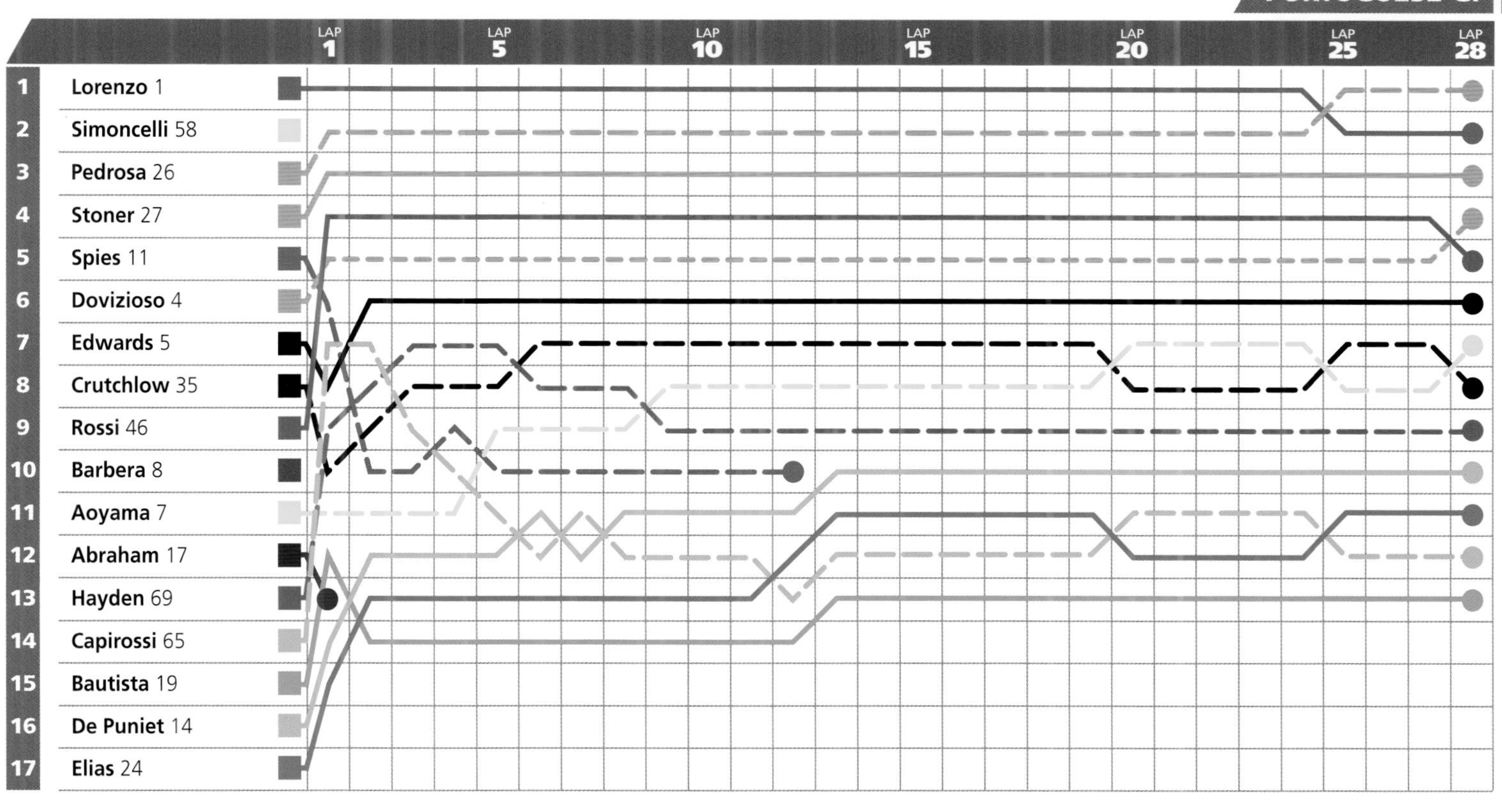

RACE

	Rider	Motorcycle	Race Time	Time +	Fastest Lap	Av Speed	B
1	Pedrosa	Honda	45m 51.483s		1m 37.629s	95.201mph	M/M
2	Lorenzo	Yamaha	45m 54.534s	3.051s	1m 37.865s	95.094mph	M/M
3	Stoner	Honda	45m 59.141s	7.658s	1m 37.853s	94.936mph	M/M
4	Dovizioso	Honda	46m 08.013s	16.530s	1m 38.263s	94.632mph	M/M
5	Rossi	Ducati	46m 08.038s	16.555s	1m 38.318s	94.631mph	M/M
6	Edwards	Yamaha	46m 24.058s	32.575s	1m 38.489s	94.087mph	M/M
7	Aoyama	Honda	46m 30.232s	38.749s	1m 38.783s	93.879mph	M/M
8	Crutchlow	Yamaha	46m 32.395s	40.912s	1m 38.736s	93.806mph	M/M
9	Hayden	Ducati	46m 46.370s	54.887s	1m 38.877s	93.339mph	S/M
10	De Puniet	Ducati	46m 51.180s	59.697s	1m 39.131s	93.179mph	M/M
11	Elias	Honda	46m 51.857s	1m 00.374s	1m 39.648s	93.157mph	S/M
12	Capirossi	Ducati	46m 53.276s	1m 01.793s	1m 39.720s	93.110mph	S/M
13	Bautista	Suzuki	47m 15.853s	1m 24.370s	1m 39.720s	92.368mph	M/M
NF	Spies	Yamaha	20m 06.256s	16 laps	1m 39.078s	93.066mph	M/M
NF	Abraham	Ducati	1m 50.239s	27 laps	1m 50.239s	84.862mph	M/M
NF	Simoncelli	Honda					M/M
NF	Barbera	Ducati					S/M

CHAMPIONSHIP

	Rider	Team	Points
1	Lorenzo	Yamaha Factory Racing	65
2	Pedrosa	Repsol Honda Team	61
3	Stoner	Repsol Honda Team	41
4	Rossi	Ducati Team	31
5	Hayden	Ducati Team	30
6	Dovizioso	Repsol Honda Team	30
7	Aoyama	San Carlo Honda Gresini	28
8	Crutchlow	Monster Yamaha Tech 3	21
9	Edwards	Monster Yamaha Tech 3	18
10	Barbera	Mapfre Aspar Team MotoGP	14
11	Abraham	Cardion AB Motoracing	12
12	Elias	LCR Honda MotoGP	12
13	Simoncelli	San Carlo Honda Gresini	11
14	Spies	Yamaha Factory Racing	10
15	Capirossi	Pramac Racing Team	9
16	De Puniet	Pramac Racing Team	6
17	Hopkins	Rizla Suzuki MotoGP	6
18	Bautista	Rizla Suzuki MotoGP	3

enlivened the second part of the race. Again cautious in the opening laps, but passed three riders on his way up to Cal's back wheel.

8 CAL CRUTCHLOW Another impressive result, despite not being fully recovered from surgery after Jerez to relieve arm pump, which meant his still recovering left shoulder took more load than was ideal. Despite a brave attempt to re-pass Aoyama on the last lap, he had to settle for eighth – a fine result given his physical condition.

9 NICKY HAYDEN Not a good weekend at a track where in 2010 he started from the front row and just missed the rostrum. Nearly changed bikes on the grid because of a problem with downshifts that persisted in the race. Being sideswiped by Spies didn't help either.

10 RANDY DE PUNIET First points of the year. Suffered serious pain in his knee – he'd had a pin removed from his left leg after Jerez – then collapsed in the pit afterwards and didn't take part in the Monday test. Ligament damage was suspected and he returned to Paris for tests.

11 TONI ELIAS Still having trouble getting heat into the tyres, obviously not helped by the low track temperatures. However, he was able to overhaul Capirossi and nearly got de Puniet.

12 LORIS CAPIROSSI Started the race in his usual aggressive fashion but ran into front-end problems that slowed him by a second a lap.

13 ALVARO BAUTISTA Even being on the bike 42 days after breaking his femur in Qatar was a miracle. His pace at the end would have put him in the top ten but a third-lap incident saw him in the gravel, avoiding the falling Abraham, after which it was a lonely race to his first points of the season.

NON-FINISHERS

BEN SPIES The damp that blocks the fuel-tank breather was left on for the race, and he was seen removing it in the first laps. As if that wasn't enough to destroy his concentration, he noticed another hose flapping loose. Worried about the brakes, he didn't want to ride near anyone, finally crashing when he ran wide and hit a bump.

KAREL ABRAHAM Lost it on the brakes for the first left-hander, Turn 4, on the second lap. Suffered a bruised hand.

MARCO SIMONCELLI Crashed out at the first left-hander on the first lap. Had a warning from the rear tyre, as did several others, coming out of the first corner, so took the first left a gear higher than normal. That didn't save him from an off-throttle highside.

HECTOR BARBERA Suffered the same crash as Simoncelli, an off-throttle highside at the first left-hander of the race. Sustained a small crack to a lumbar vertebra, but rode in the Monday test.

FRENCH GP
LE MANS

ROUND 4

May 15

THE BLAME GAME

Stoner won and Rossi got on the rostrum, but nobody was taking much notice after Simoncelli and Pedrosa clashed

Casey Stoner was fined 5,000 Euros, then dominated the race. Valentino Rossi got the Ducati on the rostrum for the first time, and Jorge Lorenzo lost one of his six engines in a nasty Sunday morning crash. On a normal race weekend any of these incidents would have dominated the headlines. Not this time.

The weekend started with an attempt to revive the verbals that had preceded the Portuguese GP. Rossi had made a remark about young riders being 'pussies' – obviously a dig at Lorenzo for criticising his mate Marco Simoncelli. When this was put to Jorge he produced a studied reply and delivered it with a hard stare: 'It must be a shame to be beaten by kids every weekend.' After which things settled down to what promised to be a weekend of Honda domination. Stoner was fastest in every session and Hondas filled the first four slots on the grid for the first time since the Pacific GP of October 2003.

Stoner also provided the first major talking point on his way to being fastest in warm-up. After de Puniet scarily drifted across his path at the end of the back straight, Casey pulled alongside and punched him in the shoulder. Race Direction summoned both riders and hit the Aussie with a fine, despite the riders apologising to each other and de Puniet arguing against any punishment for Stoner. Casey's only other problem came just before the start as his crew had trouble firing up the RCV, and then he struggled to find neutral on the line and overheated the clutch. Once the race started, though, Stoner's only fight was with Dani Pedrosa in what looked like being a rerun of the Qatar GP. Dani led the

first lap but when Casey went past it took him ten laps to shake off his team-mate – riding, as he later admitted, harder than he wanted to on a full tank.

By half-distance it looked as if Pedrosa's oft-repaired shoulder was starting to affect him; scarcely surprising on a track with three hard, downhill braking efforts. That put him into the clutches of Marco Simoncelli, who was well clear of the fraught tussle for fourth between Dovizioso, Lorenzo and Rossi. Impatient as ever, Simoncelli attacked straight away. When Pedrosa retook second coming out of La Chapelle, Simoncelli tried to go round the outside into the Chemin aux Boeufs Esses. There was a coming-together that sent the Italian across the gravel trap and the Spaniard to the medical centre with his other collarbone broken. Marco regained the track, still with a handy lead over the three pursuers, but five minutes later, to the surprise of most people, he was called in for a ride-through penalty. The most immediate effect of this was that Marco's chances of a first ever rostrum finish in MotoGP evaporated, although he did carve his way back to fifth.

Once Simoncelli had taken his penalty, Stoner was nearly 15 seconds clear of the dice for second, which was now between Rossi and Dovizioso, Lorenzo having lost touch after an off-track excursion. For the second race running Dovizioso calmly dealt with Rossi's challenge. Valentino claimed he attacked too early, thinking it was the last lap, because he misread his pit board, but Dovi looked to have the bases covered and Vale followed him over the line at a respectable distance. Rossi was delighted not just with the rostrum but also with the race.

'I CONTINUED TO PUSH MORE THAN I PREFER TO'

CASEY STONER

Opposite Rock 'n' roll royalty Slash from *Guns & Roses* toured pit lane

Above Rossi raced with the Yamaha of Lorenzo and the Honda of Dovizioso

Below The factory Hondas dominated Le Mans in practice and the race

Above Rossi was happy to be on the rostrum, but nobody was talking about him after the Pedrosa crash

Spending the whole distance in fights with a factory Yamaha and a Repsol Honda had taught him more about the Ducati, he said, than any number of tests. He did use the new, softer chassis but the engine modifications tested after the previous race couldn't be incorporated as the engines in play from his allocation still had plenty of mileage to do.

Dovizioso, who had a better view of the Desmosedici than anyone, said that the bike looked 'very stiff', that the rear still pumped significantly and that the rear spun up not once but 'two or even three times' in long corners. He also remarked that it wasn't the strongest rostrum of Rossi's career – not that Valentino or the team cared. Dovi had another curt remark ready when asked if he'd seen a TV replay of the Simoncelli incident. 'I no see – but I can imagine…' Casey Stoner hadn't seen the TV either, so refused to comment. But he did say he was pleased that Race Direction were at last making some decisions – and that included his own fine. Just in case anyone thought he was contemplating a career in the diplomatic service, Casey remarked waspishly that they hadn't looked him in the eye when issuing the fine – 'just read off a piece of paper'.

Significantly, Rossi declined to defend his friend this time, calling Simoncelli's move 'too hard'. The consensus over the incident, but not the penalty, was that Marco had left Pedrosa nowhere to go when he cut across him, something more than one rider had complained about before the French GP. Ironically, Pedrosa hadn't been one of them. At Estoril, when Dani was asked if he'd had any problems with the Italian, he replied with a grin: 'No, not me. But other riders, yes.' Pedrosa wasn't grinning this time. He went home to consider his options, deciding to have yet another operation to pin the bone in the hope of being fit for his home race. There was genuine sympathy for him from every quarter; given his history of horrible injuries, how could it be otherwise? None of which could rescue Dani's championship hopes.

Below Le Mans has never been kind to Randy de Puniet; he crashed on the first lap

JUDGEMENT

So why did Race Direction decide to inflict a ride-through penalty on Marco Simoncelli at Le Mans and not, for instance, on Valentino Rossi when he torpedoed Casey Stoner at Jerez? The answer is not simple and comes in several parts. One crucial point, well articulated by Stoner himself, is that no-one wants to penalise an honest mistake or the sort of 'racing incident' that is seen at every Grand Prix.

In many ways the rules governing on-track behaviour are written, or rather unwritten, by the riders themselves. As in any sport, there is a line that should not be crossed, whatever is written in the rule book. Call it fair play. In bike racing the unwritten rule is that a rider leaves the other guy room to race. This, historically, was the complaint about Simoncelli. Even determined neutral Nicky Hayden said that Marco 'does tend to shut the door'. Old 250 adversary Alvaro Bautista was at the other end of the diplomatic scale; he just used the word 'dangerous'.

To try to understand what happened at Le Mans it's necessary to see at least a sequence of photos – one frame is no use. Race Direction had several security cameras as well as the TV coverage to consult. The evidence does appear to show Marco cutting Dani's nose off and Pedrosa standing his bike up either as his front wheel was hit by Simoncelli's knee or as he realised a collision was inevitable.

The question about the penalty and whether it was or should have been influenced by earlier incidents or lobbying is more difficult to answer. While riders have received bans in recent years, Lorenzo and John Hopkins being two, no-one can remember a ride-through penalty. However, if Marco did feel contrition it must have occurred during a very, very long meeting in the HRC truck to which he was conducted, still in his leathers, a couple of hours after the race.

FRENCH GP

LE MANS

ROUND 4

May 15

RACE RESULTS

CIRCUIT LENGTH 2.600 miles
NO. OF LAPS 28
RACE DISTANCE 72.816 miles
WEATHER Dry, 17°C
TRACK TEMPERATURE 29°C
WINNER Casey Stoner
FASTEST LAP 1m 33.617s, 99.979mph, Dani Pedrosa (Record)
PREVIOUS LAP RECORD 1m 34.215s, 99.363mph, Valentino Rossi, 2008

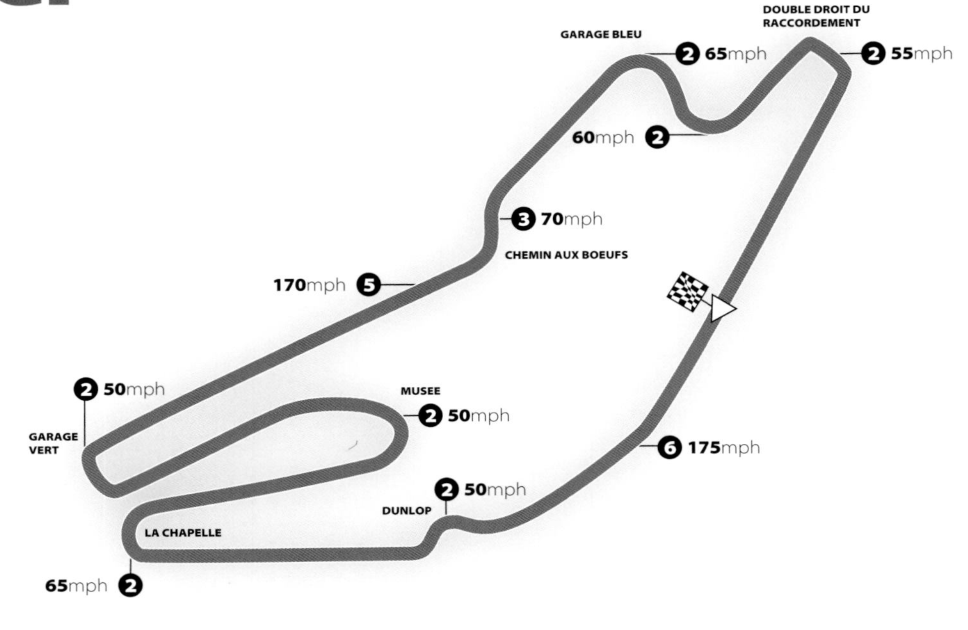

QUALIFYING

	Rider	Nationality	Team	Qualifying	Pole +	Gap
1	Stoner	AUS	Repsol Honda Team	1m 33.153s		
2	Simoncelli	ITA	San Carlo Honda Gresini	1m 33.212s	0.059s	0.059s
3	Dovizioso	ITA	Repsol Honda Team	1m 33.621s	0.468s	0.409s
4	Pedrosa	SPA	Repsol Honda Team	1m 33.683s	0.530s	0.062s
5	Lorenzo	SPA	Yamaha Factory Racing	1m 33.706s	0.553s	0.023s
6	Crutchlow	GBR	Monster Yamaha Tech 3	1m 33.804s	0.651s	0.098s
7	Edwards	USA	Monster Yamaha Tech 3	1m 34.063s	0.910	0.259s
8	Spies	USA	Yamaha Factory Racing	1m 34.206s	1.053s	0.143s
9	Rossi	ITA	Ducati Team	1m 34.206s	1.053s	–
10	Hayden	USA	Ducati Team	1m 34.277s	1.124s	0.071s
11	De Puniet	FRA	Pramac Racing Team	1m 34.351s	1.198s	0.074s
12	Bautista	SPA	Rizla Suzuki MotoGP	1m 34.513s	1.360s	0.162s
13	Aoyama	JPN	San Carlo Honda Gresini	1m 34.612s	1.459s	0.099s
14	Barbera	SPA	Mapfre Aspar Team	1m 34.650s	0.497s	0.038s
15	Capirossi	ITA	Pramac Racing Team	1m 34.866s	1.713s	0.216s
16	Abraham	CZE	Cardion AB Motoracing	1m 35.010s	1.857s	0.144s
17	Elias	SPA	LCR Honda MotoGP	1m 35.433s	2.280s	0.423s

FINISHERS

1 CASEY STONER An even more dominant win than at the opening race of the year, although again had to work hard to shake off a very persistent Pedrosa. Started from pole, his first at Le Mans in any class, and led every lap but the first on his way to winning by over 14 seconds.

2 ANDREA DOVIZIOSO Started from the front row for only the fourth time in his MotoGP career and, until the events of lap 18, was involved in a three-way fight for fourth with Rossi and Lorenzo. That became the fight for second, and for the second race running Andrea was able to deal with Valentino in the closing laps.

3 VALENTINO ROSSI Using the new 'softer' chassis, he took advantage of the misfortunes of others to score his first rostrum on the Ducati. Made progress with the bike in every session, including warm-up, and 'had fun' in the race, but had no answer to Dovizioso's speed in the final laps.

4 JORGE LORENZO Top Yamaha by over 10s but over 20s behind the winner. Destroyed an engine in a big warm-up crash, and also damaged a finger. Fought with Dovizioso for third after the Pedrosa/Simoncelli incident but lost touch when he ran wide. Not happy with his bike's potential, but events meant he extended his title lead.

5 MARCO SIMONCELLI Lying third mid-race and closing fast on Pedrosa, then tried to get past on the outside as soon as he caught him but appeared to leave Dani nowhere to go. Ran through the gravel to rejoin the race but was later hit with a ride-through penalty and a very long meeting in the HRC truck.

6 BEN SPIES Qualified in eighth, his worst grid position in nearly a year. Made two mistakes on the opening lap but was reeling in Edwards when the Tech 3 rider crashed, and Ben lost 2s taking avoiding action. That put him into Hayden's clutches and they fought for the rest of the race.

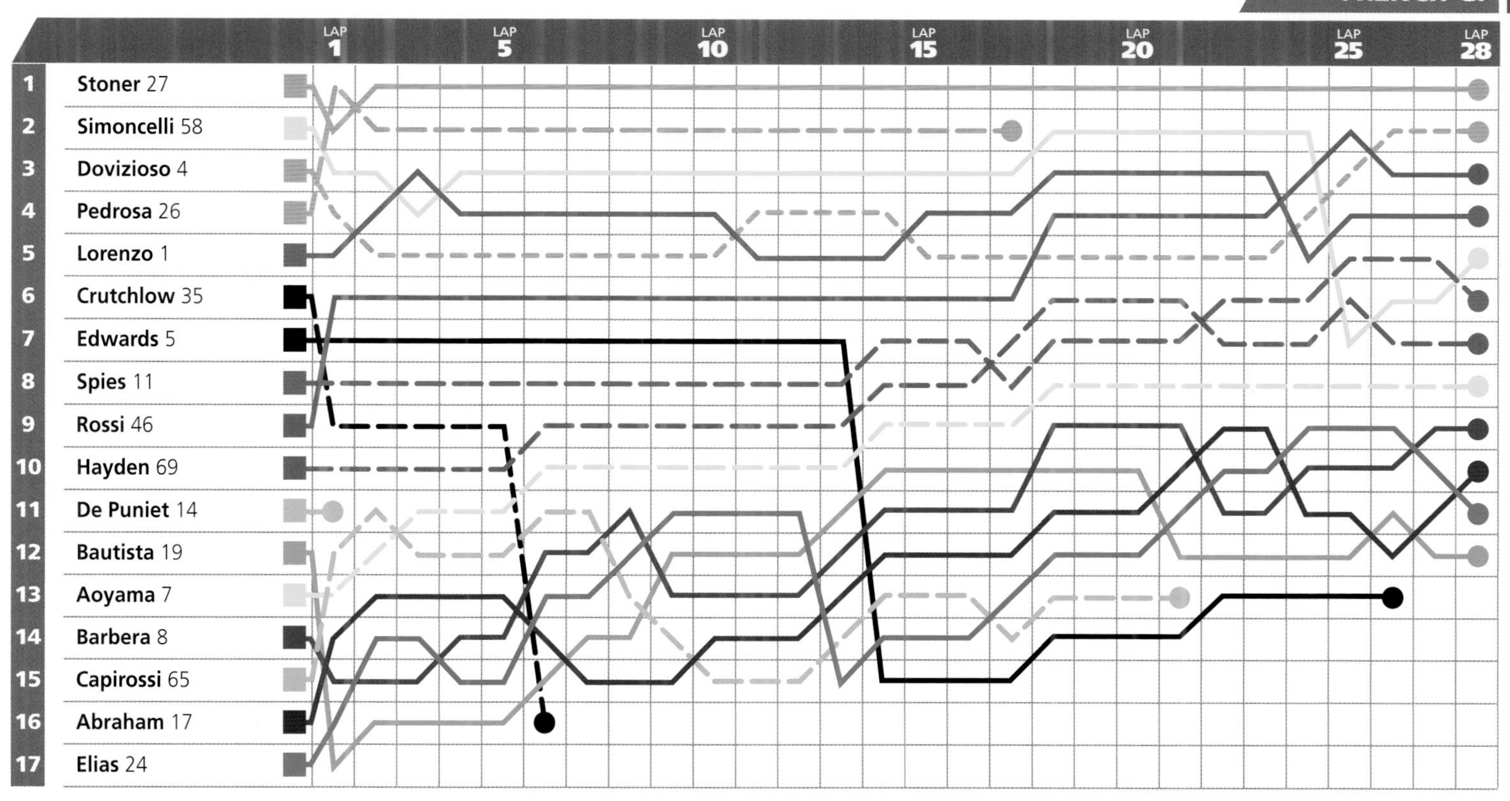

RACE

	Rider	Motorcycle	Race Time	Time +	Fastest Lap	Av Speed	B
1	Stoner	Honda	44m 03.955s		1m 33.617s	99.143mph	M/S
2	Dovizioso	Honda	44m 18.169s	14.214s	1m 34.304s	98.613mph	M/S
3	Rossi	Ducati	44m 18.519s	14.564s	1m 34.273s	98.600mph	M/S
4	Lorenzo	Yamaha	44m 25.030s	21.075s	1m 34.269s	98.360mph	M/S
5	Simoncelli	Honda	44m 35.200s	31.245s	1m 33.840s	97.986mph	M/S
6	Spies	Yamaha	44m 35.564s	31.609s	1m 34.462s	97.972mph	M/S
7	Hayden	Ducati	44m 39.521s	35.566s	1m 34.730s	97.828mph	M/S
8	Aoyama	Honda	44m 55.457s	51.502s	1m 35.400s	97.249mph	M/S
9	Barbera	Ducati	45m 07.686s	1m 03.731s	1m 35.736s	96.810mph	M/S
10	Abraham	Ducati	45m 07.840s	1m 03.885s	1m 35.604s	96.804mph	M/S
11	Elias	Honda	45m 08.023s	1m 04.068s	1m 35.740s	96.798mph	M/S
12	Bautista	Suzuki	45m 08.147s	1m 04.192s	1m 35.740s	96.793mph	M/S
13	Edwards	Yamaha	45m 03.007s	2 laps	1m 34.529s	90.050mph	M/S
NF	Capirossi	Ducati	33m 55.169s	7 laps	1m 35.828s	96.600mph	M/S
NF	Pedrosa	Honda	26m 47.714s	11 laps	1m 33.617s	98.992mph	M/S
NF	Crutchlow	Yamaha	10m 27.276s	22 laps	1m 34.805s	89.547mph	M/S
NF	De Puniet	Ducati	1m 43.987s	27 laps	1m 43.987s	90.029mph	M/S

CHAMPIONSHIP

	Rider	Team	Points
1	Lorenzo	Yamaha Factory Racing	78
2	Stoner	Repsol Honda Team	66
3	Pedrosa	Repsol Honda Team	61
4	Dovizioso	Repsol Honda Team	50
5	Rossi	Ducati Team	47
6	Hayden	Ducati Team	39
7	Aoyama	San Carlo Honda Gresini	36
8	Simoncelli	San Carlo Honda Gresini	22
9	Edwards	Monster Yamaha Tech 3	21
10	Barbera	Mapfre Aspar Team MotoGP	21
11	Crutchlow	Monster Yamaha Tech 3	21
12	Spies	Yamaha Factory Racing	20
13	Abraham	Cardion AB Motoracing	18
14	Elias	LCR Honda MotoGP	17
15	Capirossi	Pramac Racing Team	9
16	Bautista	Rizla Suzuki MotoGP	7
17	De Puniet	Pramac Racing Team	6
18	Hopkins	Rizla Suzuki MotoGP	6

7 NICKY HAYDEN Like team-mate Rossi, Nicky made progress with the bike over the whole weekend but gave himself a lot to do by qualifying down in tenth. Didn't start well but was able to make progress and spent the last half of the race fighting over sixth place with Spies.

8 HIROSHI AOYAMA Looked good on Friday, didn't improve in qualifying, but escaped from the group early on in the race. Then had a lonely ride as he was never in range of the Hayden/Spies dice.

9 HECTOR BARBERA Only got comfortable with his Ducati on race day but then had fun and won the big group fight, despite running off the track on the first lap. A good recovery from what he called 'the disaster' of Estoril.

10 KAREL ABRAHAM Involved in the big dice for the whole race. Looked to have been pushed to the back but overtook Bautista and Elias on the last two laps for a satisfactory finish. However, he was not happy with the gap to the leaders, which he'd expected to be smaller.

11 TONI ELIAS His best race of the season, and it could have been better. Despite qualifying last and being nervous about getting heat into the tyres, he was leading the group when he was flicked out of the seat hard enough to activate the airbag in his leathers, preventing him riding properly for a couple of laps as it deflated.

12 ALVARO BAUTISTA Enjoyed the race but not the result. Described it as his 'first race of the year' because, unlike Portugal, he was involved in the scrap with Barbera, Abraham and the Pramac Ducatis. Lost time when he knocked it into neutral but, as he wasn't supposed to come back before Catalunya, it was a good weekend.

13 COLIN EDWARDS Crashed when he lost the front on lap 14 while lying seventh but got the bike back to the pits to replace a broken footrest and went out again two laps down on the leaders to collect three points. A tough weekend for the team, but Colin worked tirelessly behind the scenes to hold things together.

NON-FINISHERS

LORIS CAPIROSSI Fell when he tagged the back wheel of the Suzuki after Bautista missed a gear.

DANI PEDROSA Tangled with Simoncelli going into the Esses at the end of the back straight as the pair were fighting for second on lap 18, the incident for which the Italian was penalised. Suffered a broken right collarbone (his left had just healed) and was certainly not passing the crash off as a racing incident.

CAL CRUTCHLOW Fell at Garage Vert when he put the rear wheel over the kerb as he was closing on Spies. A sticking throttle prevented him from rejoining the race.

RANDY DE PUNIET Fell on the first lap when he lost the front.

CATALAN GP
CIRCUIT DE CATALUNYA
ROUND 5
June 5
BRIDGESTONE
alpinestars
REPSO

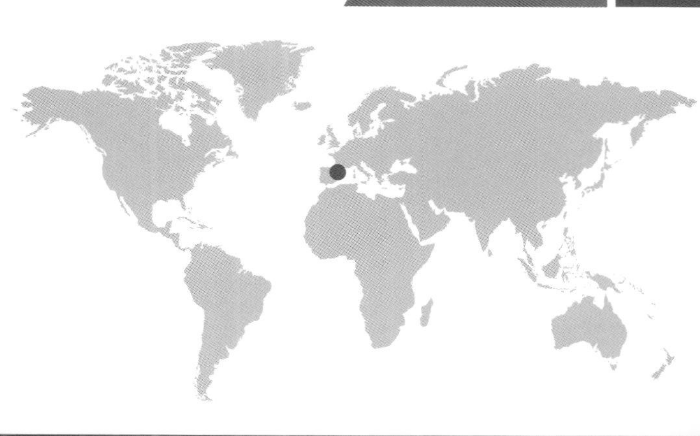

ONE BY ONE

Casey Stoner dominated again as Marco Simoncelli failed to capitalise on his first pole position

It was a weekend of multiple anticlimaxes at a circuit that rarely produces cut-and-thrust racing. That glorious last lap in 2009 was the exception, not the rule. The race this year was all the more disappointing given that Marco Simoncelli had bounced back from the public going-over he received at Le Mans to take pole position for the first time in MotoGP. In the event, what excitement there was mainly happened away from the track.

Simoncelli was summoned to appear before Race Direction prior to the race, an apparently strange decision but one that didn't bother him as he'd had no chance to put his case in France. He made various politically correct statements about thinking a little more, but he seemed more influenced by the opinion of his friend Valentino Rossi that he had 'closed the door too hard' on Pedrosa. As for Dani, there was no sign of him at his home race. His crew did go and see him at home and reported that he still had his arm in a sling, but the Spanish press was alive with rumours of further injury due to a training accident on a supermoto bike and speculation about his desire to return to racing. In Pedrosa's absence the crowd made sure that Marco knew of Catalunya's displeasure, although the two burly bodyguards might have been a bit over the top.

There was another notable absentee. Colin Edwards missed a Grand Prix for the first time since he arrived in 2003, an uninterrupted run of 141 races. The Texan became another victim of the cold-tyre syndrome, the left-hander at Turn 5 also claiming Valentino Rossi, although the Doctor wasn't hurt. Edwards broke his collarbone on Friday, had

EROL
Circuit de Catalunya
Circuit de Catalunya
APEROL
SAN CARLO
Honda Gresini
GOODYEAR
SAN CARLO
HONDA
58
BRIDGESTONE
DAINESE
Honda Italia
58

it plated on Saturday and was back at the track on Sunday determined to race. Actually, he just wanted to do a couple of laps to maintain his streak but the medical authorities denied him the opportunity. It was doubtless the right decision but it was no fun and Colin did not take it well.

The mixed weather that had followed the GP circus around since it arrived in Europe again made its presence felt on Friday and Saturday, and also had an effect on Sunday. Morning warm-up was wet, which meant that the improvement Rossi's crew had found gave them a problem when the track dried out for the race. They decided to go with the change anyway, which turned out to be a mistake, but Valentino was distinctly upbeat about his bike after the race. The factory Ducatis used the new high-inertia crankshaft, which Rossi and Hayden reported as a small improvement because it made getting back on the throttle easier. Rossi was complimentary about the front end, usually the source of all the problems, but he did say that the back of the 2012 bike he had tested was massively better than his current Desmosedici. Unfortunately, that design could not be used on the 2011 machine.

In the race Rossi first diced with and then shadowed Dovizioso. The set-up change, he said, reduced rear grip going into corners and therefore compromised his braking. There was no way he could put a move on the hard-braking Honda rider. He was also pleased that he could actually see the winner at the finish. Casey Stoner was only just over seven seconds in front of fifth-placed Rossi. The gaps between the leaders were never large, but nobody appeared to be able to do anything about them, a situation that wasn't helped when there was a sprinkling of rain with 14 laps to go. It was heavy enough, though, for Race Direction to put out the white flags, signifying that riders could change bikes. No-one did, but it definitely grabbed the racers' attention.

Above Cal Crutchlow impressed with a season's best finish of seventh

Opposite Marco Simoncelli did not take advantage of his first pole position

Below Bautista on the grid

'I WAS ABLE TO OPEN UP AN ADVANTAGE WITHOUT PUSHING TOO HARD OR FEELING TOO MUCH PRESSURE'
CASEY STONER

Stoner allowed the gap between himself and second-placed Lorenzo to drop to under two seconds before responding. 'I gauged it from the guys behind me,' he said, after admitting that there was enough water in the final corner to affect his bike's behaviour. If Lorenzo could do those lap times, he reasoned, then so could he. Casey might have had to deal with some stress but he rode superbly, and from trackside it was impossible to see anything other than an easy win. Happily, the latest super-slow-motion TV cameras at least gave viewers at home an insight into how hard the Aussie was working, showing the RCV spinning and sliding at maximum lean angle as the rider's elbow brushed the painted kerbs.

Lorenzo was content with his second place; he'd led off the line but knew that Stoner would come past sooner rather than later. It was sooner – the end of the first lap – and Jorge spent the rest of the race keeping Casey honest. Spies backed up the World Champion with his own first rostrum of the year. In his usual laconic style, Ben didn't think anything had gone particularly well, just that nothing had gone wrong. Yamaha were further cheered by rookie Cal Crutchlow's seventh place, his best of the season so far. Cal made one of the few passes in the top eight to demote Nicky Hayden. Like the rest of the field he subsequently spent the remainder of the race worrying about the rain and struggling for grip on a track surface that always reacts in an extreme fashion to temperature and damp conditions.

Not even Marco Simoncelli managed to liven things up. Once he'd made a mess of his start and was swamped going into the first corner it was all he could do to pull back up to fifth. Maybe he should get the blame for a dull race.

Above Nicky Hayden showing you can get an 800 sideways

Opposite Spies congratulates Stoner on the slow-down lap

Below Loris Capirossi won the battle of the satellite Ducatis. Here he leads Abraham and Barbera

HONDA'S Moto3 BENCHMARK

It has been a long time since anyone has launched a new, over-the-counter racing machine. The Honda NSF250R is more than just the basis for a Moto3 Grand Prix machine. It is, Honda claim, the next racing standard. The reaction when the covers were taken off in the Catalunya paddock would suggest that this was no idle boast.

The base model NSF will cost £20,000 plus taxes and Honda will make 450. It is constructed around the old RS125 chassis parts, but somehow Honda have fitted in a 250 four-stroke motor without increasing the frontal area. The engine is an all-new DOHC single with the cylinder inclined back at 15 degrees and the intake at the front. The packaging of the exhaust is particularly neat, but the NSF bristles with clever solutions such as the offset cylinder. Tech 3's technical genius Guy Coulon summed it up nicely: 'Difficult to do better for the money.'

HRC will not support teams competing in GPs, but Geo-Tech – who currently supply the Moto2 control engines – will be providing support and parts.

CATALAN GP

CIRCUIT DE CATALUNYA

ROUND 5

June 5

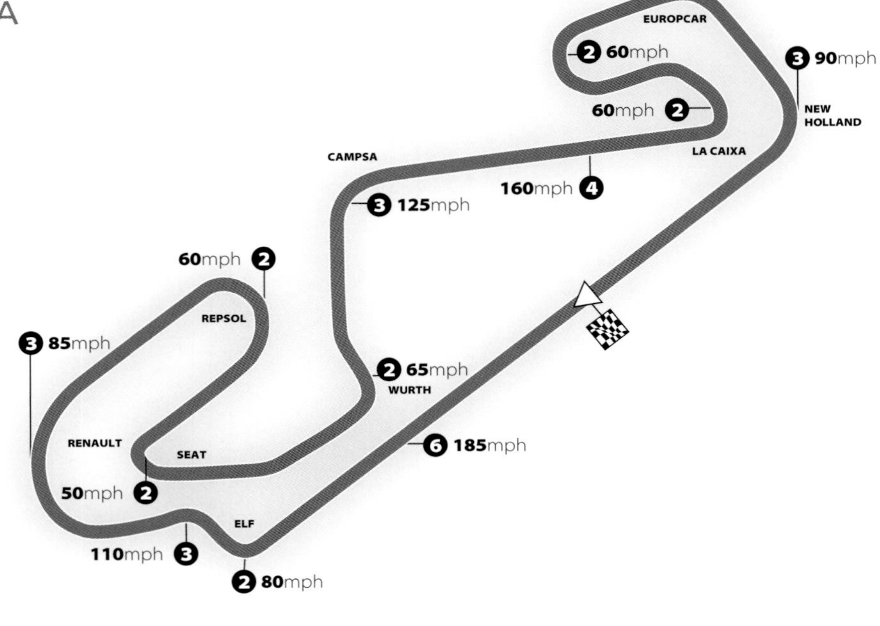

RACE RESULTS

CIRCUIT LENGTH 2.937 miles
NO. OF LAPS 25
RACE DISTANCE 73.425 miles
WEATHER Dry, 20°C
TRACK TEMPERATURE 25°C
WINNER Casey Stoner
FASTEST LAP 1m 43.084s, 102.588mph, Casey Stoner
LAP RECORD 1m 42.358s, 103.304mph, Dani Pedrosa, 2008

QUALIFYING

	Rider	Nationality	Team	Qualifying	Pole +	Gap
1	Simoncelli	ITA	San Carlo Honda Gresini	1m 42.413s		
2	Stoner	AUS	Repsol Honda Team	1m 42.429s	0.016s	0.016s
3	Lorenzo	SPA	Yamaha Factory Racing	1m 42.728s	0.315s	0.299s
4	Spies	USA	Yamaha Factory Racing	1m 42.742s	0.329s	0.014s
5	Dovizioso	ITA	Repsol Honda Team	1m 42.749s	0.336s	0.007s
6	Crutchlow	GBR	Monster Yamaha Tech 3	1m 43.202s	0.789s	0.453s
7	Rossi	ITA	Ducati Team	1m 43.223s	0.810s	0.021s
8	Hayden	USA	Ducati Team	1m 43.228s	0.815s	0.005s
9	Bautista	SPA	Rizla Suzuki MotoGP	1m 43.447s	1.034s	0.219s
10	Barbera	SPA	Mapfre Aspar Team	1m 43.656s	1.243s	0.209s
11	Aoyama	JPN	San Carlo Honda Gresini	1m 43.734s	1.321s	0.078s
12	De Puniet	FRA	Pramac Racing Team	1m 43.764s	1.351s	0.030s
13	Capirossi	ITA	Pramac Racing Team	1m 44.068s	1.655s	0.304s
14	Elias	SPA	LCR Honda MotoGP	1m 44.510s	2.097s	0.442s
15	Abraham	CZE	Cardion AB Motoracing	1m 45.661s	3.248s	1.151s
*	Edwards	USA	Monster Yamaha Tech 3			

FINISHERS

1 CASEY STONER Controlled the race brilliantly from the front once he'd passed fast-starting Lorenzo. Not pushing hard or feeling pressure until the showers made the last corner slippery, then paid close attention to his pit board. Speeded up when Jorge closed, but backed off if the lead went up. Very relieved to see the chequered flag.

2 JORGE LORENZO Led for the first lap before Stoner came past, then hung on to the Honda until the rain came. Found it difficult to maintain concentration in the fast final sector, but happy that he'd done his best and retained the championship lead.

3 BEN SPIES First rostrum of the year followed a fourth second-row start. Said it was a weekend when nothing went wrong rather than anything going especially well. Slotted into third off the start and stayed there, closing the gap to Lorenzo, but more concerned with staying ahead of Dovizioso than attacking his team-mate.

4 ANDREA DOVIZIOSO Suffered at the start of the race as his harder tyre choice compromised front stability with a full tank, and didn't have the traction of the top three, who were all on softer Bridgestones. Not happy, but did move into third place in the championship.

5 VALENTINO ROSSI Closer to the winner and the guys in front and much happier with the bike. Felt he could have fought for third, but a set-up change that worked in wet warm-up and left in for the race turned out to be the wrong decision (or guess). The problem was rear grip on corner entry, which compromised his braking.

6 MARCO SIMONCELLI Bounced back from controversy at Le Mans with his first pole position in MotoGP, but made a mess of the start and was swamped by the pack in the first corner. Managed to close down the gap to Rossi but decided it was safer not to press any harder because some parts of the track were damp.

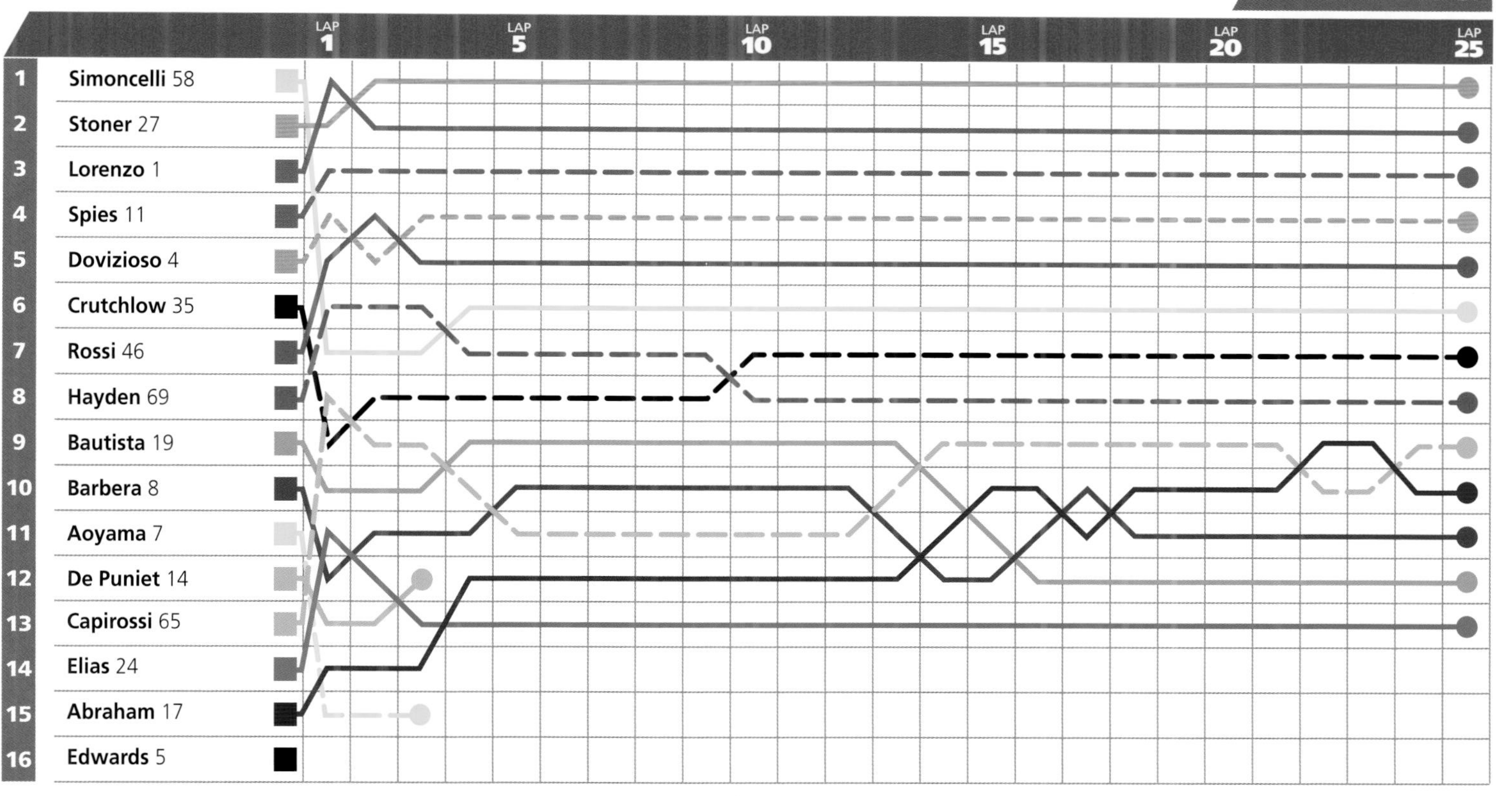

RACE

	Rider	Motorcycle	Race Time	Time +	Fastest Lap	Av Speed	B
1	Stoner	Honda	43m 19.779s		1m 43.084s	101.684mph	H/H
2	Lorenzo	Yamaha	43m 22.182s	2.403s	1m 43.416s	101.590mph	H/M
3	Spies	Yamaha	43m 24.070s	4.291s	1m 43.637s	101.517mph	H/M
4	Dovizioso	Honda	43m 25.034s	5.255s	1m 43.506s	101.479mph	H/H
5	Rossi	Ducati	43m 27.150s	7.371s	1m 43.709s	101.397mph	H/M
6	Simoncelli	Honda	43m 31.610s	11.831s	1m 43.684s	101.224mph	H/M
7	Crutchlow	Yamaha	43m 46.262s	26.483s	1m 44.049s	100.659mph	H/H
8	Hayden	Ducati	43m 53.022s	33.243s	1m 44.263s	100.400mph	H/M
9	Capirossi	Ducati	44m 02.871s	43.092s	1m 44.723s	100.026mph	H/M
10	Abraham	Ducati	44m 02.892s	43.113s	1m 44.453s	100.026mph	M/M
11	Barbera	Ducati	44m 04.003s	44.224s	1m 44.505s	99.983mph	H/M
12	Bautista	Suzuki	44m 05.018s	45.239s	1m 44.653s	99.945mph	M/M
13	Elias	Honda	44m 18.047s	58.268s	1m 45.011s	99.455mph	H/M
NF	De Puniet	Ducati	5m 23.714s	22 laps	1m 45.317s	97.997mph	H/M
NF	Aoyama	Honda	5m 24.395s	22 laps	1m 45.626s	97.790mph	H/M

CHAMPIONSHIP

	Rider	Team	Points
1	Lorenzo	Yamaha Factory Racing	98
2	Stoner	Repsol Honda Team	91
3	Dovizioso	Repsol Honda Team	63
4	Pedrosa	Repsol Honda Team	61
5	Rossi	Ducati Team	58
6	Hayden	Ducati Team	47
7	Spies	Yamaha Factory Racing	36
8	Aoyama	San Carlo Honda Gresini	36
9	Simoncelli	San Carlo Honda Gresini	32
10	Crutchlow	Monster Yamaha Tech 3	30
11	Barbera	Mapfre Aspar Team MotoGP	26
12	Abraham	Cardion AB Motoracing	24
13	Edwards	Monster Yamaha Tech 3	21
14	Elias	LCR Honda MotoGP	20
15	Capirossi	Pramac Racing Team	16
16	Bautista	Rizla Suzuki MotoGP	11
17	De Puniet	Pramac Racing Team	6
18	Hopkins	Rizla Suzuki MotoGP	6

7 CAL CRUTCHLOW Another impressive ride – a season's best result and top satellite team rider. Caught, passed and pulled away from Hayden but used up his tyres doing it and had a lonely race thereafter: 'Not too bad considering I'd never seen this place before.'

8 NICKY HAYDEN Started well and felt the tyres came in quickly, but was soon spinning up in the long corners. Had some ideas about countering the problem but wet warm-up meant they couldn't be tested. The first time this season he didn't finish the race in a higher position than qualifying.

9 LORIS CAPIROSSI Best result of the season so far off the back of the best set-up he'd yet found. Got a good start and spent most of the race controlling the big group dice, which he won by taking Abraham out of the final corner.

10 KAREL ABRAHAM After a big front-end crash in qualifying he started with a hand injury and a lack of confidence. Ran off the track on lap three, then got back up to the dice, where he was finally frustrated by Capirossi's experience.

11 HECTOR BARBERA Had his usual problems with rear grip – fine on entry to the fast corners but after six laps he couldn't get on the throttle early without the rear stepping out. Didn't have much fun, despite being in the group dice.

12 ALVARO BAUTISTA More was expected from Alvaro, who was finally fully fit. Everything went well in qualifying and the race until light rain fell and the old Suzuki problem of grip levels returned. Lost three places in the closing stages.

13 TONI ELIAS Despite a modified chassis he had what he called 'one of the worst races of my career'. Couldn't match his lap times from qualifying and managed to have problems not just with rear grip, as usual, but with the front too. A horrible home race.

NON-FINISHERS

RANDY DE PUNIET More proof that when your luck is out, it's really out. Taken out at the start of lap three by Aoyama. Worried about damage to his right ankle: 'It makes a strange noise when I walk.' Ligament damage was feared and a scan scheduled.

HIROSHI AOYAMA Crashed at the first corner of the third lap and took de Puniet with him; Hiro admitted responsibility. It was his first non-scoring race of the season.

NON-STARTERS

COLIN EDWARDS Cold tyres claimed another victim, with Colin crashing on Friday and breaking his right collarbone. Had it plated on Saturday and wanted to race on Sunday. Seriously.

DANI PEDROSA No surprise that Dani couldn't take part two weeks after breaking his collarbone, but he didn't put in an appearance at his local race either, leading to much speculation about further injury or worse.

BRITISH GP
SILVERSTONE
ROUND 6
June 12
Red Bull
NOLAN
REPSOL
HONDA
REPSOL

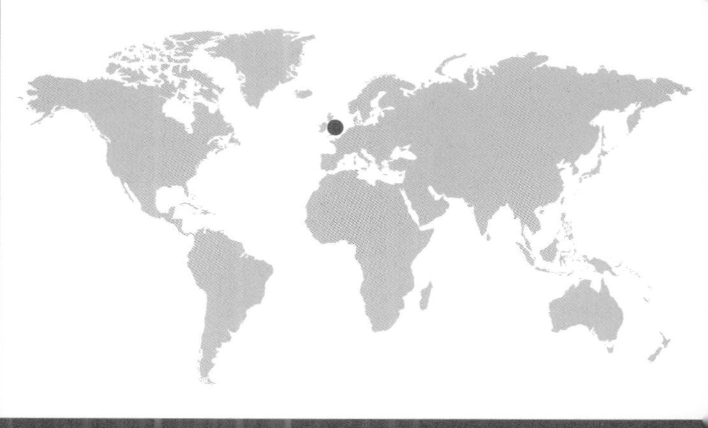

LOST IN SPACE

Wet or dry, it didn't matter. Casey Stoner won again as his main rivals crashed and Rossi had his worst weekend of the year

There was a sense of inevitability about Silverstone 2011. The circuit's infrastructure had filled out in the previous 12 months and, judging by the fans' reaction, the other improvements made them feel at home on what many had previously regarded as a car circuit. Despite conditions that felt more like November than June, well over 70,000 spectators turned up to witness Casey Stoner continue his regal progress not just to the win, but to the top of the championship table. He was quickest in every session, only headed on the first lap and just lost the fastest lap to Hayden's late push. It was Casey's 27th victory in MotoGP, nicely matching his race number. Inevitable, really.

As usual with the Aussie, he was the only one who saw any problems with his win. He claimed not to have made a good start, which since he was third for a short while is a statement that might stand up to examination, and then he had visibility problems for the first five laps. After that it was a matter of concentration and cold, of not letting the latter affect the former.

After his 'bad start', Stoner followed his team-mate Dovizioso past Lorenzo at Woodcote, the Hondas putting the power down out of the corner with astonishing ease and breezing past the Yamaha. Just to rub it in, Simoncelli also got past Jorge before the end of the first lap. At the start of the second lap Casey got round the outside of Dovi going into Farm and the race was effectively won. That left an interesting three-way tussle for second. Dovizioso made himself so difficult to pass that Lorenzo and Simoncelli both crashed while looking

M POWER
BMW
M
M PO

for an opening. Andrea went deep on the brakes, consequently carrying less corner speed, but then used the Honda's ability to get the power down and frustrate his pursuers.

The departure of Jorge and Marco left third place up for grabs. Nicky Hayden was an early candidate but a massive near-highside crash dropped him behind Spies and Edwards. When Spies crashed that left Colin Edwards in a most unlikely rostrum position just eight days after having his collarbone pinned. The weather certainly reduced the physical demands on him, but it was an heroic display that lifted the spirits of the crowd and his Tech 3 team after Cal Crutchlow's accident in qualifying. The Texan's real problem wasn't his collarbone but torn muscles in his side that were giving him real pain as well as restricting his movement on the bike. He'd treated the whole weekend like any other GP, qualifying eighth and making some major suspension changes for race day, and he kept everyone entertained along the way.

Colin's bravery kept the Yamaha flag flying ahead of all the Ducatis and a very lively Alvaro

Left A tricky start. Toni Elias takes a wide line, Jorge Lorenzo leads Casey Stoner

Above Ben Spies was the first rider to fall, followed by team-mate Lorenzo

'I WAS JUST HAPPY TO STAY ON THE BIKE. IT WAS INCREDIBLY COLD AND I WAS SO NERVOUS'
CASEY STONER

Bautista on the Suzuki. Bologna's chance of a rostrum disappeared with Hayden's massive moment, while Valentino Rossi's anticipated charge through the field just never happened. He'd started from 13th after his worst qualifying since he broke his hand at Valencia in 2007. Even more puzzling, rookie Karel Abraham had qualified top Ducati, in sixth. The Czech put his improvement down to being able to push in the final stages of qualifying for the first time.

Afterwards Rossi's crew simply said that they hadn't given Valentino the bike he needed. The contrast with all the optimism after the Catalunya race just a week earlier was marked, but surely he should have been able to fight for the rostrum in the wet, just as he would certainly have done in Jerez but for that incident with Stoner. It didn't happen, though, leaving Valentino and his crew wondering how they had been comprehensively outperformed by the other side of the garage. Sixth at the flag might not look too bad, but the old litany so familiar from Stoner's time on the Ducati resurfaced: understeer and lack of front-end feel plus inability to get heat into the tyres. Rossi admitted that the weather had made things look better for him than they really were, and that once he had big gaps both in front and behind he took a safety-first approach. The really bad news was that Valentino didn't expect any major improvements until Brno, at the earliest.

Rossi, Hayden and the test team all agreed that the 2012 chassis would be a considerable improvement, especially the behaviour of the rear.

Above Rossi was expected to take advantage of the conditions; it didn't happen

Below Colin Edwards about to take third from Nicky Hayden and revenge for Jerez

PRIVATE PLANS

Following the announcement of the Claiming Rule Team regulations after the Portuguese GP, the paddock had been waiting for the list of teams accepted to race under the new regulations. After a few weeks' delay, it finally appeared after Silverstone. The six names on the list were all current Moto2 entrants: BQR, which runs under Blusens sponsorship in 125 and Moto2; Paddock Racing, long-time entrants of Thomas Luthi with Interwetten sponsorship; Forward Racing; Andrea Iannone's Speed Master squad; Marc VDS; and Kiefer Racing, who run Stefan Bradl with Viessman as the sponsor. JiR, who run Alex de Angelis, had been expected to declare their interest but were understood to have withdrawn.

This list, it was pointed out, contained teams who had been accepted for MotoGP and who would be new to the class. They would not necessarily run as Claiming Rule Teams, but they could, as Paddock Racing was known to intend, decide to lease satellite bikes. The only team actually to have put a bike on track so far was Marc VDS who, in co-operation with their Moto2 chassis supplier Suter, tested a BMW-powered machine at Mugello with Mika Kallio riding.

The announcement also stated that other factory entries would continue to be evaluated. However, the much-touted entry – by some sections of the UK press, if no-one else – from Norton had not materialised. As a motorcycle maker Norton would, of course, have had to race as a constructor with an allowance of 21 litres of petrol for the race and nine engines for the season (the six-engine rule only kicks in after a dry-weather win). Any team not wanting to put their technology at risk of investigation could also elect to enter as a constructor.

It was now a question of how many of these prospective MotoGP entrants could – and would – come up with the sponsorship needed to get on the grid in 2012.

Above Mark Marquez, Stefan Bradl and Aleix Espargaro on the Moto2 rostrum. At this point in the season it was expected that the first two would move up to MotoGP for 2012 but things changed

Unfortunately, it could not be bolted on to the current mounting points cast into the engine cases. With an allocation of just six engines for the season, the implications were obvious – not a comfortable feeling with the home race at Mugello only three weeks away.

Jorge Lorenzo was sanguine about losing his points lead, now casting himself in the role of the hound rather than the hare. He said the crash had been his mistake, and it was doubly galling as the Yamaha did look capable of giving Stoner some competition on a circuit where its ability to get into a corner better and maintain high corner speeds should have negated the Honda's strengths in putting power down in the lower gears. None of which made Stoner's inexorable progress any less impressive – or predictable. All those fans might have been shivering in the cold and wet, much like the riders, but they knew they'd just seen something special: a racer at the peak of his powers, riding the best bike on the grid in impossible conditions, and making it look easy.

Right Colin Edwards reacts in typically serious fashion to his first rostrum since Donington Park 2009

BRITISH GP
SILVERSTONE

ROUND 6
June 12

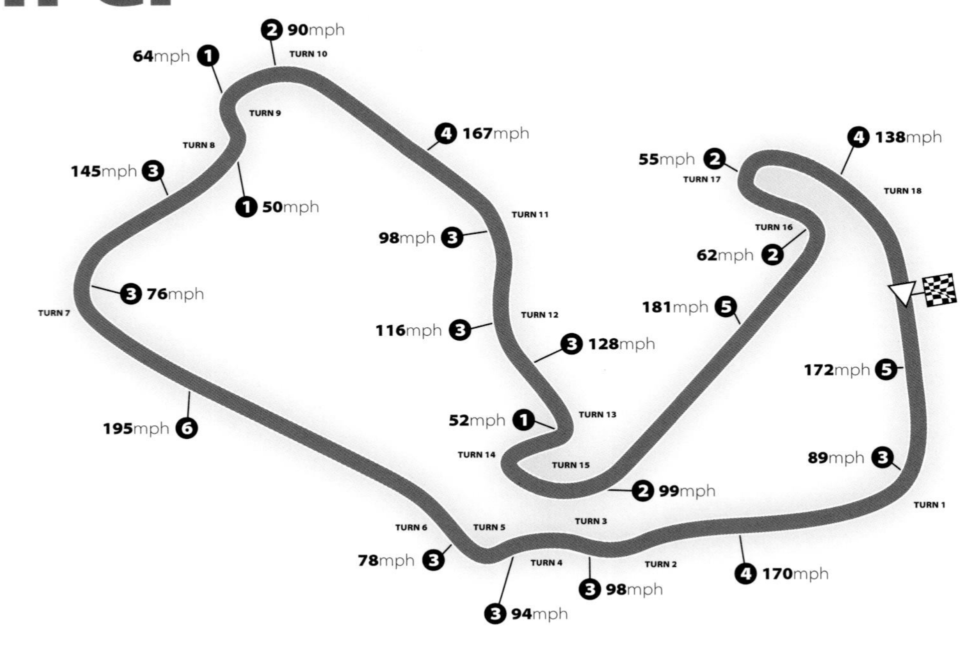

RACE RESULTS

CIRCUIT LENGTH 3.667 miles
NO. OF LAPS 20
RACE DISTANCE 73.340 miles
WEATHER Wet, 11°C
TRACK TEMPERATURE 10°C
WINNER Casey Stoner
FASTEST LAP 2m 21.432s, 93.330mph, Nicky Hayden
LAP RECORD 2m 03.526s, 105.874mph, Jorge Lorenzo, 2010

QUALIFYING

	Rider	Nationality	Team	Qualifying	Pole +	Gap
1	Stoner	AUS	Repsol Honda Team	2m 02.020s		
2	Simoncelli	ITA	San Carlo Honda Gresini	2m 02.208s	0.188s	0.188s
3	Lorenzo	SPA	Yamaha Factory Racing	2m 02.237s	0.217s	0.029s
4	Spies	USA	Yamaha Factory Racing	2m 02.677s	0.657s	0.440s
5	Dovizioso	ITA	Repsol Honda Team	2m 03.212s	1.192s	0.535s
6	Abraham	CZE	Cardion AB Motoracing	2m 04.151s	2.131s	0.939s
7	Hayden	USA	Ducati Team	2m 04.304s	2.284s	0.153s
8	Edwards	USA	Monster Yamaha Tech 3	2m 04.508s	2.488s	0.204s
9	Bautista	SPA	Rizla Suzuki MotoGP	2m 04.520s	2.500s	0.012s
10	De Puniet	FRA	Pramac Racing Team	2m 04.589s	2.569s	0.069s
11	Aoyama	JPN	San Carlo Honda Gresini	2m 04.919s	2.899s	0.330s
12	Barbera	SPA	Mapfre Aspar Team	2m 05.164s	3.144s	0.245s
13	Rossi	ITA	Ducati Team	2m 05.781s	3.761s	0.617s
14	Elias	SPA	LCR Honda MotoGP	2m 05.862s	3.842s	0.081s
15	Capirossi	ITA	Pramac Racing Team	2m 06.256s	4.236s	0.394s
16	Crutchlow	GBR	Monster Yamaha Tech 3	2m 07.911s	5.891s	1.655s

FINISHERS

1 CASEY STONER His fourth win took him to the top of the table, but he had early problems with vision and cold tyres, and then with the cold weather after he'd been out in front on his own. Took team-mate Dovizioso on the second lap and was never headed, opening up a massive lead but only relaxing in the last five laps, by which time he had a 15s lead.

2 ANDREA DOVIZIOSO Led the first lap but couldn't do anything about his team-mate. Frustrated Lorenzo and Simoncelli with his late braking and, once they'd fallen, had a lonely race to the rostrum.

3 COLIN EDWARDS The story of the weekend. Eight days after having his collarbone pinned he scored the first satellite-team rostrum of the season. Eighth in qualifying was impressive enough, but a big set-up gamble and experience paid off and turned what looked like a nightmare weekend for his team into a triumph.

4 NICKY HAYDEN Had a good set-up and thought he had rostrum potential. But for a massive near-highside on lap three that lost him two places, he might have spoiled Edwards' day. Still, he set the fastest lap of the race, the first time he'd done that on a Ducati.

5 ALVARO BAUTISTA Equalled his best MotoGP finishes of 2010, at Catalunya and Malaysia, races run in very different conditions. Felt fit and competitive for the first time since his Qatar crash, making a couple of early passes as well as benefiting from the misfortune of others, then held off Rossi's late pressure.

6 VALENTINO ROSSI The result looks better than the weekend's reality. Penultimate Ducati in qualifying, and then the expected charge through the field, as in the wet at Jerez, never materialised. The better performance of his team-mate was also a matter of concern, so blame was equally apportioned between rider, team and bike.

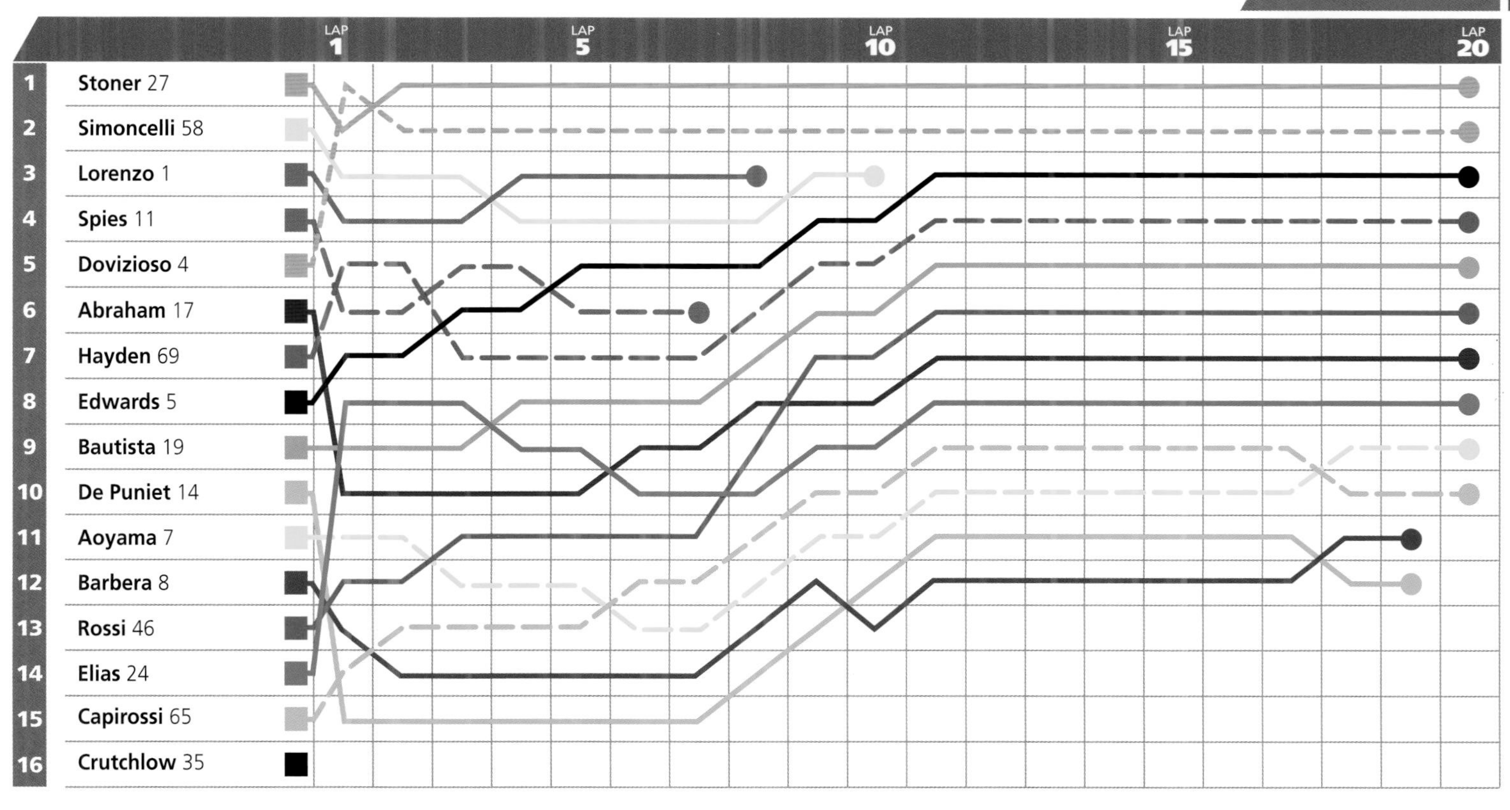

RACE

	Rider	Motorcycle	Race Time	Time +	Fastest Lap	Av Speed	
1	Stoner	Honda	47m 53.459s		2m 21.723s	91.894mph	ws/ws
2	Dovizioso	Honda	48m 08.618s	15.159s	2m 22.723s	91.412mph	ws/ws
3	Edwards	Yamaha	48m 14.939s	21.480s	2m 21.823s	91.212mph	ws/ws
4	Hayden	Ducati	48m 20.443s	26.984s	2m 21.432s	91.040mph	ws/ws
5	Bautista	Suzuki	48m 29.028s	35.569s	2m 23.025s	90.771mph	ws/ws
6	Rossi	Ducati	48m 57.985s	1m 04.526s	2m 24.421s	89.876mph	ws/ws
7	Abraham	Ducati	49m 26.109s	1m 32.650s	2m 25.182s	89.024mph	ws/ws
8	Elias	Honda	49m 45.397s	1m 51.938s	2m 26.302s	88.448mph	ws/ws
9	Aoyama	Honda	49m 45.809s	1m 52.350s	2m 25.287s	88.437mph	ws/ws
10	Capirossi	Ducati	49m 56.771s	2m 03.312s	2m 27.843s	88.113mph	ws/ws
11	Barbera	Ducati	48m 10.582s	1 lap	2m 27.485s	86.783mph	ws/ws
12	De Puniet	Ducati	48m 13.094s	1 lap	2m 29.065s	86.707mph	ws/ws
NF	Simoncelli	Honda	24m 04.277s	10 laps	2m 22.189s	91.414mph	ws/ws
NF	Lorenzo	Yamaha	19m 18.287s	12 laps	2m 22.752s	91.189mph	ws/ws
NF	Spies	Yamaha	17m 14.283s	13 laps	2m 25.292s	89.356mph	ws/ws

CHAMPIONSHIP

	Rider	Team	Points
1	Stoner	Repsol Honda Team	116
2	Lorenzo	Yamaha Factory Racing	98
3	Dovizioso	Repsol Honda Team	83
4	Rossi	Ducati Team	68
5	Pedrosa	Repsol Honda Team	61
6	Hayden	Ducati Team	60
7	Aoyama	San Carlo Honda Gresini	43
8	Edwards	Monster Yamaha Tech 3	37
9	Spies	Yamaha Factory Racing	36
10	Abraham	Cardion AB Motoracing	33
11	Simoncelli	San Carlo Honda Gresini	32
12	Barbera	Mapfre Aspar Team	31
13	Crutchlow	Monster Yamaha Tech 3	30
14	Elias	LCR Honda MotoGP	28
15	Bautista	Rizla Suzuki MotoGP	22
16	Capirossi	Pramac Racing Team	22
17	De Puniet	Pramac Racing Team	10
18	Hopkins	Rizla Suzuki MotoGP	6

7 KAREL ABRAHAM Astonished the paddock by being top Ducati in qualifying. Nervous on race-day morning and made a mess of the start, then couldn't match Rossi in the race. Nevertheless, went tenth and best satellite Ducati in the championship.

8 TONI ELIAS Actually wanted a wet race because, as usual, he couldn't make the Honda work in the dry. The key was a great start but he ran wide at the first corner. Fortunately able to get back on track in eighth and, after a scrap in the first ten laps, climbed back to eighth for his best result of the season so far.

9 HIROSHI AOYAMA Took a while to get a feel for the bike on a track where he hadn't raced before (due to a back injury sustained in warm-up at last year's event). Not surprisingly, he was happy to finish and learn something about the wet set-up.

10 LORIS CAPIROSSI Lack of feeling with the front in dry qualifying as well as the race. Never got the front up to temperature and only ever thought about finishing rather than racing.

11 HECTOR BARBERA The team went too soft on the suspension – with a full tank he was nearly bottoming the forks every time he touched the brakes and the front was tucking on every corner. If it had been a practice session he said he would have come in after one lap, but managed to stay upright and score some points.

12 RANDY DE PUNIET At least he finished, for only the second time this year, but he described it as the worst race of his life. A big crash in warm-up didn't help, but the old front-end problems were there in the wet as well as the dry: 'I came close to crashing at least two times a lap.'

NON-FINISHERS

MARCO SIMONCELLI Started from the front row for the fourth consecutive race and it seemed like that elusive first rostrum was within sight. Running third and looking for a way past Dovizioso, however, he lost the front on the brakes.

JORGE LORENZO Lost the back on lap nine going into Copse Corner. He'd led off the start and looked to be able to go with Stoner, then couldn't find a way past Dovizioso. It was Jorge's first DNF in 25 races and lost him the championship lead.

BEN SPIES Lost the front going into the first corner on lap eight, hitting the fence hard and severely damaging his back protector. Taken to hospital for a check-up but thankfully no damage.

NON-STARTERS

CAL CRUTCHLOW Yet another victim of cold-tyre syndrome. Crashed early in qualifying and broke his left collarbone as well as collecting a nasty concussion. Multiple breaks were pinned the Tuesday after the race.

DANI PEDROSA Still not recovered from his collarbone operation after the French Grand Prix. The Repsol Honda team decided not to replace him here.

DUTCH TT

TT CIRCUIT ASSEN

ROUND 7

June 25

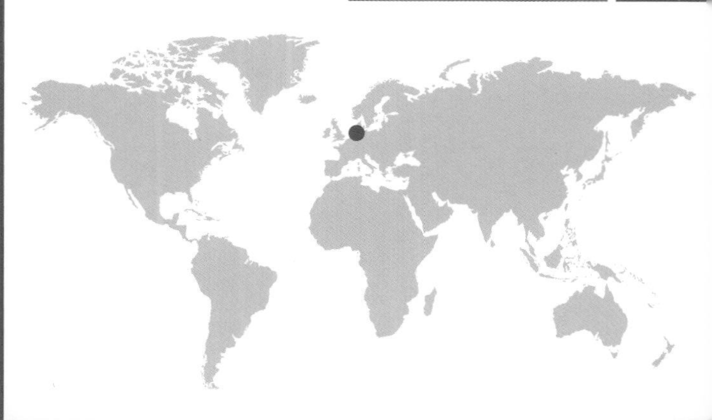

THE ICE MAN COMETH

Ben Spies broke the stranglehold of the four 'Aliens' with his maiden victory, but Stoner extended his championship lead

All of the season's talking points got a good airing at Assen: tyres, Ducati's dilemmas and Marco Simoncelli's riding. The debates nearly, but not quite, overshadowed a breakthrough performance by Ben Spies. For the first time in the 800cc MotoGP era a dry race was won by someone other than the 'Aliens' – Valentino Rossi, Jorge Lorenzo, Casey Stoner or Dani Pedrosa. It was a fittingly dominant victory for Yamaha as they celebrated the 50th year in Grand Prix racing with a retro red and white livery and in the presence of many of their champions.

The only subjects that received a proper airing on the first day of practice were theoretical. Exploding Moto2 machines left enough oil on track for the afternoon's session to be cancelled, so the paddock had a little fret over whether Ducati's move in bringing in what was effectively their 2012 bike with its 1,000cc motor de-stroked to 800cc was strictly within the rules that severely restrict testing. These rules apply only to machines eligible for MotoGP, and as the 1,000cc bike was not legal to race then Ducati did nothing outside the letter of the law. And as it didn't appear to be any faster than the 2011 bike, nobody was seriously bothered about whether it contravened the spirit of those laws either.

When the specially extended third free practice started there was plenty to talk about. All three Repsol Hondas hit the deck in quick succession on a cold, drying track. Cue much muttering about the Bridgestone control tyres. Stoner went so far as to say the session should have been red-flagged. When Loris Capirossi had a big crash in qualifying and put himself out of the race the situation came to a head. Bridgestone were prepared to ship in a new rear slick with a softer left side, as is permitted by the regulations when safety is compromised. The truck was ready to leave

Above Lorenzo and Simoncelli run for their machines after the coming together on lap one

Below Ben Spies knew the field had been split by the Simoncelli/Lorenzo crash and took advantage to pull out a two-and-a-half-second lead by the end of the first lap

Germany when it was turned back as the teams weren't in unanimous agreement. Some riders felt their safety was not compromised and were happy to race with the original allocation. Given that track temperatures were at times 30 degrees cooler than the previous year it is not surprising that many riders had to abandon their usual preference for the harder front tyre. This resulted in both Tech 3 Yamahas having serious problems: by the end of the race their fronts looked as bad as the old qualifiers used to and Crutchlow had to pit to change his. Andrea Dovizioso was also affected by front-tyre wear.

So who didn't want the softer rears? Obviously not Suzuki, who suffered from their old problems with generating grip in cold conditions. Marco Simoncelli was the only top rider who used the harder front tyre in the race, so it is fair to assume that the Gresini team didn't think there was a safety issue. Ben Spies, who was narrowly pipped for pole by Simoncelli, was more worried about having to use the softer front.

They nearly didn't have to worry about the choice at all. Most of the MotoGP field went to the grid on wet tyres after rain-affected 125 and Moto2 races. Some frantic spanner work after the sighting lap then put everyone back on slicks for the race. All the cold-tyre problems manifested themselves in left-handers and, sure enough, first time round at Turn 5, the slowest corner on the track, Simoncelli gave it too much gas and flicked himself off and into the path of Jorge Lorenzo. Both riders fell but were able to restart.

Spies saw the incident on one of the big screens and seized the chance to escape, promptly ripping four seconds out of the pursuing Repsol Hondas in three laps. From then on Ben controlled things, pressing harder if Stoner got within three-and-a-half seconds, and went on to win with ease. Well, that's what it looked like from the side of the track. It was the sort of demolition job at which Ben had specialised in both the World and American Superbike Championships.

There was a danger that Spies's first win in MotoGP would be overshadowed by the latest instalment of the Marco Simoncelli saga. That would have been unjust, because this was the performance we've been waiting for from the Silent One. The American's start to the

Below Colin Edwards ran into serious front tyre issues and was the last rider to be passed by Lorenzo on his charge back through the field

season was puzzlingly subdued, but he could have been on the rostrum at Jerez, while a crew error at Estoril ruined his chances there. Le Mans? Just get that one out of the way. Spies's first rostrum came in Catalunya, the first front row at Assen. Was the win a surprise? A look at the times from qualifying shows that the race should have been between Ben and Marco; indeed, but for the yellow flags for Capirossi's crash, Spies might have been on pole. In the race he was in front when Simoncelli took Lorenzo out, and then Casey said he couldn't have matched Ben's pace (or Marco's), no matter what. Like most of the field, the mixed conditions on Thursday and Friday plus a wet warm-up didn't help, and in Stoner's case neither did a big Friday morning crash. The Aussie was never quite on the pace of the front two all weekend – by his standards third on the grid and a distant second in the race meant a bad day at the office, as had happened in Portugal – but he emerged with an increased championship lead and a smile on his face.

The other riders were more sympathetic to Simoncelli than expected. Casey refused to take a direct dig, saying he thought it was best to stay away from him on track. 'I think I'll take Casey's advice,' said Spies. Andrea Dovizioso, historically a major critic, thought this was a racing incident that could have happened to anyone. The dissenter, as usual, was Lorenzo, who thought it was time for a suspension.

'AT LEAST WE'VE WON A RACE NOW!'

BEN SPIES

A TALE OF TWO DUCATIS

After they tested Ducati's 2012 bike at Mugello, both Valentino Rossi and Nicky Hayden declared it a major improvement over the 2011 Desmosedici GP11. The layout of the GP12 is sufficiently different from the current bike to preclude improvements, specifically to the rear of the bike, from being incorporated. Nevertheless, after the disaster of Silverstone it was decided to bring the new bike to Assen for Rossi and to the Sachsenring for Hayden.

To make it legal under current regulations, the 1,000cc motor was destroked to 800cc, a modification so major it almost guaranteed the two bikes would behave very differently on a racetrack. Also, it meant that Rossi had to take another engine from his allocation of six. The crankcases and cylinder heads incorporated the mountings for the rear suspension system and were obviously very different bike to bike. Given that Hayden lost one of the motors from his allocation of six early on, this decision suggested that the Ducati team were quite prepared to take a penalty later in the year, a prospect that didn't worry Rossi: 'If we start from the back of the grid, we start from the back of the grid.'

It is almost unprecedented for a factory team to make these sorts of changes during the season, and underlines the fact that the situation with the 2011 bike is so serious that Ducati is effectively just testing for 2012.

Opposite top Simoncelli, here passing temporary team-mate Akiyoshi, cut back up the field despite the damage

Opposite bottom Spies ends up on the top step in what was his 28th Grand Prix start

Below Valentino Rossi raced the 2012 chassis, but it didn't seem to make much difference

DUTCH TT

TT CIRCUIT ASSEN

ROUND 7
June 25

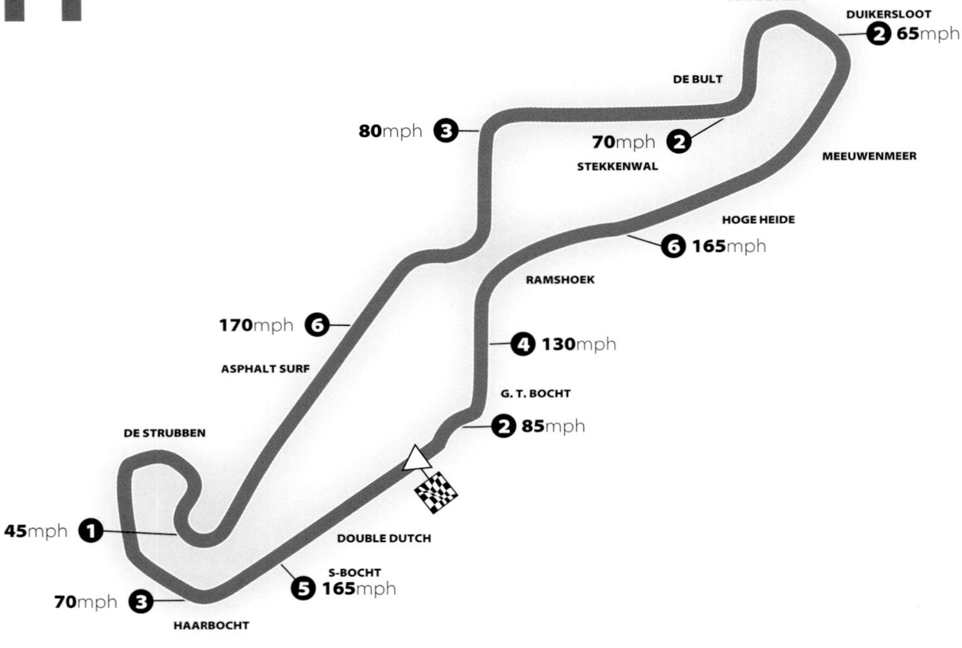

RACE RESULTS

CIRCUIT LENGTH 2.830 miles
NO. OF LAPS 26
RACE DISTANCE 73.592 miles
WEATHER Dry, 14°C
TRACK TEMPERATURE 16°C
WINNER Ben Spies
FASTEST LAP 1m 35.240s, 106.689mph, Ben Spies (Record)
LAP RECORD 1m 34.525s, 106.455mph, Dani Pedrosa, 2010

QUALIFYING

	Rider	Nationality	Team	Qualifying	Pole +	Gap
1	Simoncelli	ITA	San Carlo Honda Gresini	1m 34.718s		
2	Spies	USA	Yamaha Factory Racing	1m 34.727s	0.009s	0.009s
3	Stoner	AUS	Repsol Honda Team	1m 35.008s	0.290s	0.281s
4	Lorenzo	SPA	Yamaha Factory Racing	1m 35.143s	0.425s	0.135s
5	Dovizioso	ITA	Repsol Honda Team	1m 35.244s	0.526s	0.101s
6	Crutchlow	GBR	Monster Yamaha Tech 3	1m 35.329s	0.611s	0.085s
7	Abraham	CZE	Cardion AB Motoracing	1m 35.742s	1.024s	0.413s
8	Edwards	USA	Monster Yamaha Tech 3	1m 35.818s	1.100s	0.076s
9	Hayden	USA	Ducati Team	1m 35.866s	1.148s	0.048s
10	De Puniet	FRA	Pramac Racing Team	1m 36.435s	1.717s	0.569s
11	Rossi	ITA	Ducati Team	1m 36.564s	1.846s	0.129s
12	Aoyama	JPN	Repsol Honda Team	1m 36.580s	1.862s	0.016s
13	Barbera	SPA	Mapfre Aspar Team	1m 36.590s	1.872s	0.010s
14	Bautista	SPA	Rizla Suzuki MotoGP	1m 36.820s	2.102s	0.230s
15	Capirossi	ITA	Pramac Racing Team	1m 37.130s	2.412s	0.310s
16	Elias	SPA	LCR Honda MotoGP	1m 37.651s	2.933s	0.521s
17	Akiyoshi	JPN	San Carlo Honda Gresini	1m 39.006s	4.288s	1.355s

FINISHERS

1 BEN SPIES First win in MotoGP, the first in the dry by a 'non-Alien' in the 800cc era, and reminiscent of his domination in US racing: perfect lap after lap, always with a little in hand to push when Stoner closed. And the fact it was at Assen, in Yamaha's red and white 50th anniversary livery, made it all the more special.

2 CASEY STONER Sore after a heavy crash on Friday morning, unhappy about his set-up after qualifying and honest enough to say he couldn't have caught Spies. By his standards that's a bad day; but just like his bad weekend in Portugal, it merely meant a trip to one of the lower steps on the rostrum.

3 ANDREA DOVIZIOSO Happy with third after hitting problems with the right side of the front tyre. Second after the first-lap incident and stayed with his team-mate for ten laps until he felt a vibration from the rear of the bike. Dovi then controlled the gap to Rossi.

4 VALENTINO ROSSI Came to Assen with a completely new motorcycle based on the chassis being tested for 2012. Not surprisingly, mixed conditions hampered its development, and although Vale was fast in wet practice the team was clearly flat-out trying to find the feel he needs. Under the circumstances, fourth was a good result.

5 NICKY HAYDEN Only used a new frame, not the completely new bike of his team-mate. Happy with the feel in the opening laps but made a couple of mistakes, including one run-on when he lost the front. That let Edwards past, but he was able to regain the place. Best dry result of the year, but refused to get excited about fifth.

6 JORGE LORENZO Taken down when Simoncelli crashed on the first lap, but the engine didn't stop and Jorge was able to get back in the action. He then put in a determined ride through the field and with another lap would have caught Hayden. Lost vital ground to Stoner in the championship.

7 COLIN EDWARDS Like his team-mate, Colin ran into front-tyre problems. Also had trouble with arm pump as he was forced to compensate for his lack of core strength. Things got so bad he contemplated pulling in but, typically, hung tough for a good result.

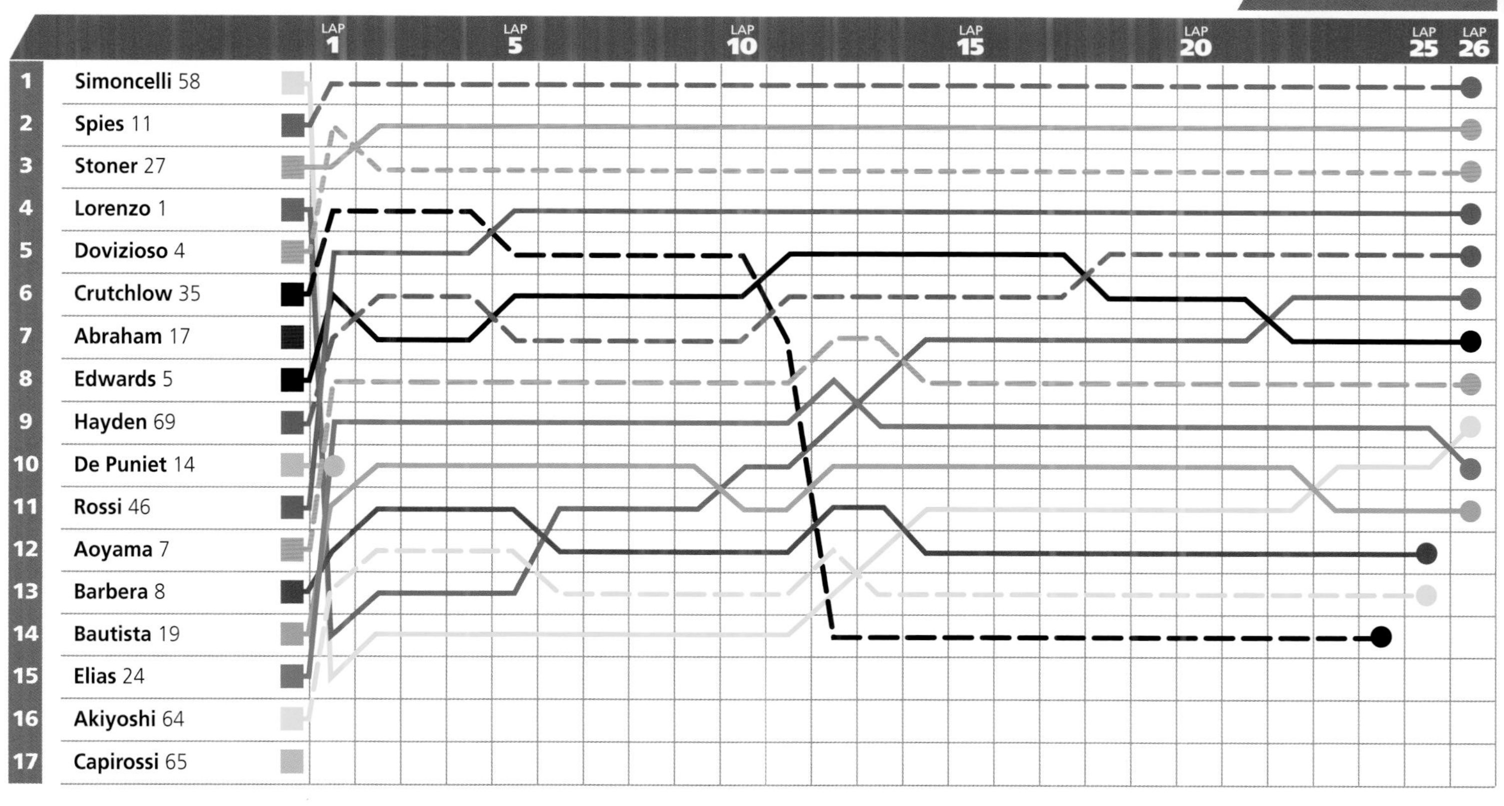

RACE

	Rider	Motorcycle	Race Time	Time +	Fastest Lap	Av Speed	
1	Spies	Yamaha	41m 44.659s		1m 35.240s	105.472mph	S/M
2	Stoner	Honda	41m 44.659s	7.697s	1m 35.422s	105.149mph	S/M
3	Dovizioso	Honda	42m 12.165s	27.506s	1m 35.673s	104.326mph	S/M
4	Rossi	Ducati	42m 15.343s	30.684s	1m 36.700s	104.195mph	S/M
5	Hayden	Ducati	42m 27.831s	43.172s	1m 36.764s	103.685mph	S/M
6	Lorenzo	Yamaha	42m 29.195s	44.536s	1m 35.641s	103.629mph	S/M
7	Edwards	Yamaha	42m 52.771s	1m 08.112s	1m 36.320s	102.680mph	S/M
8	Aoyama	Honda	42m 55.412s	1m 10.753s	1m 37.561s	102.575mph	S/M
9	Simoncelli	Honda	43m 09.584s	1m 24.925s	1m 35.962s	102.013mph	S/M
10	Elias	Honda	43m 10.875s	1m 26.216s	1m 38.516s	101.962mph	S/M
11	Bautista	Suzuki	43m 23.125s	1m 38.466s	1m 38.567s	101.482mph	S/M
12	Barbera	Ducati	42m 11.017s	1 lap	1m 39.040s	100.359mph	S/M
13	Akiyoshi	Honda	42m 58.437s	1 lap	1m 40.512s	98.513mph	S/M
14	Crutchlow	Yamaha	43m 07.755s	2 laps	1m 36.727s	94.232mph	S/M
NF	De Puniet	Ducati	1m 52.494s	25 laps	–	90.319mph	S/M
NF	Abraham	Ducati					M/M

CHAMPIONSHIP

	Rider	Team	Points
1	Stoner	Repsol Honda Team	136
2	Lorenzo	Yamaha Factory Racing	108
3	Dovizioso	Repsol Honda Team	99
4	Rossi	Ducati Team	81
5	Hayden	Ducati Team	71
6	Pedrosa	Repsol Honda Team	61
7	Spies	Yamaha Factory Racing	61
8	Aoyama	Repsol Honda Team	51
9	Edwards	Monster Yamaha Tech 3	46
10	Simoncelli	San Carlo Honda Gresini	39
11	Barbera	Mapfre Aspar Team MotoGP	35
12	Elias	LCR Honda MotoGP	34
13	Abraham	Cardion AB Motoracing	33
14	Crutchlow	Monster Yamaha Tech 3	32
15	Bautista	Rizla Suzuki MotoGP	27
16	Capirossi	Pramac Racing Team	22
17	De Puniet	Pramac Racing Team	10
18	Hopkins	Rizla Suzuki MotoGP	6
19	Akiyoshi	San Carlo Honda Gresini	3

8 HIROSHI AOYAMA Replaced Pedrosa in the Repsol team. Had a high-speed crash on Friday morning which meant sharp back pain on race day. Unsurprisingly, given his recent back injury, he was a little tentative at the start but his lap times were consistent from mid-race and he improved on his qualifying position by four places.

9 MARCO SIMONCELLI Started from pole but flicked himself off in the first left-hander and took Lorenzo down. Had to push start his Honda but then laid down some impressive lap times. Used the word 'naive' about his crash and apologised to Jorge. Looked very deflated back in his garage.

10 TONI ELIAS Despite another horrible qualifying session, including a crash, he made a decent fist of race day. Got a really good start and was up to ninth until he had to avoid Abraham's crash at the end of the first lap. Rear grip still his major issue, but at least Toni was content with this result.

11 ALVARO BAUTISTA The softer rear tyre was much too hard for the Suzuki, which never likes cold conditions. Alvaro simply couldn't get any heat into, and therefore grip from, the rear slick. Not happy when the emergency swap to softer rubber was vetoed.

12 HECTOR BARBERA Suffered the indignity of being lapped. Never managed to get any heat in the tyres in qualifying or the race despite some radical experiments with chassis geometry. Keeping it upright under braking was hard enough, never mind leaning it over.

13 KOUSUKE AKIYOSHI Just as at the previous Assen GP, Honda's senior test rider rode as a replacement, this time for Aoyama, who moved up to Pedrosa's factory bike.

14 CAL CRUTCHLOW A brilliant start followed by his first extended run at the front of a MotoGP race. Was having no problems staying with Rossi when he was forced to pit for a harder front tyre; he'd started with the softer option and the injured right shoulder couldn't cope. Went out again to collect a couple of points.

NON-FINISHERS

RANDY DE PUNIET Ran wide at Turn 1 on the second lap and was flicked off. Blamed himself, despite the lack of dry testing time, because he thought he could and should have been inside the top ten.

KAREL ABRAHAM Pushed on to the still wet kerbs by Aoyama at the chicane on the first lap, which resulted in the inevitable crash and a very painful finger. One of only two riders who started with the harder front tyre.

NON-STARTERS

LORIS CAPIROSSI Another victim of an off-throttle highside. Went down hard at the end of qualifying and was hit by his own bike, dislocating his right shoulder and taking a big hit to his back and ribs.

DANI PEDROSA Still recovering after yet another operation to re-attach a bone fragment from the collarbone he broke in France.

ITALIAN GP
MUGELLO
ROUND 8
July 3

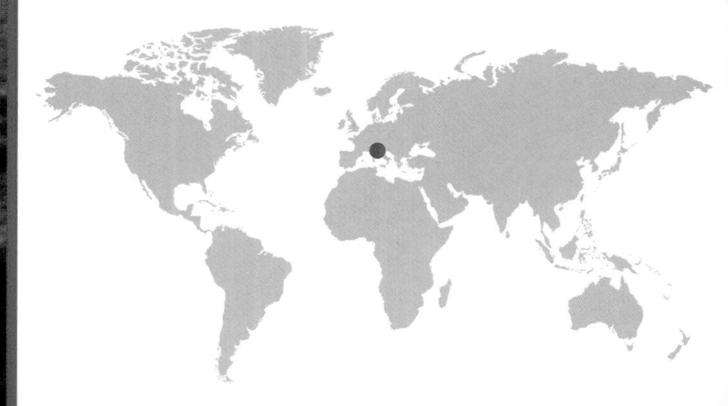

RETURN OF THE HAMMER

Jorge Lorenzo reminded everyone why he's World Champion, as Ducati foundered in front of their home crowd

The year 2011 was Italy's 150th birthday, and Mugello was spruced up to celebrate: new tarmac, kerbs painted in the colour of the Italian flag, and a brand-new stylish grandstand on the home straight. All that was needed was for Valentino Rossi, in his first race with Ducati on home soil, to win at the track where he'd won every year from 2002 to 2008. Not long ago you'd have put money on it. Not any more.

The absence of Jerry Burgess, back home in Australia for family reasons, didn't help; neither did the weather. Rossi had both bikes stop on him in the first free practice, and then the afternoon session was all but wiped out by rain, as was the last 20 minutes of qualifying. Despite the lack of track time, one thing was now horribly obvious: the 11.1 version of the Ducati, having had a GP's worth of testing in Holland, and now running on a track where the 1,000cc version had tested successfully, was not going to be the answer Rossi and his fans were hoping for. In every session Valentino was 1.8 seconds slower than the fastest rider and he still couldn't get any feel out of the front. A selection of quotes:

'We don't improve a lot.'

'We don't understand the bike.'

'With Jerry is better.'

'I cannot push the front.'

With very little in the way of good news coming out of the Ducati camp, Italian attention turned to Marco Simoncelli. He probably thought he was in for a gentle start to the weekend at the Thursday press conference; he hadn't counted on Dani Pedrosa, back in action for the first time since the Le Mans incident and not in a conciliatory mood. Pedrosa kicked it off outside the press conference room when he refused Marco's proffered hand. It wasn't

Left Lorenzo leads Stoner and Dovizioso through Mugello's high-speed swoops

subtle either; it was both arms raised and a solid 'No'.

Dani warmed up on a journalist who felt he had to enquire if the stories about him going bowling and riding a supermoto bike after his first collarbone operation were true. 'Do you think I'm stupid?' came the forceful response. And then came the main course: Simoncelli. What did Dani think about the criticism of Marco's riding style after Assen? 'Is someone still in doubt about this? Unbelievable… On his head there is nothing but hair.'

Marco's retort, after various references to Alberto Puig's comments after Le Mans and some straight talking on Dani's blog, was simply: 'The things he and his manager say are stupid. It's better to say nothing.'

Jorge Lorenzo had been dealing with Simoncelli fallout as well. An interview in an Italian magazine was inflammatory enough for one of Super Sic's team to come and find Jorge to explain that it wasn't a true reflection of Marco's views and that he really wanted to calm his riding down. 'I would prefer him to come to the Safety Commission and say this,' was Jorge's considered reaction.

The race, thankfully run in glorious sunshine, transcended the – admittedly entertaining – squabbling. Lorenzo reminded everyone how world champions ride. After being outqualified by his team-mate, Jorge hunted down two Repsol Hondas, passing both on the frightening downhill sweeps of Casanova-Savelli: this is the place that gave Rossi the inspiration for that open-mouthed expression which decorated the top of his crash helmet a couple of years ago. Ben Spies added a little more joy to Yamaha's weekend with a last-corner pass on Simoncelli for fourth, an incisive inside move, and then he made a point of saying what a clean race it had been.

Lorenzo described the win as even better than his home win at Jerez, but second-placed Andrea Dovizioso seemed even happier. He pushed his way past Casey Stoner late on, then climbed the wire on the slow-down lap to celebrate with his fans. Dovi later reverted to his usual family-man self and proudly showed his little daughter to the cameras in *parc fermé*. Stoner wasn't too happy. He knew he'd had the bike and the pace to win, but a decision to increase the tyre pressures to cope with higher temperatures had led to overheating. Casey had no complaints about his

Above Jorge Lorenzo was back on the 2010 chassis and confident again

Below Dani Pedrosa returned from injury and he wasn't happy

but he got into the first corner of the second lap way too hot and took a trip across the giant gravel trap. Rossi did end up sixth but he was a long way back, and he'd spent an inordinate amount of time behind Barbera and Bautista before making any progress.

All of Ducati's top brass – owners and management – were present, and one can only imagine what was said behind closed doors when Rossi had the chance. He even missed the Safety Commission on Friday because he was 'too busy'. Still we get talk of the bike being 'different' and the need to 'understand'. The team put a positive gloss on the weekend but it needed some creative manipulation of the numbers to claim an improvement. The truth is that Rossi's best lap was 0.9s slower than Lorenzo's record fastest race lap, and over the 23 laps Valentino lost 1.15s per lap. Better than qualifying, as we've come to expect, but still a long way off what's needed.

By contrast, there was an air of renewed confidence in the Yamaha camp. Jorge had won for the first time since Portugal and set his first fastest lap of the season. Going back to the 2010 chassis after Le Mans had given him the feel he'd been missing, and the confidence to go round the outside of two Hondas at Casanova-Savelli. 'X-fuera' at his best.

Above Spies cuts inside Simoncelli to take fourth place in the final corner

Opposite The fans under the rostrum refused to disperse until Valentino took a bow

Below Dovizioso was top Italian and top Honda rider in second place

team-mate's move, however; quite the reverse, and he congratulated Dovi fulsomely afterwards.

One strange thing was that the race was conducted in relative silence compared to the noise over 80,000 Italians usually make. They eventually got excited about Dovizioso's race, but nothing any Ducati managed gave them anything to cheer about. It had looked like Nicky Hayden, the fastest Duke through practice and qualifying, was going to go with Spies and Simoncelli,

'I COULDN'T PASS ON THE BRAKES, BUT I FOUND ANOTHER PLACE'
JORGE LORENZO

COMPARE AND CONTRAST

Mugello was the place where it was supposed to come right for Valentino and Ducati. The track where he was unbeaten for so long, the track where Ducati do much of their development.

The Silverstone debacle had persuaded Ducati to bring forward their 2012 chassis design. Rossi raced it in Holland, and now here it was on home ground in front of his adoring public. At the 2011 race Casey Stoner, then Ducati's lead rider, was in the midst of his problems with the feeling the bike's front end gave him and was way down in 13th place in the championship. Nevertheless, Casey started from the front row with a qualifying time of 1m 49.432s. A year later on a supposedly improved motorcycle, Valentino managed 1m 49.902s. That would have put him eighth on the grid in 2010 but only got him 12th this year. The gap to the front went up from 0.613s to a disturbing 1.868s.

In the 2010 race, Casey won the fight for fourth place with a best lap of 1m 50.996s to finish 25.703s behind runaway race winner Dani Pedrosa, with a race time of 42m 53.769s. This year Valentino finished sixth with a best lap of 1m 49.301s, 26.450s behind Jorge Lorenzo and with a race time of 42m 16.539s.

As usual this season, Valentino's race performances looked better than qualifying. However, the numbers from the Italian Grand Prix and other races demonstrate a worrying lack of progress. Several questions were now being asked. The new chassis was supposed to be a magic bullet. It clearly wasn't, so what was to be done now?

The fans still called Valentino out onto the podium but he didn't look comfortable after what was, frankly, a humiliating weekend. How far would their loyalty stretch? And that of the sponsors?

Above Machinery trouble in practice didn't help Valentino; both bikes coasted to a halt in one session

ITALIAN GP

MUGELLO

ROUND 8

July 3

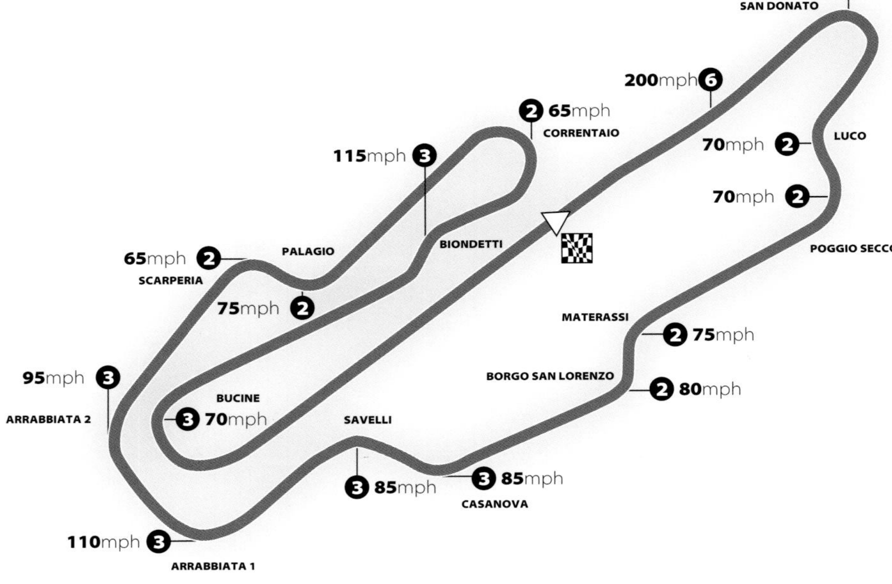

RACE RESULTS

CIRCUIT LENGTH 3.259 miles
NO. OF LAPS 23
RACE DISTANCE 74.794 miles
WEATHER Dry, 29°C
TRACK TEMPERATURE 54°C
WINNER Jorge Lorenzo
FASTEST LAP 1m 48.402s, 108.243mph, Jorge Lorenzo (Record)
PREVIOUS LAP RECORD 1m 49.531s, 105.909mph, Dani Pedrosa, 2010

QUALIFYING

	Rider	Nationality	Team	Qualifying	Pole +	Gap
1	Stoner	AUS	Repsol Honda Team	1m 48.034s		
2	Spies	USA	Yamaha Factory Racing	1m 48.479s	0.445s	0.445s
3	Simoncelli	ITA	San Carlo Honda Gresini	1m 48.485s	0.451s	0.006s
4	Dovizioso	ITA	Repsol Honda Team	1m 48.694s	0.660s	0.209s
5	Lorenzo	SPA	Yamaha Factory Racing	1m 48.756s	0.722s	0.062s
6	Edwards	USA	Monster Yamaha Tech 3	1m 48.974s	0.940s	0.218s
7	Crutchlow	GBR	Monster Yamaha Tech 3	1m 49.021s	0.987s	0.047s
8	Pedrosa	SPA	Repsol Honda Team	1m 49.398s	1.364s	0.377s
9	Hayden	USA	Ducati Team	1m 49.509s	1.475s	0.111s
10	Barbera	SPA	Mapfre Aspar Team	1m 49.663s	1.629s	0.154s
11	Abraham	CZE	Cardion AB Motoracing	1m 49.678s	1.644s	0.015s
12	Rossi	ITA	Ducati Team	1m 49.902s	1.868s	0.224s
13	Aoyama	JPN	San Carlo Honda Gresini	1m 50.156s	2.122s	0.254s
14	Bautista	SPA	Rizla Suzuki MotoGP	1m 50.460s	2.426s	0.304s
15	De Puniet	FRA	Pramac Racing Team	1m 50.651s	2.617s	0.191s
16	Elias	SPA	LCR Honda MotoGP	1m 50.742s	2.708s	0.091s

FINISHERS

1 JORGE LORENZO Even better than his win at home in Jerez. After being outqualified by his team-mate he hunted down the Hondas of Dovizioso and Stoner, passing them both with identical moves at Casanova-Savelli. The most impressive aspect was the run of near-perfect laps that closed the gap to Casey.

2 ANDREA DOVIZIOSO Top Honda for the first time this year. Woke the crowd up by taking second off Stoner at Turn 1 on the last lap. Forgot his reputation as the quiet man and climbed the wire fence on the slow-down lap to celebrate with the fans.

3 CASEY STONER Looked as if he was going to run away from the field until half-distance: his lead was over 2.5s when Lorenzo started to close him down. The team hadn't reduced the tyre pressure enough to cope with the much higher race-day temperatures, so what he'd seen as a good chance of victory was wasted.

4 BEN SPIES A couple of mistakes early on meant he lost touch with the top three. Ben then battled with Simoncelli, decided to follow him, and used the knowledge gained to sweep inside on the final corner. Made a point of saying that the race with Marco had been completely clean.

5 MARCO SIMONCELLI Started from the front row for the sixth consecutive race but the changed conditions meant he never had the same feel he'd enjoyed in practice. Hung on to the top three for half a dozen laps, then it was a fight for fourth with Spies, who had noted his tendency to run wide at the last corner and took advantage.

6 VALENTINO ROSSI A horrible weekend. Failed to get a good start from 12th on the grid, his worst qualifying at Mugello by a whole eight places, then took nearly half the race to work up to sixth. Top Ducati again, but it was shocking to watch him working so hard just to get through the midfield on a circuit he'd dominated for years.

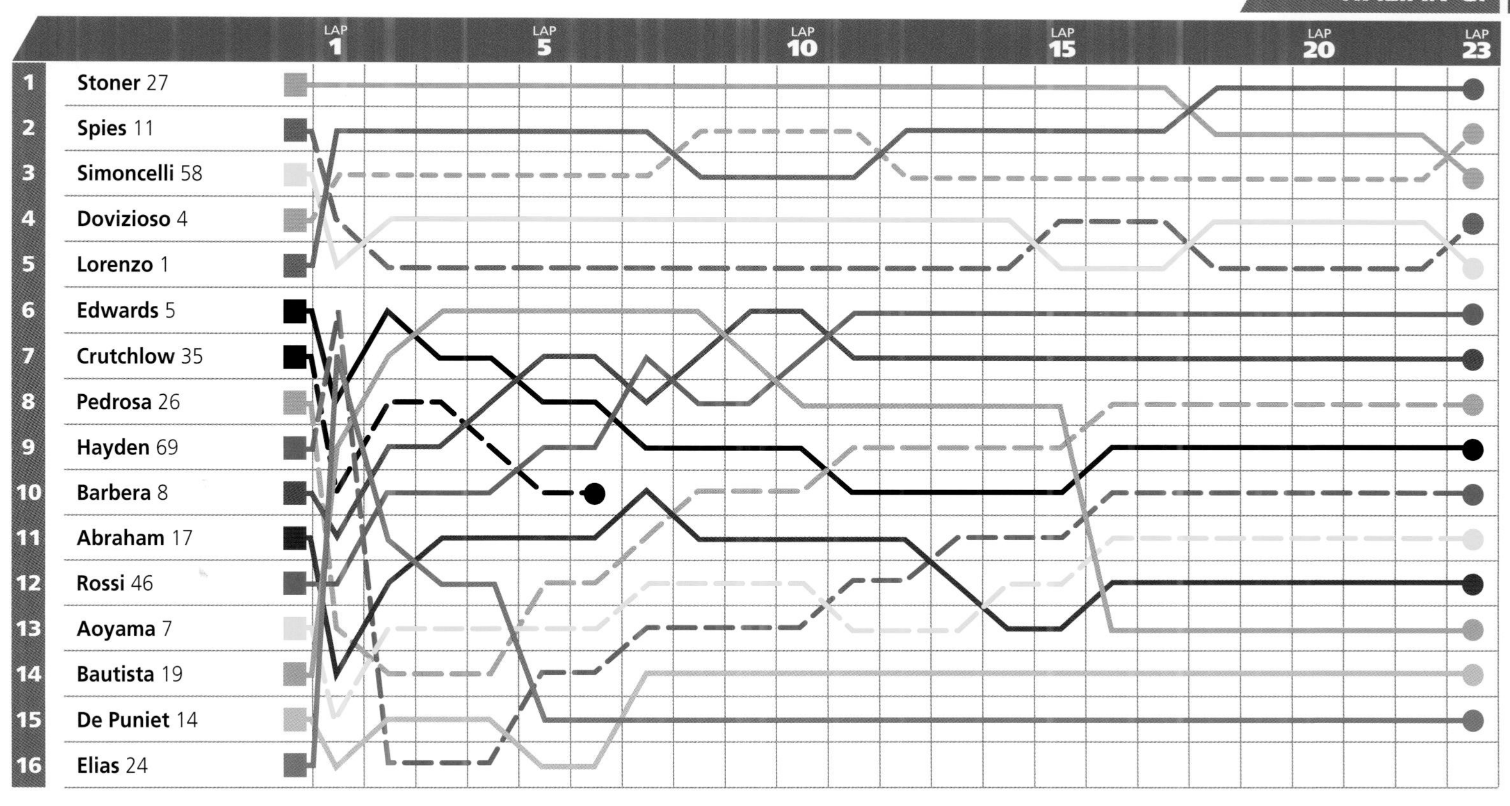

RACE

	Rider	Motorcycle	Race Time	Time +	Fastest Lap	Av Speed	
1	Lorenzo	Yamaha	41m 50.089s		1m 48.402s	107.510mph	H/H
2	Dovizioso	Honda	41m 51.086s	0.997s	1m 48.678s	107.467mph	H/H
3	Stoner	Honda	41m 51.232s	1.143s	1m 48.577s	107.461mph	H/H
4	Spies	Yamaha	41m 59.069s	8.980s	1m 48.647s	107.127mph	H/H
5	Simoncelli	Honda	41m 59.165s	9.076s	1m 48.833s	107.122mph	H/H
6	Rossi	Ducati	42m 16.539s	26.450s	1m 49.301s	106.389mph	H/H
7	Barbera	Ducati	42m 18.834s	28.745s	1m 49.468s	106.293mph	H/M
8	Pedrosa	Honda	42m 22.132s	32.043s	1m 49.226s	106.155mph	H/M
9	Edwards	Yamaha	42m 23.510s	33.421s	1m 49.909s	106.097mph	H/M
10	Hayden	Ducati	42m 24.813s	34.724s	1m 49.524s	106.043mph	H/H
11	Aoyama	Honda	42m 27.448s	37.359s	1m 49.791s	105.933mph	H/M
12	Abraham	Ducati	42m 34.053s	43.964s	1m 49.731s	105.659mph	H/M
13	Bautista	Suzuki	42m 37.743s	47.654s	1m 49.448s	105.507mph	H/M
14	De Puniet	Ducati	42m 38.929s	48.840s	1m 50.342s	105.458mph	H/M
15	Elias	Honda	43m 05.288s	1m 15.199s	1m 51.271s	104.383mph	H/H
NF	Crutchlow	Yamaha	11m 10.247s	17 laps	1m 50.117s	105.033mph	H/M

CHAMPIONSHIP

	Rider	Team	Points
1	Stoner	Repsol Honda Team	152
2	Lorenzo	Yamaha Factory Racing	133
3	Dovizioso	Repsol Honda Team	119
4	Rossi	Ducati Team	91
5	Hayden	Ducati Team	77
6	Spies	Yamaha Factory Racing	74
7	Pedrosa	Repsol Honda Team	69
8	Aoyama	San Carlo Honda Gresini	56
9	Edwards	Monster Yamaha Tech 3	53
10	Simoncelli	San Carlo Honda Gresini	50
11	Barbera	Mapfre Aspar Team MotoGP	44
12	Abraham	Cardion AB Motoracing	37
13	Elias	LCR Honda MotoGP	35
14	Crutchlow	Monster Yamaha Tech 3	32
15	Bautista	Rizla Suzuki MotoGP	30
16	Capirossi	Pramac Racing Team	22
17	De Puniet	Pramac Racing Team	12
18	Hopkins	Rizla Suzuki MotoGP	6
19	Akiyoshi	San Carlo Honda Gresini	3

7 HECTOR BARBERA Much happier after a run of races where he'd appeared lost. Helped by the arrival of a softer and more flexible chassis, and reverting to settings that he knew worked. Described it as his best race in MotoGP.

8 DANI PEDROSA A very impressive return to action after missing the previous three GPs. It looked as if he wasn't ready when he dropped back early on, but that was a transmission problem. Happy and surprised by his race pace, but very tired and hurting a lot at the flag.

9 COLIN EDWARDS His best qualifying of the season so far, but the softer option tyre proved to be a mistake. As the afternoon sessions had been all but wiped out by rain this was guesswork, and he never had the grip he expected in the higher temperatures.

10 NICKY HAYDEN Top Ducati in qualifying for the first time this season and should have had a better race. Got away with the leaders but ran on at the start of the second lap and dropped to the back of the field. Should have been racing with his team-mate, judging by lap times.

11 HIROSHI AOYAMA Severely handicapped by his injuries from Assen, especially in the first half of the race.

12 KAREL ABRAHAM Another rider who was affected by the lack of dry set-up time. Started well but soon found both tyres moving, so unable to fight with the others in his group.

13 ALVARO BAUTISTA Race-day conditions suited the Suzuki well and he was up to sixth quickly and leading the group for six laps until lap 16 when he had a massive front-end slide and ran off the track. Went one second faster than he'd done in qualifying and had the pace to be fighting with Rossi.

14 RANDY DE PUNIET Another morale-sapping outing, losing the front every time he pushed to pass someone and ending the race with his rear slick totally destroyed.

15 TONI ELIAS Qualified last, so with nothing to lose he took a risk on a major change to the front end for the race. Got a great start but realised on the first flying lap that the change was not for the better. Finished nearly 30 seconds behind de Puniet.

NON-FINISHERS

CAL CRUTCHLOW Pulled in because of lack of feel from the front tyre combined with worry about what would happen to his recently plated collarbone if he crashed.

NON-STARTERS

LORIS CAPIROSSI Unfit following his crash at Assen. The Pramac team decided not to replace him.

GERMAN GP
SACHSENRING CIRCUIT
ROUND 9
July 17
REPSOL
HONDA
Arai

LOOK WHO'S BACK AGAIN

Dani Pedrosa reminds the championship leaders that he is still a force to be reckoned with

For the second race running, slight tyre problems prevented Casey Stoner from achieving what had looked like a certain victory. Starting from pole, he led most of the first half of the race despite, as usual, not feeling entirely happy on a full tank, and finished third.

Stoner had another reason for not feeling too great – a massive crash on Friday in the very fast downhill corner that leads on to the back straight. Along with Dani Pedrosa, Toni Elias and Valentino Rossi, he was a victim of the dreaded cold-tyre syndrome. This time the right side of the front tyre had had no chance to heat up on a chilly day; as the right-hander is preceded by seven lefts, all it needed was a misty morning to ensure the front tyre didn't get enough heat into it. Stoner bruised his forearm badly while Rossi put a hole in his, but Pedrosa did manage to avoid aggravating his recently repaired collarbone.

Not that Valentino could use that as an excuse for his qualifying position: he was down in 16th, with only Pramac Ducati's replacement rider Sylvain Guintoli behind him. Again without Jerry Burgess, the team had failed to find any balance between the improved traction from the redesigned rear end and the flaky front end, which simply wasn't giving the rider any feel or confidence. On the standard bike, Nicky Hayden was top Ducati in eighth. The Desmosedici 11.1 that appeared on Sunday morning looked very different; in fact it looked odd – low to the ground with the forks at a steep angle. There had been a lot of email traffic between Germany and Australia overnight.

The changes did indeed enable Valentino to become competitive, but only with his team-mate and a very lively Alvaro Bautista on the Suzuki. However,

Above Toni Elias's season got even worse; he failed to score points for the first time since Qatar

Below Sylvain Guintoli returned to MotoGP as a replacement for the injured Loris Capirossi

Opposite Alvaro Bautista and Suzuki impressed, finishing ahead of the factory Ducatis

this was just one of the crowd-pleasing fights taking place at a respectful distance from the leaders.

Lorenzo led from the start but he was soon to be passed by Stoner, with Pedrosa, Dovizioso and Simoncelli in close attendance. The two Italians were soon left to fight among themselves as Lorenzo took up the running and Stoner faded to third. Then Pedrosa started to charge. He set the fastest lap of the race on lap 20 and two laps later steamrollered past the Yamaha, up the hill out of the final corner – the Honda getting its power down so much better than the Yamaha – and pulled away. When Stoner repassed Lorenzo it looked like all the interest would now be in the two scraps behind the leaders. Ben Spies, full of cold and after a lonely race, was closing fast on Dovizioso and Simoncelli, and Bautista and the Ducatis were still battling.

But Lorenzo had one last move left. In terms of the championship, Pedrosa was irrelevant; that fight was between Stoner and himself. The difference between second and third – four points – was enough to encourage Jorge to mount a last-lap charge. It looked as if it would be in vain when he had a major moment at the top of the hill and lost touch with Casey. Lorenzo must have been the only person in the packed-to-capacity Sachsenring who thought he still had a chance of second place. He was frighteningly quick into the penultimate left-hander as the Aussie took a defensive inside line and was slow out, giving Jorge the opportunity to carry his momentum and make a daring inside pass on the last corner. It was reminiscent of the move Casey had made on

46
TIM
Arai
69
TIM
SHOEI
SUZUKI
MOTUL
19
RIZLA
SUZUKI

'BIG THANKS TO MY FAMILY AND DOCTORS… THEY ALL KNOW HOW HARD IT HAS BEEN'
DANI PEDROSA

Valentino Rossi for the final rostrum position 12 months previously, a swoop from way out on the dirty part of the track. Now in trouble with grip on the left side of his rear tyre, Stoner had no answer. Jorge, never one for understatement, called it 'a miracle pass'.

A number of other dices were resolved at the last corner as well. Spies passed a disconsolate Simoncelli, while Bautista came out on top of a frantic three-way mix-up in front of the Ducatis, with Hayden beating his team-mate for the first time this year in a dry race. There was an immediate flurry of speculation about whether Rossi would use the 11 or 11.1 version of the Ducati in the next race – much of it from the rider. None of that would have been allowed if Jerry Burgess had been in the pit, and the arm-waving merely emphasised the depth of the predicament in which Ducati found themselves.

Amid all the last-lap drama it would be easy to overlook the winner. Dani Pedrosa's main emotion seemed to be surprise, and he also reported an unusual feeling of calm when things weren't going too well early on, 'a strange feeling, something I've never had before'. It was easy to forget that this was only his second race back from injury, albeit at a track that gave his still-healing collarbone an easier time than any other on the calendar. It was noticeable that the praise from his competitors was wholehearted and genuine. Dani obviously has the respect, as well as the sympathy, of the rest of the grid. Did this reinstate him as a title contender? 'I know it's almost impossible.' Though Pedrosa was not a threat for the championship, Germany showed that he would have a big say in who would eventually come out on top.

SOFTLY, SOFTLY

Following the growing number of complaints about cold-tyre crashes, Bridgestone proposed a new system that was intended to give riders more soft-tyre options.

After the rash of crashes at Assen, Loris Capirossi suggested at the Safety Commission that slicks should be cut to help get heat into them. This would have been tenable before the control-tyre system was introduced, and indeed in times past it was common for teams to get out the soldering iron and do their own work. However, the whole ethos of a control-tyre rule is that everyone uses the same tyre; clearly, allowing individual modifications that not every team might want to implement contradicts that basic principle.

Bridgestone's proposal was to supplement the existing allocation of eight front tyres split between two compounds with an extra tyre featuring a softer compound specifically intended for use, if required, during Friday morning's first free practice session. Riders would therefore get two each of the harder and medium tyres plus the new soft on Thursday and then decide on how they wanted to make up the remaining four on Friday evening after the first day of practice. The number of rear tyres was not changed, but the allocation process was to mimic the system for the front: four of either compound on Thursday and the final two chosen after second free practice.

Bridgestone also moved the entire rear-tyre allocation one compound softer, so where it used to be, for instance, medium and hard, it would now be soft and medium. This had already happened in Catalunya and Germany and would be effective for all races after Laguna Seca. The exceptions would be where the extremes of the compound spectrum had already been selected, as in the softest option front that is part of the allocation at Valencia and Australia. Conversely, at Malaysia, the choices are hard and extra-hard, and adding a softer choice would be meaningless as its wear rate and stability wouldn't cope with the conditions.

Opposite top The top three charge over the crest before the back straight, under the bubble and on the gas

Opposite bottom The new-model Dani Pedrosa allows himself to express a bit of emotion on the rostrum

Below Ben Spies rounds the Omega in front of the packed grandstands; he just failed to catch the top three

GERMAN GP

SACHSENRING CIRCUIT

ROUND 9

July 17

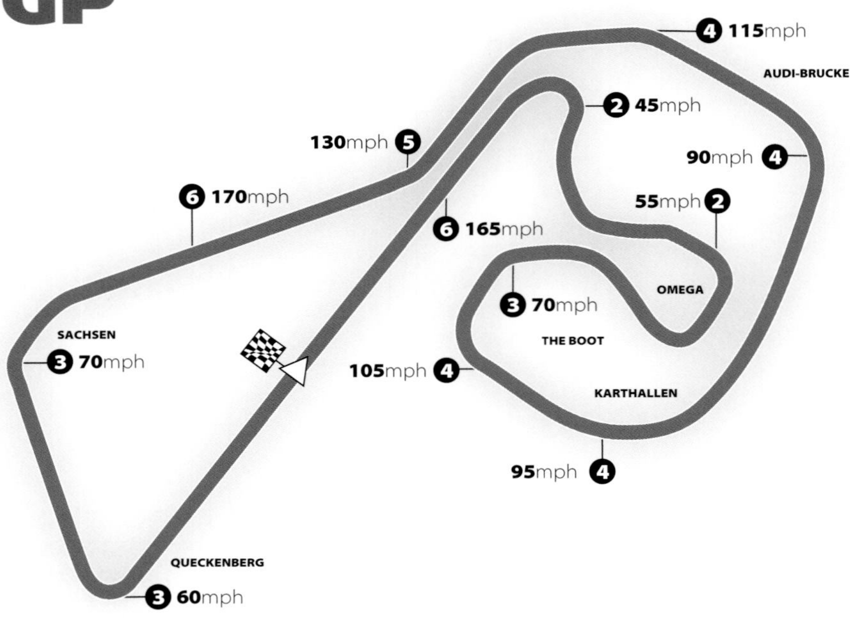

RACE RESULTS

CIRCUIT LENGTH 2.281 miles
NO. OF LAPS 30
RACE DISTANCE 68.430 miles
WEATHER Dry, 21°C
TRACK TEMPERATURE 29°C
WINNER Dani Pedrosa
FASTEST LAP 1m 21.846s, 100.351mph, Dani Pedrosa (Record)
PREVIOUS LAP RECORD 1m 21.882s, 99.657mph, Dani Pedrosa, 2010

QUALIFYING

	Rider	Nationality	Team	Qualifying	Pole +	Gap
1	Stoner	AUS	Repsol Honda Team	1m 21.681s		
2	Pedrosa	SPA	Repsol Honda Team	1m 21.933s	0.252s	0.252s
3	Lorenzo	SPA	Yamaha Factory Racing	1m 21.944s	0.263s	0.011s
4	Simoncelli	ITA	San Carlo Honda Gresini	1m 21.954s	0.273s	0.010s
5	Spies	USA	Yamaha Factory Racing	1m 22.056s	0.375s	0.102s
6	Dovizioso	ITA	Repsol Honda Team	1m 22.157s	0.476s	0.101s
7	Edwards	USA	Monster Yamaha Tech 3	1m 22.368s	0.687s	0.211s
8	Hayden	USA	Ducati Team	1m 22.388s	0.707s	0.020s
9	De Puniet	FRA	Pramac Racing Team	1m 22.503s	0.822s	0.115s
10	Bautista	SPA	Rizla Suzuki MotoGP	1m 22.604s	0.923s	0.101s
11	Barbera	SPA	Mapfre Aspar Team	1m 22.676s	0.995s	0.072s
12	Crutchlow	GBR	Monster Yamaha Tech 3	1m 22.676s	0.995s	–
13	Abraham	CZE	Cardion AB Motoracing	1m 23.164s	1.483s	0.488s
14	Elias	SPA	LCR Honda MotoGP	1m 23.201s	1.520s	0.037s
15	Aoyama	JPN	San Carlo Honda Gresini	1m 23.248s	1.567s	0.047s
16	Rossi	ITA	Ducati Team	1m 23.320s	1.639s	0.072s
17	Guintoli	FRA	Pramac Racing Team	1m 24.707s	3.026s	1.387s

FINISHERS

1 DANI PEDROSA Waited until the fuel load had gone down and the tyres were sliding to make his move, with amazing drive out of the last corner to motor past Lorenzo. Said he'd felt strangely calm despite not feeling great at the start. This 14th win in the top class made him the most successful rider never to have won the title.

2 JORGE LORENZO A World Champion's display. Took risks to lead early on and ended the race with what he called 'a miracle pass' on Stoner to wrest second place on the very last corner. Reduced the Aussie's lead in the title chase to 15 points.

3 CASEY STONER Limited by tyre problems for the second race running: TV pictures from Dani's on-board camera showed how much his rear tyre was spinning. Like the rest of them, he knew tyre management would be an issue and eased his pace after a few laps in front, but didn't have the grip to catch Pedrosa or fend off Lorenzo.

4 ANDREA DOVIZIOSO Not too happy with fourth place but pointed to a major improvement in his pace compared to previous outings here. Again raced better than he qualified, after a great start from the second row, and was definitely happy about maintaining his record of beating Simoncelli in every race.

5 BEN SPIES Didn't start well and was worried by a lack of rear grip. Settled into a steady rhythm that got him up to Dovizioso and Simoncelli by the end of the race, but again able to pass Marco on the last corner, for the second race in a row.

6 MARCO SIMONCELLI Another victim of wear on the left side of the rear tyre. Spent the first part of the race dicing with Dovizioso, the pair falling slightly off the pace of the three leaders, but unable to defend against Spies's late charge and last-corner pass.

7 ALVARO BAUTISTA Not his best result of the year but definitely his best race. Fought with the factory Ducatis throughout and won the battle for seventh on the

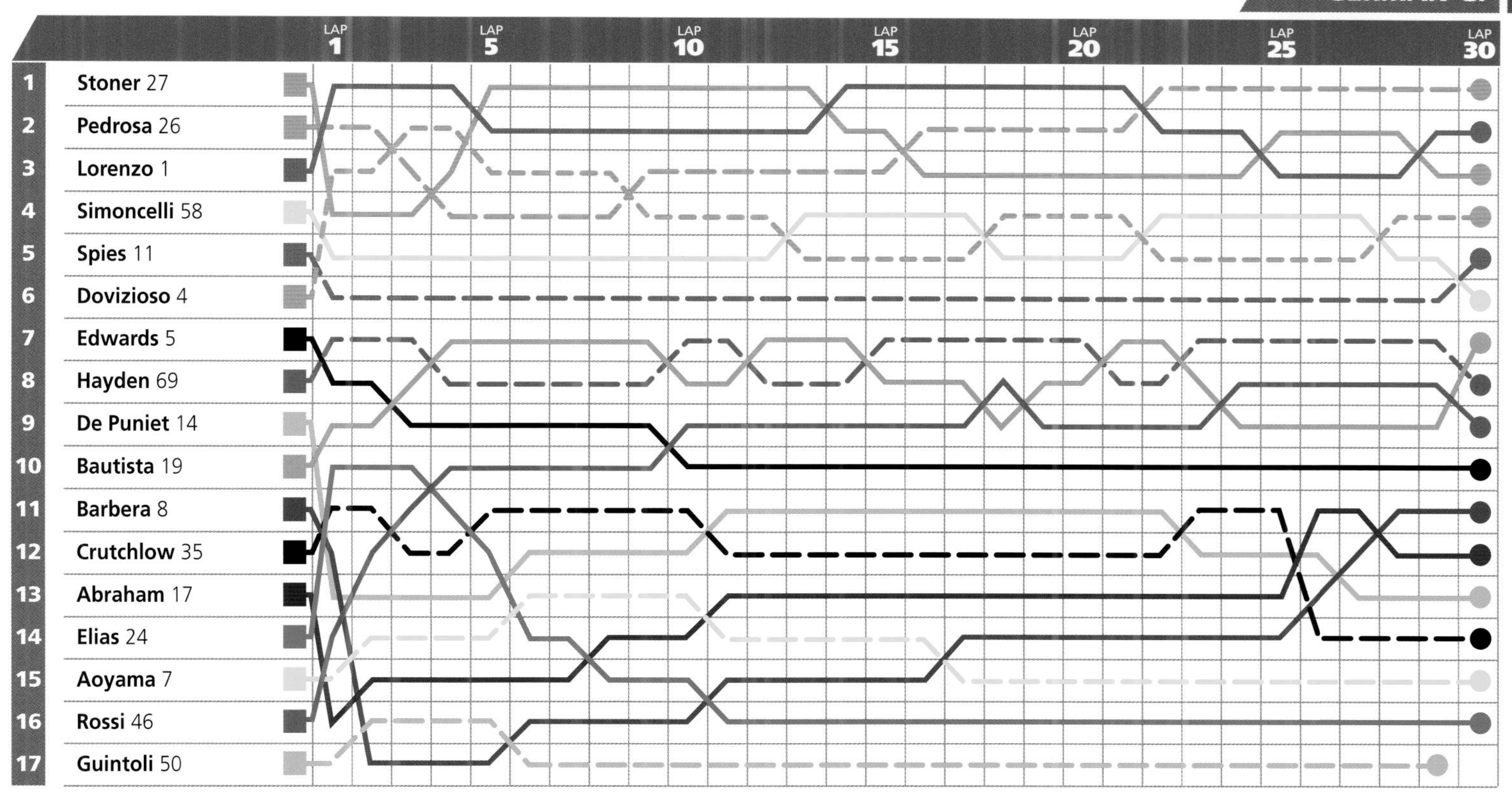

RACE

	Rider	Motorcycle	Race Time	Time +	Fastest Lap	Av Speed	B
1	Pedrosa	Honda	41m 12.482s		1m 21.846s	99.641mph	XH/H
2	Lorenzo	Yamaha	41m 13.959s	1.477s	1m 22.024s	99.581mph	XH/H
3	Stoner	Honda	41m 14.050s	1.568s	1m 22.070s	99.578mph	XH/H
4	Dovizioso	Honda	41m 22.995s	10.513s	1m 22.218s	99.219mph	XH/H
5	Spies	Yamaha	41m 23.201s	10.719s	1m 22.406s	99.211mph	XH/H
6	Simoncelli	Honda	41m 23.405s	10.923s	1m 22.125s	99.202mph	XH/H
7	Bautista	Suzuki	41m 39.933s	27.451s	1m 22.780s	98.547mph	H/M
8	Hayden	Ducati	41m 39.992s	27.510s	1m 22.787s	98.544mph	XH/H
9	Rossi	Ducati	41m 40.058s	27.576s	1m 22.802s	98.541mph	XH/H
10	Edwards	Yamaha	41m 45.973s	33.491s	1m 22.923s	98.309mph	XH/H
11	Barbera	Ducati	41m 51.426s	38.944s	1m 22.588s	98.096mph	H/M
12	Abraham	Ducati	41m 51.630s	39.148s	1m 22.897s	98.087mph	H/H
13	De Puniet	Ducati	41m 51.897s	39.415s	1m 23.065s	98.078mph	XH/H
14	Crutchlow	Yamaha	41m 51.959s	39.477s	1m 22.984s	98.075mph	XH/H
15	Aoyama	Honda	42m 06.998s	54.516s	1m 23.398s	97.491mph	H/H
16	Elias	Honda	42m 24.817s	1m 12.335s	1m 23.797s	96.809mph	H/H
17	Guintoli	Ducati	41m 28.441s	1 lap	1m 24.683s	95.702mph	H/M

CHAMPIONSHIP

	Rider	Team	Points
1	Stoner	Repsol Honda Team	168
2	Lorenzo	Yamaha Factory Racing	153
3	Dovizioso	Repsol Honda Team	132
4	Rossi	Ducati Team	98
5	Pedrosa	Repsol Honda Team	94
6	Spies	Yamaha Factory Racing	85
7	Hayden	Ducati Team	85
8	Simoncelli	San Carlo Honda Gresini	60
9	Edwards	Monster Yamaha Tech 3	59
10	Aoyama	Repsol Honda Team	57
11	Barbera	Mapfre Aspar Team MotoGP	49
12	Abraham	Cardion AB Motoracing	41
13	Bautista	Rizla Suzuki MotoGP	39
14	Elias	LCR Honda MotoGP	35
15	Crutchlow	Monster Yamaha Tech 3	34
16	Capirossi	Pramac Racing Team	22
17	De Puniet	Pramac Racing Team	15
18	Hopkins	Rizla Suzuki MotoGP	6
19	Akiyoshi	San Carlo Honda Gresini	3

final corner with a daring move on Hayden, having passed Rossi earlier in the lap. Had the confidence to go with the softer tyres and set his fastest time on the penultimate lap.

8 NICKY HAYDEN Stuck with the flexier version of the GP11 and finished as top Ducati. Things looked better in qualifying, but a big moment on the bumps at Turn 1 early on meant he lost touch with the leaders, afterwards dicing with his team-mate and Bautista. With hindsight, he would have used the softer tyre.

9 VALENTINO ROSSI The weekend started with a big crash on Friday morning and continued with his worst qualifying since his broken wrist at Valencia in 2007. A major set-up change improved his pace by nearly 0.5s on race day, but all he could do was fight with his team-mate, who beat him in the dry for the first time this year.

10 COLIN EDWARDS On the tail of the Ducatis and the Suzuki until three laps from the finish when the rear came round off-throttle in Turn 2. After that he felt a vibration and settled for tenth. Took consolation from going faster than ever at a track where usually he has 'a disaster'.

11 HECTOR BARBERA Backed up the massive improvement of Mugello with another good race. It would have been even better but for an early incident when he ran off-track avoiding another rider at Turn 1, which put him down to last. His pace fighting back showed he could have been up with Bautista.

12 KAREL ABRAHAM Crashed three times in practice and qualifying but improved throughout the race and set his fastest lap on the 23rd of 30 laps. Went past Barbera on the last lap, only to be retaken.

13 RANDY DE PUNIET Lacked confidence at the start and hit front grip problems mid-race despite getting a modified, more flexible chassis.

14 CAL CRUTCHLOW Frustrated as he struggled with grip problems front and rear. Doubly frustrated to lose three places when he couldn't hold his line at Turn 3, three laps from the flag, and was unable to repass.

15 HIROSHI AOYAMA Still suffering as a result of his crash at Assen and lacking in confidence, especially in the first half of the race.

16 TONI ELIAS Started well but soon ran into his usual problems with a full tank. Finished outside the points for the first time since he crashed in Qatar.

17 SYLVAIN GUINTOLI Tested the Pramac Ducati on the Monday after Mugello but didn't get to ride it until the second free practice session, as Capirossi wanted to test his fitness. Not surprisingly, the Frenchman improved his times every session but could only qualify and race at the back of the field.

NON-STARTERS

LORIS CAPIROSSI Rode the first free practice session but realised his injuries from Assen still prevented him from racing, so the bike was handed over to Guintoli.

UNITED STATES GP
LAGUNA SECA
ROUND 10
July 24

THE PERFECT STORM

Casey Stoner produced a near-perfect race after a fraught qualifying as the 'Aliens' dominated

Casey Stoner really enjoyed this one, and with good reason. His win left the opposition heading for the summer break contemplating his lead of 20 points over Lorenzo, not to mention the manner in which he achieved it.

Remember that Stoner was coming off two races where he had suffered tyre woes and last-lap passes, despite starting both from pole position. Things didn't seem to be improving after qualifying. Sure, Casey had taken second place, only a fraction of a second behind Jorge Lorenzo's Yamaha, but it was down to one very brave lap compared to Lorenzo's astonishing run of eight 1m 21s laps on one run and six in another. Casey only dipped into the 1m 21s bracket on his last flying lap.

Things started to look better on Sunday morning when a front-end modification for warm-up gave the Aussie some feel. But perhaps the most impressive aspect of Stoner's victory was the way he managed the race and made two of the best passes one could hope to see in a whole season's racing. Lorenzo bolted from the start, followed by Pedrosa, with Casey third. Still not happy with the bike's feel with a full tank, Stoner was nevertheless into 1m 21s on the third lap and stayed there for seven laps, save for two very low 1m 22s circuits. He then dropped into the low 22s for a few laps, watching Pedrosa, before passing him on the run into the Corkscrew, a move that one former World Champion, Wayne Gardner, described as 'already the pass of the year'. It is true that Dani was suffering more from his shoulder surgeries here than he had at the Sachsenring, but it was still

a sublime move. Another run of 21s saw Casey cross the one-second gap to Jorge in just six laps. In another display of the sort of tactical thinking he's displayed for much of the year, Stoner shadowed Lorenzo until the 27th lap of 32.

Lorenzo was suffering from a very sore hip, thanks to a massive highside at the close of third free practice. Actually, it happened after the end of the session. He did a practice start but was flipped over the bars at Turn 5. For once this wasn't a cold-tyre crash but an electronics issue. The Yamaha's traction control is switched off for a start and only re-engages after the first downshift; unfortunately Jorge cruised up to the corner and got on the throttle without the requisite downchange. The on-board camera's microphone picked up perfectly the insane rate at which the revs went up as soon as Lorenzo touched the throttle. When he finally stopped bouncing, Jorge grasped his right thigh in a manner all too reminiscent of Bautista at Qatar, but thankfully he was able to walk away. His race day was obviously compromised by the crash, and he also had trouble with his tyre. Like the rest of the top men he'd chosen the harder option but, unlike the rest, Jorge found it faded badly in the closing laps.

The other factory Yamaha rider also suffered from an electronics glitch. Ben Spies got a good start but it didn't last long. His engine-management system refused to give him the power he was asking for in the lower gears and Ben was swamped going down to Turn 2. He then had to get by the Ducatis – Rossi is never an easy man to pass – and close the gap to Dovizioso, which he did with his usual efficiency on worn tyres,

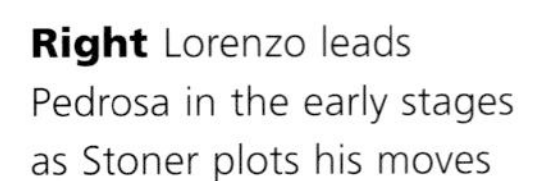

Right Lorenzo leads Pedrosa in the early stages as Stoner plots his moves

Below Family time in the Tech 3 garage: Colin Edwards, wife Alyssia, daughter Gracie and son Hayes

REPSOL
25
X-lite
PETRONAS
YAMAHA
PETRONAS
YAMAHA

to finish fourth. If he'd had the correct setting on the bike, who knows where he would have been. By his own admission the front two riders were untouchable, but you have to believe Ben would have taken advantage of Pedrosa's lack of fitness to seize the final rostrum position.

Stoner saved another breathtaking overtaking move for five laps from the flag, after Lorenzo lost a little momentum wheelieing out of the final corner. Casey went round the outside at Turn 1 and squeezed across Jorge's nose going into the second corner. It's actually a bit of an exaggeration to call Turn 1 a corner; it's a slight kink in a straight, and the kink is over a blind crest. The Aussie went round the outside on the white line, with a concrete wall not far from his right elbow, at around 170mph. Yet another ex-World Champion, Kevin Schwantz, later said it was one of the bravest passes he'd ever seen. Stoner even apologised to Lorenzo on the rostrum for the way he'd cut across him. Jorge accepted without demur, remarking that Stoner was always a clean rider, although he did have to get off the throttle. It was the decisive move. Lorenzo was in trouble with his injury, and very soon with his rear tyre too, and he had no answer.

Meanwhile, 30 seconds behind the winner, the factory Ducatis were busy racing each other, or they were once Bautista had again closed on them but then crashed. Jerry Burgess returned to Rossi's pit after a two-race hiatus and concentrated on the new bike – Valentino rode the GP11.1 all weekend, whereas Nicky Hayden rode both the 11.1 and the 11 on Friday before deciding to stick with the older bike until the test on

Above Local hero Ben Bostrum rode as a wild-card entry on Toni Elias's second LCR Honda

Below Impressive rookie Karel Abraham increased his lead over Cal Crutchlow in the Rookie of the Year table

Opposite Casey Stoner acknowledges the fans at the Corkscrew

'WE WEREN'T TOO CONFIDENT THAT WE COULD RUN WITH JORGE AND DANI'

CASEY STONER

the Monday after the Czech GP. It didn't seem to matter much either way. Valentino just held off a very determined Hayden, who dismissed the idea that Rossi was in any way taking it easy. 'I saw his right foot a couple of times,' he said, referring to front-end tucks bad enough for the nine-times champion's foot to come off the rest. Valentino later made all the right noises about the bike getting better and Ducati working hard, but there was also a whisper about Ducati building an aluminium frame, the origins of which appeared to be traceable back to Rossi.

It was hard not to believe that Casey Stoner's obvious enjoyment of such a well-worked victory didn't have something to do with the race here in 2008. That was the pivotal moment of the season, when Rossi pulled off a couple of breathtaking moves on Casey, the fairness of at least one later being questioned by the Aussie. Indeed, Valentino refers to the defeat as something Casey has never been able to get over. Well, he looked fine about it after this one.

THE JOY OF SIX

MotoGP takes its summer break after Laguna Seca so that seemed an appropriate point to check on how teams were dealing with their allowance of six engines for the season. In 2010, the first year of the rule, only Suzuki had to take extra motors. This year they didn't appear to be in trouble – reliability as well as competitiveness had improved – with Alvaro Bautista having had only one motor removed from his allocation and yet to take the final two.

As was evident last season, the Hondas were ahead of the rest. Factory men Dovizioso and Stoner both had one engine withdrawn after using it in four races and still had three to take. Simoncelli had also had one withdrawn, but after it was used in five races. Aoyama and Elias each had a motor withdrawn after Estoril. As Aoyama had a motor withdrawn at the same time last year, for no apparent reason, it was tempting to think this was HRC's way of having a look inside to check their calculations. Dani Pedrosa, having missed two races, had not lost a motor and only took his third at the Sachsenring.

At Tech 3 Yamaha, Edwards took his fourth motor on Sunday morning at Laguna, Crutchlow his a week earlier in Germany. Ben Spies took his fourth motor at Assen, but Lorenzo lost a motor in his warm-up crash at Le Mans and was forced to take his fourth on Friday at Catalunya. That meant a little extra pressure for the World Champion, who wasn't in a position to afford any more problems.

Ducati's satellite teams looked to be on the same schedule as most of the paddock, with de Puniet taking his fourth motor in Germany, Barbera and Capirossi taking theirs in Laguna Seca, while Abraham was still on his third. All of them had had one engine withdrawn.

The situation at the factory team was not so simple. The introduction of the 11.1 chassis meant new engines to fit revised engine mountings. Rossi therefore took his fourth and fifth motors at Assen when the new bike arrived. Nicky Hayden lost a motor at Estoril and took his fifth at Laguna when he had the 11.1 for the first time and would have to take his sixth when two of the new bikes arrived in his pit at Brno. Surely a factory Ducati will start a race from pit lane before the end of the year?

Above A Desmosedici engine awaits the attention of the Ducati mechanics. How many motors would they fit for Rossi before the end of the year?

UNITED STATES GP

LAGUNA SECA

ROUND 10

July 24

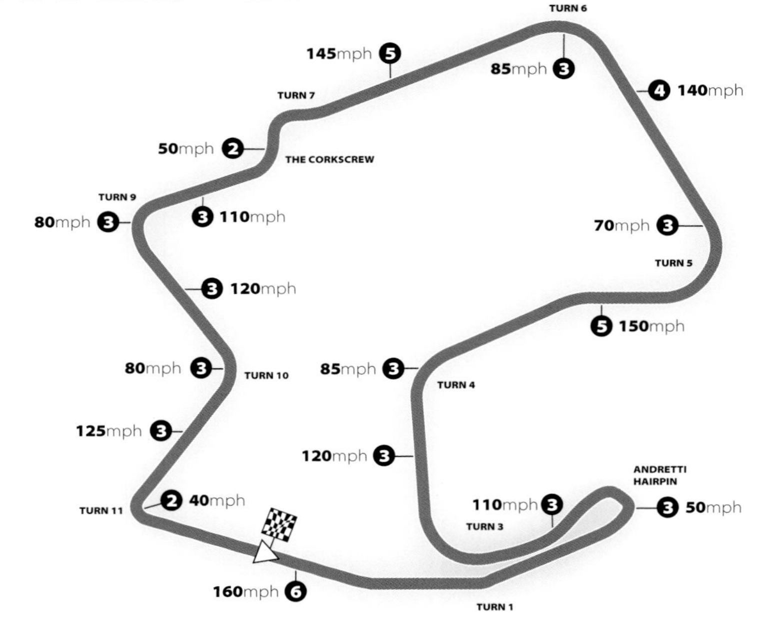

RACE RESULTS

CIRCUIT LENGTH 2.243 miles
NO. OF LAPS 32
RACE DISTANCE 71.776 miles
WEATHER Dry, 23°C
TRACK TEMPERATURE 44°C
WINNER Casey Stoner
FASTEST LAP 1m 21.673s, 98.860mph, Casey Stoner (Record)
LAP RECORD 1m 21.376s, 97.946mph, Casey Stoner, 2010

QUALIFYING

	Rider	Nationality	Team	Qualifying	Pole +	Gap
1	Lorenzo	SPA	Yamaha Factory Racing	1m 21.202s		
2	Stoner	AUS	Repsol Honda Team	1m 21.274s	0.072s	0.072s
3	Pedrosa	SPA	Repsol Honda Team	1m 21.385s	0.183s	0.111s
4	Spies	USA	Yamaha Factory Racing	1m 21.578s	0.376s	0.193s
5	Simoncelli	ITA	San Carlo Honda Gresini	1m 21.696s	0.494s	0.118s
6	Dovizioso	ITA	Repsol Honda Team	1m 21.731s	0.529s	0.035s
7	Rossi	ITA	Ducati Team	1m 22.235s	1.033s	0.504s
8	Barbera	SPA	Mapfre Aspar Team	1m 22.238s	1.036s	0.003s
9	Hayden	USA	Ducati Team	1m 22.271s	1.069s	0.033s
10	Crutchlow	GBR	Monster Yamaha Tech 3	1m 22.385s	1.183s	0.114s
11	Edwards	USA	Monster Yamaha Tech 3	1m 22.520s	1.318s	0.135s
12	Bautista	SPA	Rizla Suzuki MotoGP	1m 22.669s	1.467s	0.149s
13	Abraham	CZE	Cardion AB Motoracing	1m 22.893s	1.691s	0.224s
14	Aoyama	JPN	San Carlo Honda Gresini	1m 22.937s	1.735s	0.044s
15	De Puniet	FRA	Pramac Racing Team	1m 22.961s	1.759s	0.024s
16	Capirossi	ITA	Pramac Racing Team	1m 23.876s	2.674s	0.915s
17	Elias	SPA	LCR Honda MotoGP	1m 24.156s	2.954s	0.280s
18	Bostrom	USA	LCR Honda MotoGP	1m 25.291s	4.089s	1.135s

FINISHERS

1 CASEY STONER Found something overnight to banish the tyre woes of the previous two races and give him the consistency he lacked in qualifying. Started carefully, then put two of the best passes ever on Pedrosa and Lorenzo to win and extend his lead in the championship to 20 points.

2 JORGE LORENZO Amazingly fast and consistent in qualifying and took pole after a massive highside at the end of third free practice. Hurting on race day but didn't use that as an excuse. Ran into tyre trouble in the closing laps but admitted that on the day everyone except Casey was racing for second place.

3 DANI PEDROSA His fitness problems – specifically lack of strength in his left shoulder and arm – were more significant here than in Germany. Knew he was in trouble by half-distance and had to settle for third. Not helped by a general lack of grip, but went up to fourth in the championship, in front of Rossi.

4 BEN SPIES Top finisher on the softer tyre, but his podium chances were effectively ruined at the start. The launch-control electronics refused to give him the required power and he was swamped on the run through Turn 1 and then boxed in at Turn 2. Took time to get past Rossi but persevered to hunt down Dovi.

5 ANDREA DOVIZIOSO Lost a fight for the first time this season to concede fourth to Spies at the end of the race. Pushed to go with the top three but lost out in Turns 3 and 11 and had to make up lost ground on the brakes. Had the speed but not the consistency.

6 VALENTINO ROSSI Decided, with the return of crew chief Jerry Burgess, to concentrate on the GP11.1 Desmosedici. Improved through the weekend but only able to race with his team-mate and Bautista. Tried to go with the leaders, lost the front two or three times, then had to work hard to keep ahead of Hayden.

7 NICKY HAYDEN Ran back-to-back tests on the two versions of the Ducati on Friday before deciding to stick with the older version. Diced with his team-mate for most of the race, just as in Germany the previous weekend, and not exactly overjoyed with the result at a track where he has won in front of his home fans.

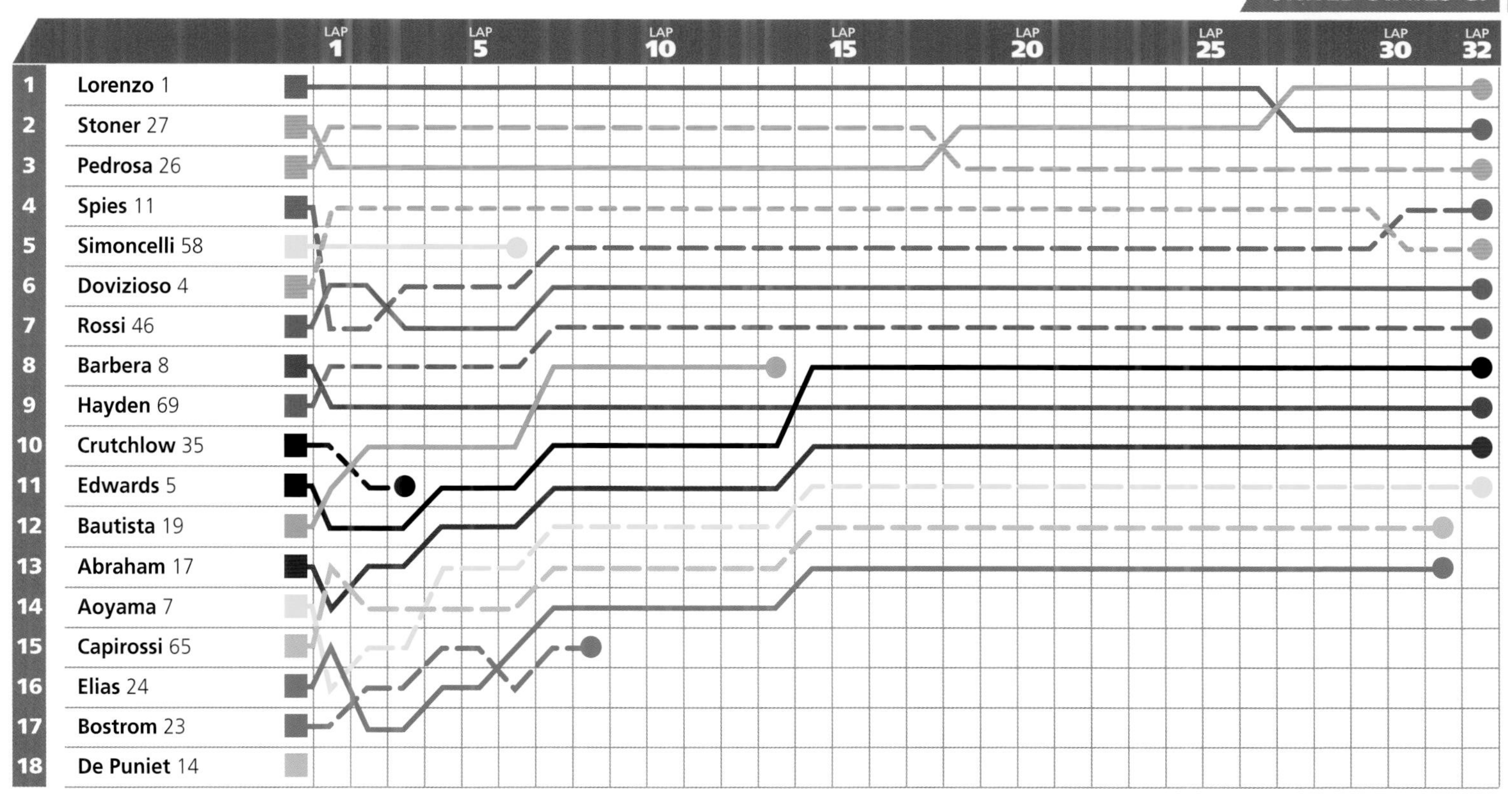

RACE

	Rider	Motorcycle	Race Time	Time +	Fastest Lap	Av Speed	
1	Stoner	Honda	43m 52.145s		1m 21.673s	98.178mph	H/M
2	Lorenzo	Yamaha	43m 57.779s	5.634s	1m 21.692s	97.968mph	H/M
3	Pedrosa	Honda	44m 01.612s	9.467s	1m 21.738s	97.826mph	H/M
4	Spies	Yamaha	44m 12.707s	20.562s	1m 22.244s	97.416mph	H/S
5	Dovizioso	Honda	44m 13.030s	20.885s	1m 21.913s	97.405mph	H/M
6	Rossi	Ducati	44m 22.496s	30.351s	1m 22.520s	97.058mph	H/S
7	Hayden	Ducati	44m 23.176s	31.031s	1m 22.704s	97.034mph	H/S
8	Edwards	Yamaha	44m 37.647s	45.502s	1m 22.952s	96.509mph	H/S
9	Barbera	Ducati	44m 43.694s	51.549s	1m 22.850s	96.292mph	H/S
10	Aoyama	Honda	45m 00.995s	1m 08.850s	1m 23.518s	95.675mph	H/S
11	Abraham	Ducati	45m 01.277s	1m 09.132s	1m 23.131s	95.665mph	H/S
12	Capirossi	Ducati	44m 05.129s	1 lap	1m 23.661s	94.642mph	M/S
13	Elias	Honda	44m 29.962s	1 lap	1m 24.200s	93.763mph	M/S
NF	Bautista	Suzuki	18m 06.782s	19 laps	1m 22.592s	96.599mph	H/S
NF	Bostrom	Honda	12m 09.042s	24 laps	1m 24.091s	88.616mph	M/S
NF	Simoncelli	Honda	8m 21.101s	26 laps	1m 22.091s	96.694mph	H/M
NF	Crutchlow	Yamaha	4m 18.554s	29 laps	1m 23.063s	93.700mph	H/S

CHAMPIONSHIP

	Rider	Team	Points
1	Stoner	Repsol Honda Team	193
2	Lorenzo	Yamaha Factory Racing	173
3	Dovizioso	Repsol Honda Team	143
4	Pedrosa	Repsol Honda Team	110
5	Rossi	Ducati Team	108
6	Spies	Yamaha Factory Racing	98
7	Hayden	Ducati Team	94
8	Edwards	Monster Yamaha Tech 3	67
9	Aoyama	San Carlo Honda Gresini	63
10	Simoncelli	San Carlo Honda Gresini	60
11	Barbera	Mapfre Aspar Team MotoGP	56
12	Abraham	Cardion AB Motoracing	46
13	Bautista	Rizla Suzuki MotoGP	39
14	Elias	LCR Honda MotoGP	38
15	Crutchlow	Monster Yamaha Tech 3	34
16	Capirossi	Pramac Racing Team	26
17	De Puniet	Pramac Racing Team	15
18	Hopkins	Rizla Suzuki MotoGP	6
19	Akiyoshi	San Carlo Honda Gresini	3

8 COLIN EDWARDS After the set-up problems of the last two races he reverted to his settings from 2010 for warm-up and the race. Lacked grip, and if he pushed his lap times got worse. Saw his team-mate crash and knew he just had to stay smooth and collect the points.

9 HECTOR BARBERA Went for the softer tyre, like the factory Ducatis, but lost touch with them when rear grip went off. Didn't quite live up to the promise of practice and qualifying but still a decent result.

10 HIROSHI AOYAMA Still affected by the Assen crash and off the pace in qualifying. Did achieve some regularity in the second half of the race but Hiro's team manager, never an easy man to impress in any case, publicly speculated about his motivation.

11 KAREL ABRAHAM Qualified and started badly but looked to be closing on Barbera in the closing stages when something failed in the rear suspension. Passed by Aoyama on the last lap.

12 LORIS CAPIROSSI Rode despite the severe handicap of the rib and shoulder injuries suffered at Assen. Managed a good start and a few fast laps before the pain was too much and he took no more risks. Just didn't want to see anyone else on his bike again.

13 TONI ELIAS Tried a major change to the rear set-up on race morning, which felt right, and got his usual good start. However, the problems with the front soon returned and he ran off-track, after which he said he felt he was riding on ice.

NON-FINISHERS

ALVARO BAUTISTA His loss of the front while chasing the Ducatis disguised what was another promising weekend for the Suzuki team. His pace had been almost good enough to race with Spies and Dovizioso, and he reported he felt better than ever on a MotoGP bike but that he should have used the softer front tyre.

BEN BOSTROM A wild card for the LCR team's second bike – Elias's spare. Not surprisingly, the 37-year-old GP rookie qualified last but in the race immediately took a second off his lap time before running off track after hitting his foot on the ground in Turn 1. Decided to pull in when he had the same problem next time round.

MARCO SIMONCELLI A little bit off the pace in qualifying, then found that the front gave him more trouble in the race than in practice. Lost the front in Turn 7 on lap one, then terminally in Turn 8 two laps later while chasing Dovizioso.

CAL CRUTCHLOW Lost the front at Turn 2 while chasing Bautista. Hotter afternoon temperatures precipitated the problem, an echo of his difficulties in recent races. Team manager Hervé Poncharal lamented the fact that such an early crash meant Cal didn't get the track time a rookie would need.

NON-STARTERS

RANDY DE PUNIET Crashed heavily in qualifying, cracking two vertebrae and his pelvis. Intended to race but his hip swelled up overnight 'like a football' – he had to get a doctor out to deal with the pain and announced on Sunday morning that he couldn't race.

CZECH REPUBLIC GP

AUTOMOTODROM BRNO

ROUND **11**

August 14

FIGHTBACK

Stoner profited from mistakes by his main rivals to extend his title lead, and Simoncelli finally made it to the rostrum

For the fourth race in a row, the form from practice and qualifying did not carry across to the race. If it had done, Dani Pedrosa would have won comfortably from his first pole position of the season. Three weeks away from racetracks and hospitals had done the Spanish rider a power of good; he felt fit and rested, and finally decided to use the latest Ohlins front forks, something he'd been dithering over since the test at Brno a year ago. There were none of the one-lap practice efforts seen in Germany. This time his pace was consistently fast. Right from the start of first free practice Dani was at the top of the timing sheets, which is not his normal way of working. If you hadn't checked the number on his bike you'd have thought it was Casey Stoner out on track.

The real Casey Stoner wasn't so happy. Of course he was quick, but he used the word 'frustrated' a lot when talking about his set-up, and matters weren't helped by a fast crash in third free practice. Casey got away with it but John Hopkins, riding as a wild card for Suzuki, wasn't so lucky. He had an identical crash on the brakes going into Turn 3 and looked to be sliding harmlessly into the gravel, well away from his bike. Cruelly, though, he had his hand in front of him to try to scrub off some speed, and the impact with the gravel trap snapped the fingers back, breaking three of them, one badly. Right up until that moment Suzuki had been having their best weekend not just of the season but for a very long time. Hopkins and Bautista had been seventh and eighth in the first free practice, and the bike was obviously working well at a track where it

used to struggle. Hopper had his career-best result, second place, at this track in 2007, and his presence here really gave the team a boost. Like Pedrosa, their weekend went from great to gruesome in the time it takes for a front tyre to lose adhesion.

The third man to suffer was Jorge Lorenzo. He looked the rider most likely to give Pedrosa and the other Hondas a fight, but his race was compromised by his choice of the softer front tyre. He'd run it in qualifying as well as on Friday, when it gave 'a good feeling and consistent pace', but in the race he felt in danger of crashing at every corner from the second lap onwards. He did lead on the first lap but was soon shuffled back after one amazing save at Turn 1 when the front tucked. The only other rider to choose the softer front was Alvaro Bautista, whose race pace was astounding, but his habit of qualifying badly masked this progress. He was the second-fastest man on track for four laps and 1.8s quicker per lap than in 2010.

Lorenzo knew by the second lap that his chance of victory had gone, and then one lap later a bemused Pedrosa was sliding out of the lead. Dani lost the front and didn't know why: 'I may have tilted the bike too much or maybe the tyre was not warm enough. Still, I don't know. The problem is that I've wasted an important race that we had prepared for very well.'

Which left a slightly bemused Casey Stoner out in front, controlling the race. He'd pushed a lot harder than he wanted to in the opening laps in order to go with the Spaniards, and after the race reported himself pleasantly surprised to take a comfortable win after a tough weekend. His Repsol team-mate Andrea

Above Marco Simoncelli finally made it to the MotoGP rostrum as part of a Honda clean sweep

Opposite top Simoncelli didn't have it easy at Brno; he had to fight back from sixth place

Below Brno is one of the best tracks for spectators, especially in the 'stadium' area

agv
58
MONSTER
SAN CARLO
HONDA
BRIDGESTONE
DAINESE
がんばれ日本!

GENERALI
GENERALI
GENERALI

Above Front wheel aviating and crossed up, out on the rumble strip and on the gas; Casey Stoner at work

Below Cal Crutchlow's run of bad luck continued with another crash

Dovizioso came through from a third-row qualifying position to take second, thanks in large part to one of his trademark starts. To complete the first all-Honda podium since Laguna Seca in 2006, Marco Simoncelli also came through from disappointing qualifying to finally claim his first rostrum finish in MotoGP.

Dovizioso lost touch with Stoner when he got into a corner far too hot and let Lorenzo past. Simoncelli thought he could catch Dovi late in the race but Andrea had enough in reserve to press over the final five laps, causing Marco to do the sensible thing. His relief was obvious. 'I need this result, all the polemic of this year – some mistakes, some confusion – I've been a little bit more careful.' Not that he had an uneventful race; a short scrap with his friend Valentino Rossi left him with tyre marks on his leathers.

Rossi's finishing position of sixth didn't really look any more impressive than most of his earlier results, but some serious progress had been made. On a track that should have punished the Ducati's front-end uncertainty more than any other on the calendar, Rossi closed the gap to the front runners from roughly one second to 0.7s per lap. Ducati had brought new parts, probably to allow for a greater range of adjustment, and possibly a new carbon 'shoebox' chassis. Valentino said he could now 'feel what the front tyre is doing, force on the entry and brake on the edge'. It was, he said, 'a small but clear step'.

Rossi's race was compromised by mistakes in the tyre warm-up procedure going to the line and also by a bad start. 'I lose two seconds, after which I have the pace to fight for the podium.' As he eased off significantly in the final two laps, this was not an idle boast. 'I heat the front tyre in a better way, remain the understeer, braking and corner entry are better.' On that evidence, Rossi and Ducati were on the way to making the Desmosedici, if only the 11.1 iteration, competitive. As Vale said, 'I was in the same TV shot as Dovizioso at the end!' True, but as he and everyone else was well aware, it was going to need a very wide-angle lens to keep Casey in sight.

RESURRECTION MAN

It's a truism that international sport doesn't hand out second chances. Get it wrong first time round, for whatever reason, and you'll be spat out never to return. By this rule, John Hopkins shouldn't have had a chance of coming back to MotoGP after he finished fourth overall on a Suzuki in 2007 and then made a big-money move to Kawasaki, which was when things started to go wrong. Injuries, painkillers and booze took over – but now he has been sober for nearly two years.

Hopper's Brno was the culmination of a remarkable sequence of three weekends of racing in three different championships. First he went to Silverstone and set pole position for the British round of the World Superbike Championship, finishing just off the podium in both races. Next it was the British Superbike Championship on the Brands Hatch long circuit and a fourth and two rostrums in three races. Then it was Brno and seventh and tenth in Friday's practices before his wet-weather crash.

To perform at that level on three different types of tyre on successive weekends is nothing short of remarkable, and indicative of his remarkable personal turnaround. John is very open about his problems and well aware of the chance Suzuki had given him, but he'd also done Suzuki some serious good. The fact he could go fast instantly on the bike demonstrated that the GSV-R had made progress and was now surely capable of running with the Ducatis and the 'non-Alien' works riders.

Hopefully, the factory will take note and be back for 2012. Bautista remarked before the race that 'if Hopkins is faster than me then I'm in trouble'. Alvaro doesn't have to worry about his race pace, just about his qualifying. He needs to be fast on Saturday as well as on Sunday.

'AFTER SUCH A HARD WEEKEND IT'S FANTASTIC TO COME OUT WITH A COMFORTABLE WIN'

CASEY STONER

Below Rossi thought he detected signs of hope in the Ducati's performance at a track it shouldn't have liked

CZECH REPUBLIC GP

AUTOMOTODROM BRNO

ROUND 11
August 14

RACE RESULTS

CIRCUIT LENGTH 3.357 miles
NO. OF LAPS 22
RACE DISTANCE 73.854 miles
WEATHER Dry, 24°C
TRACK TEMPERATURE 37°C
WINNER Casey Stoner
FASTEST LAP 1m 57.191s, 103.148mph, Casey Stoner
LAP RECORD 1m 56.670s, 103.592mph, Jorge Lorenzo, 2009

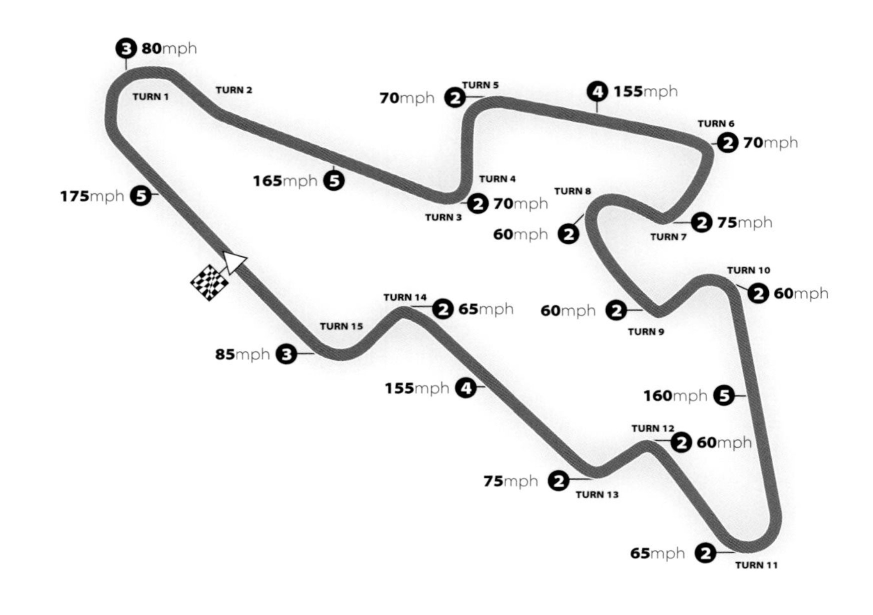

QUALIFYING

	Rider	Nationality	Team	Qualifying	Pole +	Gap
1	Pedrosa	SPA	Repsol Honda Team	1m 56.591s		
2	Lorenzo	SPA	Yamaha Factory Racing	1m 56.704s	0.113s	0.113s
3	Stoner	AUS	Repsol Honda Team	1m 56.860s	0.269s	0.156s
4	Spies	USA	Yamaha Factory Racing	1m 57.178s	0.587s	0.318s
5	Simoncelli	ITA	San Carlo Honda Gresini	1m 57.351s	0.760s	0.173s
6	Rossi	ITA	Ducati Team	1m 57.367s	0.776s	0.016s
7	Dovizioso	ITA	Repsol Honda Team	1m 57.442s	0.851s	0.075s
8	Edwards	USA	Monster Yamaha Tech 3	1m 57.676S	1.085s	0.234s
9	Hayden	USA	Ducati Team	1m 57.721s	1.130s	0.045s
10	Aoyama	JPN	San Carlo Honda Gresini	1m 57.784s	1.193s	0.063s
11	Crutchlow	GBR	Monster Yamaha Tech 3	1m 57.797s	1.206s	0.013s
12	Elias	SPA	LCR Honda MotoGP	1m 58.245s	1.654s	0.448s
13	Barbera	SPA	Mapfre Aspar Team	1m 58.273s	1.682s	0.028s
14	Bautista	SPA	Rizla Suzuki MotoGP	1m 58.274s	1.683s	0.001s
15	De Puniet	FRA	Pramac Racing Team	1m 58.889s	2.298s	0.615s
16	Capirossi	ITA	Pramac Racing Team	1m 58.938s	2.347s	0.049s
17	Abraham	CZE	Cardion AB Motoracing	1m 58.946s	2.355s	0.008s
*	Hopkins	USA	Rizla Suzuki MotoGP			

FINISHERS

1 CASEY STONER Worked through a difficult practice and qualifying looking for set-up he felt comfortable with. Had to press a lot harder than he wanted at the start to stay with Lorenzo and Pedrosa, then found the bike starting to work for him when the fuel load went down. Mildly surprised at the ease of his win.

2 ANDREA DOVIZIOSO Fourth runner-up spot of the year. Started well from bad qualifying, swapped places with Lorenzo before losing touch with Stoner, made a major mistake on the brakes and had to deal with Jorge again, then it was a matter of controlling the gap to Simoncelli, accomplished with a very rapid final five laps.

3 MARCO SIMONCELLI Relieved to get his first rostrum in MotoGP at last. Qualified badly, then didn't start well, but fought his way past Rossi and the factory Yamahas. Thought he had a chance of catching Dovizioso but declined to take too many risks as Dovi pressed in the closing five laps.

4 JORGE LORENZO Chose the softer front tyre (the only other rider to make that choice was Bautista) after doing long runs on it on Friday and Saturday. Started well but was soon in trouble. Like a few others, found the race-day conditions different. Survived a big front-end moment early on and struggled with braking and turning.

5 BEN SPIES Suffered from what he thought was a trapped nerve in his neck, spending more time in the Clinica Mobile than the rest of his career put together, and his right arm was numb after the race. Had thought he'd be unable to do more than a dozen laps at race pace so was surprised to finish fifth.

6 VALENTINO ROSSI Most promising race from his first second-row start of the year. The Ducati's front-end problems should have been cruelly exposed here – and those of the satellite bikes were – but to finish less than 5s from the rostrum was a major step forward. New parts for the front were used in the race and more tested on Monday.

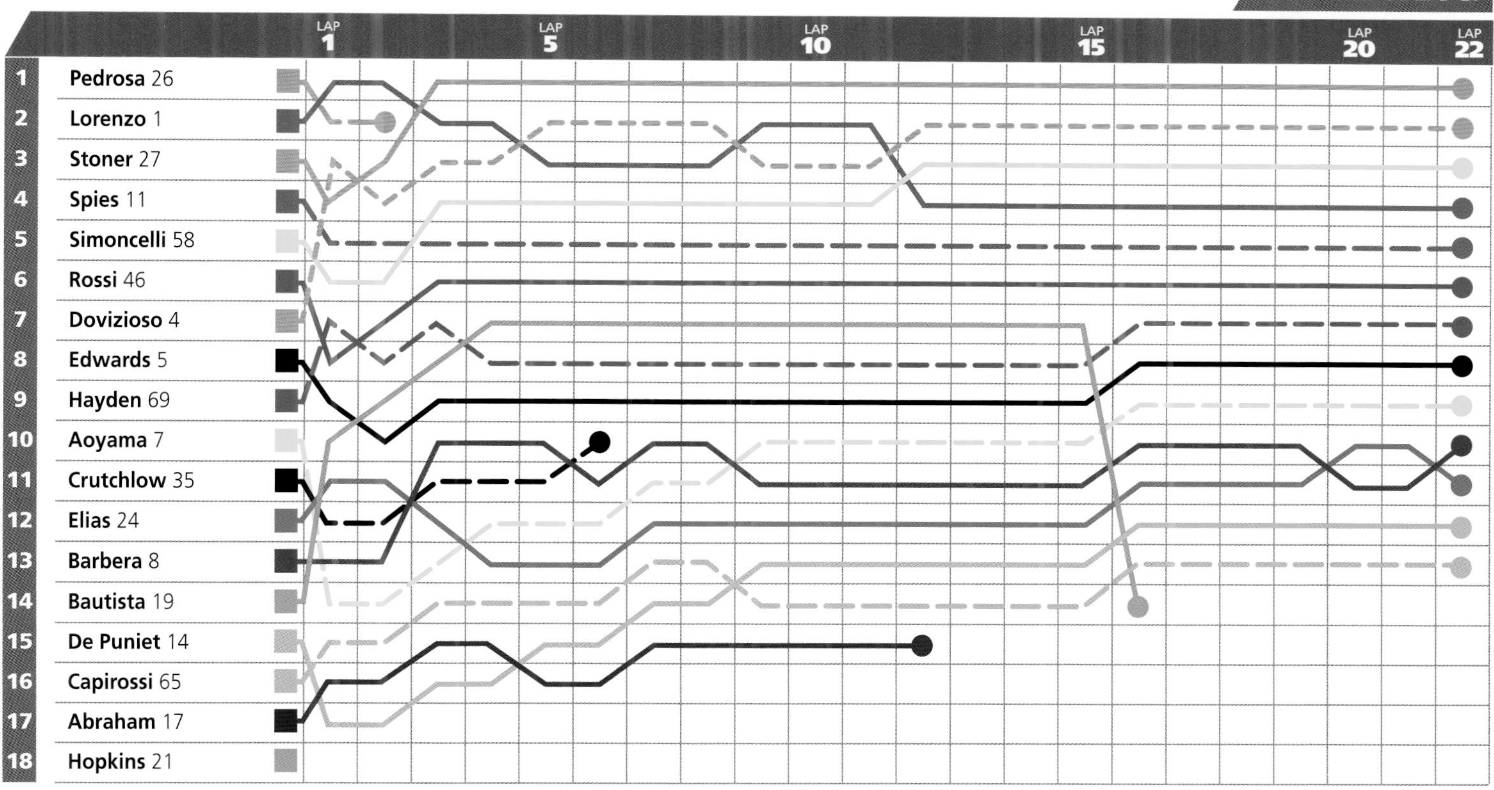

RACE

	Rider	Motorcycle	Race Time	Time +	Fastest Lap	Av Speed	
1	Stoner	Honda	43m 16.796s		1m 57.191s	102.396mph	XH/S
2	Dovizioso	Honda	43m 23.328s	6.532s	1m 57.468s	102.140mph	XH/S
3	Simoncelli	Honda	43m 24.588s	7.792s	1m 57.497s	102.090mph	XH/S
4	Lorenzo	Yamaha	43m 25.309s	8.513s	1m 57.636s	102.062mph	H/S
5	Spies	Yamaha	43m 26.982s	10.186s	1m 57.726s	101.996mph	XH/S
6	Rossi	Ducati	43m 29.428s	12.632s	1m 57.844s	101.901mph	XH/S
7	Hayden	Ducati	43m 39.833s	23.037s	1m 58.264s	101.496mph	XH/S
8	Edwards	Yamaha	43m 40.985s	24.189s	1m 58.522s	101.451mph	XH/S
9	Aoyama	Honda	43m 41.998s	25.202s	1m 58.484s	101.412mph	XH/S
10	Barbera	Ducati	43m 53.362s	36.566s	1m 58.687s	100.974mph	XH/S
11	Elias	Honda	43m 53.475s	36.679s	1m 58.971s	100.970mph	XH/S
12	De Puniet	Ducati	43m 53.905s	37.109s	1m 58.775s	100.954mph	XH/S
13	Capirossi	Ducati	44m 05.707s	48.911s	1m 59.139s	100.503mph	XH/S
NF	Bautista	Suzuki	32m 33.227s	6 laps	1m 57.821s	99.007mph	H/S
NF	Abraham	Ducati	26m 08.827s	10 laps	1m 58.978s	92.450mph	XH/S
NF	Crutchlow	Yamaha	12m 01.440s	16 laps	1m 58.362s	100.520mph	XH/S
NF	Pedrosa	Honda	4m 01.636s	20 laps	1m 57.518s	100.039mph	XH/S

CHAMPIONSHIP

	Rider	Team	Points
1	Stoner	Repsol Honda Team	218
2	Lorenzo	Yamaha Factory Racing	186
3	Dovizioso	Repsol Honda Team	163
4	Rossi	Ducati Team	118
5	Pedrosa	Repsol Honda Team	110
6	Spies	Yamaha Factory Racing	109
7	Hayden	Ducati Team	103
8	Simoncelli	San Carlo Honda Gresini	76
9	Edwards	Monster Yamaha Tech 3	75
10	Aoyama	San Carlo Honda Gresini	70
11	Barbera	Mapfre Aspar Team MotoGP	62
12	Abraham	Cardion AB Motoracing	46
13	Elias	LCR Honda MotoGP	43
14	Bautista	Rizla Suzuki MotoGP	39
15	Crutchlow	Monster Yamaha Tech 3	34
16	Capirossi	Pramac Racing Team	29
17	De Puniet	Pramac Racing Team	19
18	Hopkins	Rizla Suzuki MotoGP	6
19	Akiyoshi	San Carlo Honda Gresini	3

7 NICKY HAYDEN Rode the standard 11.0 version of the Ducati, and in his own words he 'chipped away' at its problems all weekend and made minor improvements. Spent most of the race fending off Edwards rather than threatening his team-mate. Tested the 11.1 on Monday and decide to change to it for the next race.

8 COLIN EDWARDS Said before the race that if he finished where he started he'd be happy, and that's what happened. Made a geometry change after warm-up when he had major grip problems and then ran remarkably consistent lap times in the race, but had nothing extra with which to challenge Hayden.

9 HIROSHI AOYAMA Happier with his fitness and the bike. Had a few grip problems but put in a spirited ride for his best finish since the Dutch TT. Made up for a bad start but was gifted most of the places by the crashers.

10 HECTOR BARBERA Ran into front-end problems after five laps which made him feel the front was going to go on the brakes in certain corners. Caught by Elias and de Puniet in the closing stages and did well to defend his position.

11 TONI ELIAS At last, something resembling decent form. Didn't get his usual fast start and found himself in a dice, losing touch with Aoyama and caught over the final two laps by Barbera. Encouraged by the significant reduction in the gap to the leaders.

12 RANDY DE PUNIET The injuries from his Laguna Seca crash meant Randy had to deal with severe back pain. Thought he could fight with the two in front of him but had to grit his teeth to get to the finish.

13 LORIS CAPIROSSI Like his team-mate, Loris was OK until the pain in his arm became too much and all he could do was focus on getting to the flag.

NON-FINISHERS

ALVARO BAUTISTA His crash disguised what was a very promising race for Suzuki. Lap times were on average faster than those of the factory Yamahas and Rossi's Ducati, and for four laps he was the second-fastest man out there. His race ended when he lost the front at Turn 13 while lying seventh with six laps to go.

KAREL ABRAHAM Once again, the pressure of the home race told. Karel was all over the local media and it's hard to believe he wasn't distracted. Qualified last, crashed early on while attacking Capirossi but managed to remount, only for the bike to expire.

CAL CRUTCHLOW Another front-end crash, this time while on the gas at the exit of Turn 1… just what Cal didn't need as he searched for confidence in the front.

DANI PEDROSA Lost the front on lap three just after taking the lead, having qualified in pole position for the first time this year. Couldn't understand why he'd crashed.

NON-STARTERS

JOHN HOPKINS Entered as a wild card for the second time this season. Faster than his team-mate on Friday but a wet-weather crash on Saturday resulted in three broken fingers.

INDIANAPOLIS GP
INDIANAPOLIS MOTOR SPEEDWAY
ROUND 12
August 28
DUNLOP

GROUNDHOG DAY

The only thing that got near Casey Stoner was the local wildlife, the Aussie making it three in a row as Jorge Lorenzo had another bad day

It felt like a turning point. Despite universal uncertainty over tyre life on the newly resurfaced infield of the Indianapolis Motor Speedway, Casey Stoner romped to his third win in a row as Jorge Lorenzo hit the predicted rubber trouble.

This wasn't a machinery thing, because Ben Spies on the other factory Yamaha didn't have too many problems while two of the other three factory Honda riders did. It was a matter of tyre management and riding style; some riders just gave their front tyre an easier time. Marco Simoncelli, heavier than most and with a super-aggressive style, was out of front grip before half-distance. Spies, by no means the smallest guy on the grid, had to fight his way back from a horrible start, yet he got on the rostrum. Just to show how complicated the situation was, Andrea Dovizioso reported front and rear grip issues at the start but set his best lap of the race on the final circuit.

The one thing that was clear all weekend was that Stoner was going to be the man to beat. He was half a second quicker than anyone in qualifying and was simply awesome to watch in the final corner, a tight left-hander on to the oval circuit that's vital to get right in order to carry speed on to the long front straight and down to the favourite Indy passing place at Turn 1. Casey dialled in improbable amounts of throttle as, still hanging off to the inside of the corner, he pushed the bike upright to get it on the fat part of the tyre while running up the angle-iron kerbing. The result was serious speed at the end of the straight, where he took the lead from Dani Pedrosa on lap seven. After qualifying, the Aussie had warned that the vagaries of varying grip and temperature would make for an unpredictable race; it was the one thing he got wrong all weekend, because it was business as usual on his way to a 44-point lead over Lorenzo.

The action came from the home-town heroes, Ben Spies and Nicky Hayden. Spies looked to be the man most likely to give Casey a race, but the first few corners put paid to that idea. His start, he said, wasn't bad, but what followed immediately afterwards was. Ben was already back in fifth going into Turn 4 when he had a coming-together with Andrea Dovizioso that was violent enough to shake the Texan's feet off the pegs, after which he was quickly shuffled back to ninth. At the end of the first lap, he was over 2.5s down on the leader, Pedrosa.

Dani had been strangely downbeat about his chances after the crash at Brno, and seemed relieved to get a good start and finish second. He reverted to the old design of Ohlins forks, obviously making the current design the scapegoat for his otherwise inexplicable Czech crash.

The last pass in Spies's charge through the field to finish third on the rostrum was on his team-mate Jorge Lorenzo, and it was the only time he was able to pass at the end of the straight. Nicky Hayden also had some fun, but not for long. He was the only rider to go with the softer front tyre, saying the harder option had been even worse in practice, graining more quickly, and after the race he pointed out that two Ducatis had pulled in when the harder front didn't last.

However, Nicky had looked a picture of frustration all weekend. This was his first race with the 11.1 version of the Ducati and it did at least let him ride a very competitive first few laps. There was a lot of very Italian arm-waving in the pit garage on Saturday, most of it uncharacteristically being done by Nicky, and although he argued that the soft tyre was the better choice the decision looked like an attempt to put on a show for his fans. Indianapolis is a short drive from Nicky's home town and the idea of not being

Above Alvaro Bautista wore a special crash helmet design, later auctioned for the Japanese disaster appeal

Below The Indianapolis Motor Speedway's main building dominates the sky line

Opposite Jorge Lorenzo congratulates Casey Stoner on his third consecutive victory

YAMAHA
PETRONAS
REPSOL
SEMAKIN DI DEPAN
がんばろう日

Right Hector Barbera tried a little bit too hard on the final lap

Opposite Ben Spies made a terrible start but battled his way through to a podium finish

Below Rossi had to come back from last place after gearbox problems, Simoncelli's tyres gave up, and Crutchlow split them at the flag

competitive in front of his friends and family was just too much. He let it all out in a combative opening few laps but the inevitable happened and he slid down the order, eventually pitting with a front tyre down to the carcass. 'It felt like in the dry was the first time I could put up any kind of fight. Obviously we made a mistake but we tried to do something. It wasn't the right thing but we were just destroying front tyres when you don't have front grip.'

Valentino Rossi also had problems with the front end of his Ducati, although the previously problem-free seamless-shift gearbox was the cause of most of the troubles that saw him finish 10th. It found a false neutral seven or eight times, twice sending Rossi straight on and up the banking at the first corner. The top Ducati rider was Randy de Puniet, having his best race of the year in eighth, on the satellite Pramac bike.

The only obstacle all weekend to Casey's progress came from the local wildlife. On Saturday afternoon he only just managed to avoid a large rodent on the track. There was some debate about the species. Beaver? Woodchuck? Gopher? The consensus was woodchuck – otherwise known as a groundhog. Which begged a question: how many more times would Casey dominate a race in exactly the same way?

'I WAS STRUGGLING WITH GRIP BUT I SUPPOSE IN COMPARISON WITH EVERYONE ELSE WE FELT PRETTY GOOD'

CASEY STONER

GOODBYE NUMBER 9

Motorcycle racing lost an American icon when Gary Nixon died just before the Indy GP. Nixon, who seemed to have lived at least several lives on and off track, was 70 years old when he passed away from complications of a heart attack.

There may never be a more American racer than Gary Nixon. Too scrawny for ball sports, Nixon found his tight build made for racing. He came of age in the mid-1960s, won Daytona and the AMA championship in 1967, and by 1968 was the man that racers of the era were usually measured against. 'Beating Nixon' was an achievement not taken lightly by the men who were among the fastest of the fast.

As children of the 1970s, Nixon and former World Champion Barry Sheene gravitated towards each other and enjoyed a lifelong friendship. Sheene usually raced wearing a Gary Nixon T-shirt under his leathers. It was an uncommonly – for rivals and riders – close friendship.

Nixon didn't seem to require sleep and no matter how beat up he was, or which limb he had broken, he was always blazingly fast. The record books show he was second in the 1976 F750 world championship (F750 was a precursor of Superbike). Most people think he was the winner.

In written correspondence, Nixon always referred to it as a 'disputed championship'. He never said that it was his, but wasn't shy about saying the politics of the situation were like nationalistic quicksand. On the flip side, one wonders if that season and title would be so well known today if the results were cut and dried, even if Nixon were officially given the title. Literally a hundred stories about Nixon in the last 30 years used the unjust angle of the '76 championship as a lead. Victor Palermo, who is credited with the title, is an obscure figure in motorcycle racing history.

Nixon's legend spanned generations. Both Nicky Hayden and Ben Spies call Nixon's hard-edged and undefeatable soul an inspiration and influence on their racing careers. Spies actually ran after Nixon one day in his AMA career so as to shake his hand and introduce himself. Hayden knew Nixon virtually his entire life – his father and Nixon were good friends – and can recall falling asleep as a lad with Nixon telling stories from his career.

Neither Hayden nor Spies had been born in 1976.

Above Steve Parrish, an old friend of Nixon's, did a lap at Indianapolis on Gary's championship-winning Triumph in the reverse direction – an old dirt-track tradition

INDIANAPOLIS GP

INDIANAPOLIS MOTOR SPEEDWAY

ROUND 12
August 28

RACE RESULTS

CIRCUIT LENGTH 2.620 miles
NO. OF LAPS 28
RACE DISTANCE 73.360 miles
WEATHER Dry, 27°C
TRACK TEMPERATURE 51°C
WINNER Casey Stoner
FASTEST LAP 1m 39.807s, 94.510mph, Casey Stoner
PREVIOUS LAP RECORD 1m 40.896s, 92.605mph, Dani Pedrosa, 2010

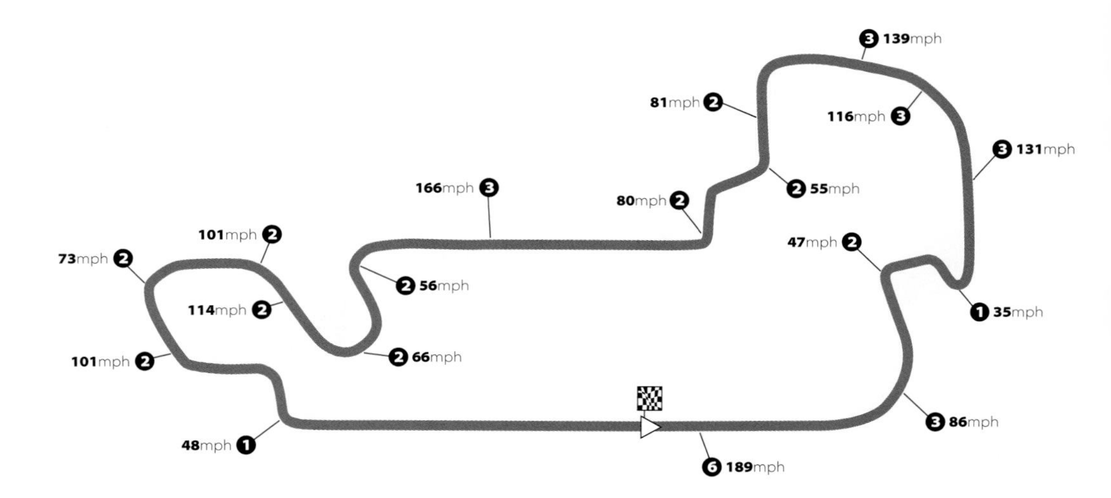

QUALIFYING

	Rider	Nationality	Team	Qualifying	Pole +	Gap
1	Stoner	AUS	Repsol Honda Team	1m 38.850s		
2	Spies	USA	Yamaha Factory Racing	1m 39.373s	0.523s	0.523s
3	Lorenzo	SPA	Yamaha Factory Racing	1m 39.629s	0.779s	0.256s
4	Pedrosa	SPA	Repsol Honda Team	1m 39.947s	1.097s	0.318s
5	Dovizioso	ITA	Repsol Honda Team	1m 40.024s	1.174s	0.077s
6	Edwards	USA	Monster Yamaha Tech 3	1m 40.098s	1.248s	0.074s
7	Simoncelli	ITA	San Carlo Honda Gresini	1m 40.204s	1.354s	0.106s
8	Hayden	USA	Ducati Team	1m 40.244s	1.394s	0.040s
9	Bautista	SPA	Rizla Suzuki MotoGP	1m 40.333s	1.483s	0.089s
10	Barbera	SPA	Mapfre Aspar Team	1m 40.360s	1.510s	0.027s
11	Crutchlow	GBR	Monster Yamaha Tech 3	1m 40.620s	1.770s	0.260s
12	De Puniet	FRA	Pramac Racing Team	1m 40.815s	1.965s	0.195s
13	Aoyama	JPN	San Carlo Honda Gresini	1m 40.925s	2.075s	0.110s
14	Rossi	ITA	Ducati Team	1m 40.975s	2.125s	0.050s
15	Elias	SPA	LCR Honda MotoGP	1m 41.030s	2.180s	0.055s
16	Abraham	CZE	Cardion AB Motoracing	1m 41.085s	2.235s	0.055s
17	Capirossi	ITA	Pramac Racing Team	1m 41.092s	2.242s	0.007s

FINISHERS

1 CASEY STONER Another masterclass and maybe the championship-clinching race – pole by 0.5s, fastest lap on the 20th of 28 laps, and the win for a 44-point lead at the top of the table. Vociferous in his complaints about the track before the race, but managed the ever-changing surface perfectly.

2 DANI PEDROSA A whole second slower than Stoner in qualifying and well over 0.5s slower than Spies, so pleasantly surprised to finish second. Reverted to the old Ohlins forks after his Brno crash. Made the holeshot but knew he couldn't go with Casey, so it became a matter of concentration and tyre management.

3 BEN SPIES Looked like the only man capable of giving Stoner a race until he got boxed in off the start, cut up by Simoncelli and sideswiped by Dovizioso, to find himself back in ninth by the fourth corner. Then put in what may have been ride of the day to get on the rostrum, proving there are no team orders at Yamaha.

4 JORGE LORENZO A great start but suffered from front-tyre problems, unlike his team-mate, and knew his race was effectively over after just four or five laps. Also very well aware that the gap at the top of the table between himself and Stoner was now a highly significant 44 points.

5 ANDREA DOVIZIOSO Had tyre troubles early on which weren't helped by some rough treatment from Hayden and a bump with Spies. Changed his style and set his fastest lap of the race last time round as he closed dramatically on Lorenzo.

6 ALVARO BAUTISTA His and Suzuki's best dry-weather result of the season, aided considerably by his joint best qualifying. Fought Hayden and Edwards before opening up a gap, reporting the bike wasn't as good as at the previous two rounds and this was the best he could achieve. Especially as he crashed in those two races…

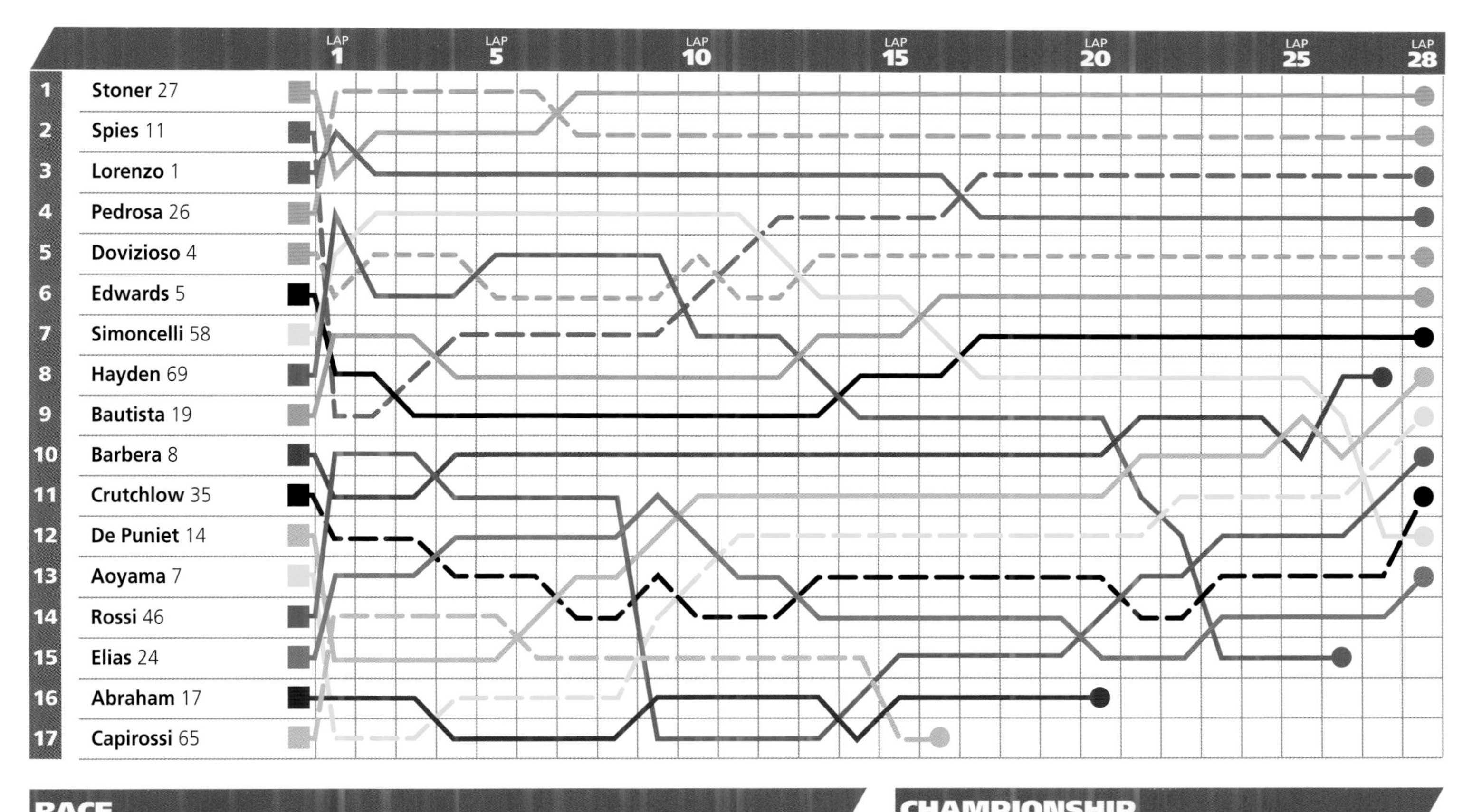

RACE

	Rider	Motorcycle	Race Time	Time +	Fastest Lap	Av Speed	B
1	Stoner	Honda	46m 52.786s		1m 39.807s	93.883mph	H/H
2	Pedrosa	Honda	46m 57.614s	4.828s	1m 40.026s	93.722mph	H/H
3	Spies	Yamaha	47m 03.389s	10.603s	1m 39.874s	93.530mph	H/H
4	Lorenzo	Yamaha	47m 09.362s	16.576s	1m 40.349s	93.333mph	H/H
5	Dovizioso	Honda	47m 09.988s	17.202s	1m 40.108s	93.312mph	H/H
6	Bautista	Suzuki	47m 23.233s	30.447s	1m 40.768s	92.878mph	H/H
7	Edwards	Yamaha	47m 32.476s	39.690s	1m 40.521s	92.576mph	H/H
8	De Puniet	Ducati	47m 46.202s	53.416s	1m 40.856s	92.133mph	H/H
9	Aoyama	Honda	47m 46.576s	53.790s	1m 40.608s	92.122mph	H/H
10	Rossi	Ducati	47m 48.131s	55.345s	1m 41.189s	92.071mph	H/H
11	Crutchlow	Yamaha	47m 49.970s	57.184s	1m 40.993s	92.012mph	H/H
12	Simoncelli	Honda	47m 52.927s	1m 00.141s	1m 40.470s	91.918mph	H/H
13	Elias	Honda	47m 54.955s	1m 02.169s	1m 41.739s	91.852mph	H/H
14	Hayden	Ducati	47m 38.936s	2 laps	1m 40.516s	85.770mph	M/H
NF	Barbera	Ducati	46m 03.510s	1 lap	1m 40.892s	92.144mph	H/H
NF	Abraham	Ducati	34m 36.516s	8 laps	1m 41.864s	90.836mph	H/H
NF	Capirossi	Ducati	27m 47.440s	12 laps	1m 41.799s	90.497mph	H/H

CHAMPIONSHIP

	Rider	Team	Points
1	Stoner	Repsol Honda Team	243
2	Lorenzo	Yamaha Factory Racing	199
3	Dovizioso	Repsol Honda Team	174
4	Pedrosa	Repsol Honda Team	130
5	Spies	Yamaha Factory Racing	125
6	Rossi	Ducati Team	124
7	Hayden	Ducati Team	105
8	Edwards	Monster Yamaha Tech 3	84
9	Simoncelli	San Carlo Honda Gresini	80
10	Aoyama	San Carlo Honda Gresini	77
11	Barbera	Mapfre Aspar Team MotoGP	62
12	Bautista	Rizla Suzuki MotoGP	49
13	Abraham	Cardion AB Motoracing	46
14	Elias	LCR Honda MotoGP	46
15	Crutchlow	Monster Yamaha Tech 3	39
16	Capirossi	Pramac Racing Team	29
17	De Puniet	Pramac Racing Team	27
18	Hopkins	Rizla Suzuki MotoGP	6
19	Akiyoshi	San Carlo Honda Gresini	3

7 COLIN EDWARDS First non-factory bike after a good fight with Bautista before the field strung itself out. Lost out to the Suzuki on the front straight but made it up in the final twisty sector before a big moment with the front end a few laps from home made Colin back off.

8 RANDY DE PUNIET His best race of the year, and even better than it looked on paper as Randy was hit by his team-mate on the first lap and lost three places. He then rode through the group, making most progress in the second half of the race thanks to a set-up that didn't lead to tyre troubles.

9 HIROSHI AOYAMA No problems with tyres or his fitness, but with a more aggressive start he might have been able to fight for a higher finish, according to his team manager.

10 VALENTINO ROSSI An awful weekend. Qualifying ruined when he crashed his preferred bike early in the session, then the seamless-shift gearbox kept finding neutrals in the race, resulting in two trips up the banking at the first corner. Seriously thought about pulling in, but came back from last place on the track.

11 CAL CRUTCHLOW The happiest he's ever been with an 11th-place finish. Ran on at the first corner when his drink tube's mouthpiece came off and tried to choke him, but after a few early worries ended up enjoying the race and taking his best result since Catalunya.

12 MARCO SIMONCELLI Knew he'd be in trouble with front-tyre wear but thought he might have found an answer in warm-up. Unfortunately the elevated afternoon track temperature meant he was in serious trouble after just five laps, but held it together for another six or seven, and then did well to stay upright to the flag.

13 TONI ELIAS Tried to follow Aoyama early on but couldn't, spinning the rear tyre for most of the race.

14 NICKY HAYDEN First race on the 11.1, but visibly frustrated and angry at his home race. Gambled on the softer front and gave his fans a show with some ruthless moves in the first half-dozen laps before the rubber started to degrade. So bad later that he pulled in, only to be sent out as there were points to be had.

NON-FINISHERS

HECTOR BARBERA Did well to adjust his riding style after the tyre degraded just a few laps in, but lost the front attempting a last-corner pass on Aoyama.

KAREL ABRAHAM Pulled in when problems with the front tyre became too great.

LORIS CAPIROSSI Pulled in at the end of lap 16 with severe front-tyre wear. Reported losing the front at every corner from the fourth lap onwards.

SAN MARINO GP
MISANO WORLD CIRCUIT
ROUND 13
September 4

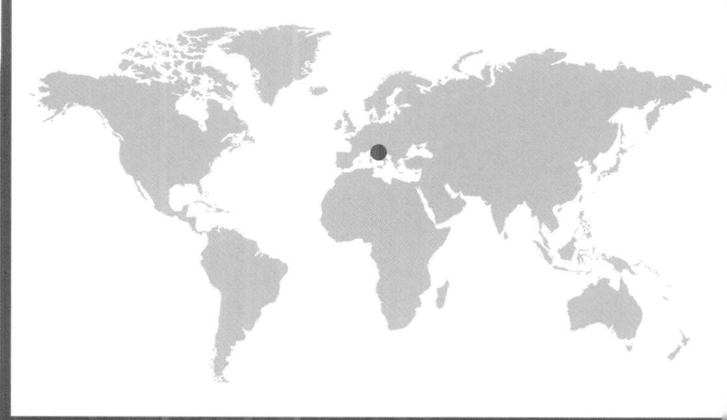

JORGE HAMMERS IT

Jorge Lorenzo struck back as Valentino Rossi and Marco Simoncelli kept the home fans happy

It was an emotional weekend for a lot of people. The return of Wayne Rainey to Misano 18 years after his career-ending crash aroused some complex feelings in a lot of people, especially the longer-serving members of the paddock. The man himself was totally unfazed. He wasn't there to lay any ghosts, he said. No regrets… except for the races that had got away. Wayne was in Italy as part of Yamaha's 50th anniversary of GP racing celebrations, and it just so happened that Misano fitted in with his family schedule. It's hard to avoid the conclusion that Wayne's presence helped inspire Jorge Lorenzo to a dominant performance. That may be fanciful, but it has been noticeable at races in the USA in previous years that Wayne has spent a lot of time in Jorge's garage.

Whatever the source of his form, the World Champion put together a near-perfect weekend. He didn't start from pole position, but even a perfunctory scan of the lap times from practice and qualifying showed that Lorenzo was the man with the best race pace. After Friday practice the TV cameras caught a telling image. Jorge was back in his pit garage and turned to face the lens, his eyes blazing with optimism and confidence. Even through the aperture of a crash helmet his state of mind was obvious. His team were actually worried that he might be over-confident, a fear fuelled by their rider's post-qualifying statements about the bike feeling like it did at Mugello.

They needn't have worried. Jorge was never headed, although it needed a very brave charge through the first chicane to keep Stoner back.

REV'IT!
RIZLA+
MICRON
SUZUKI
MOTUL
BRIDGESTONE
NGK
SUZUKI
MOTUL

REPSOL
26

Despite that pole position, Casey was never particularly optimistic about his chances. Nevertheless, he kept the pressure on Lorenzo until half-distance. Just as everyone was expecting the Aussie to ease past and make it four wins in a row for the first time in his career, he started losing ground. Slow-starting Dani Pedrosa, in third, getting over front-end problems with a full tank, scented blood. When the pass came it was at the fastest part of the track, the right-hander at the end of the back straight. Casey had no answer. What we didn't know was that he hadn't got over the jet lag from the Indianapolis trip the previous weekend and he simply ran out of strength. He wasn't helped by the lingering effects of his big crash at Assen which had hindered his training programme. Just as with his other third places so far this year – at Estoril, Mugello and the Sachsenring – a bad day at work still meant a rostrum.

As the top three pulled away in formation, attention centred on the fight for fourth. For the first half of the race the battle involved Valentino Rossi. After another woeful qualifying, Valentino rode a storming first lap from 11th place to sixth and was fastest man on the first flying lap. His home-town crowd loved it and Vale was much more like his old self in the post-race debrief with the media. Was this outbreak of optimism because of the race or the persistent rumours of a conventional aluminium twin-beam chassis to be tested the week after the race? Spy shots of a CAD drawing of the frame emerged after the race, further fuelling the rumour mill which was

Opposite At Misano Alvaro Bautista's Suzuki ran in a special silver livery

Below Lorenzo had to be brave in the first corner to keep Stoner at bay

Above Wayne Rainey went to the rostrum to accept the contructors' trophy for Yamaha

Above Loris Capirosi started a Grand Prix in Italy for the last time. Unfortunately, he didn't finish it

Below Hector Barbera beat Cal Crutchlow to the flag for ninth but both were more concerned with rebuilding their confidence

flat-out in any case after the Ducati technical chief's remarks beforehand. Filippo Preziosi said the rumours were wrong. Then he said that no factory would give advance notice of their next move and that 'sometimes we tell lies'. That remark was delivered with a grin and did nothing to calm the speculation.

Valentino was undoubtedly happy with the way he rode, but the fact remains that he still finished in seventh place and 23 seconds behind the winner. He'd been gleefully mugged by Simoncelli, but at least the bikes in front of him were the two factory Yamahas and four factory Hondas. As one of Rossi's crew remarked, 'seventh is the new first.'

Vale's good friend Marco Simoncelli was a lot happier. He came out on top of what boiled down to a three-way out-braking contest for fourth place on the last lap. Back in pit lane he celebrated like he'd won the race, doubtless because the two men he faced down were Dovizioso and Spies. Ben had taken seven or eight laps to come to terms with his set-up but couldn't do what he'd managed for most of the season – get the better of Simoncelli in the closing stages. And if that wasn't enough for Marco, he also beat Dovizioso for the first time this season.

Given that Misano is very heavy on fuel consumption, thanks to the full-bore acceleration out of second-, third- and fourth-gear corners, the assumption was that Simoncelli would be affected worst. That wasn't the case; it was Dovizioso whose engine-management system deprived him of the power to get to the flag. Dovi had to console himself with reminding the world that the score versus Simoncelli stood at 12:1 in his favour.

This was also the anniversary of the loss of Shoya Tomizawa in 2010's Moto2 race. His parents were present to see his bike raced by Tomoyoshi Koyama. They said before the race that as Shoya had not taken the chequered flag the previous year it was their wish that Koyama-san would do so this year. He did. And there wasn't a dry eye in the house.

All this, and the sight of Wayne Rainey on the rostrum to accept the constructors' award on behalf of Yamaha… it was definitely an emotional weekend.

CRT MOVED FORWARD

A privateer team's press conference is not usually expected to be of great significance, but Forward Racing's announcement of their MotoGP entry for 2012 as a CRT team was probably the most important event of the weekend. The political significance was enormous. Not only was this the first official confirmation of a CRT entry for 2012, but the personnel involved and the very public backing from Dorna CEO Carmelo Ezpeleta, who shared the stage with the rider and the team manager, underlined just how hard the new class is being pushed.

So far there have been lots of rumours about who might go down the CRT route. Remember that the list of teams issued earlier in the year – Kiefer, Interwetten, Speed Master, Forward Racing, BQR and Marc VDS – wasn't a list of CRT entrants but of new teams accepted for MotoGP. They might indeed go the CRT route or they might be intending to lease bikes from Ducati, Yamaha or Honda.

Colin Edwards may or may not get the benefit of the Yamaha World Superbike team's surplus equipment, but the Forward Racing project wanted to use an R1-based motor and Colin wanted to use a Tech 3 chassis.

That turned out not to be possible and Forward are likely to start 2012 with a BMW engine in a Suter chassis.

Whatever machinery is available to Colin and the team, they will get the support of the MotoGP power brokers. Ezpeleta gave a bullish welcome to Forward Racing's entry, saying there will be six CRT bikes on the grid next year and insisting that in due course they will form the majority of the grid. It was, he said, 'a very important day'. And it was.

Latterly the CRT concept had started to look shaky. The Marc VDS team's Suter BMW wasn't impressive in testing and the team had yet to commit officially to racing in MotoGP next year; the only other project known to be under way was the BQR team with their FTR Kawasaki. Having a name like Colin Edwards signed up to the idea is a definite coup and a leap forward for the credibility of CRT. Ezpeleta also hinted at further rule changes to 'try to improve their possibilities' and to enable privateer teams to be competitive with the factory teams. 'In the past it was possible, but no longer.'

'I DEDICATE THIS VICTORY TO WAYNE'
JORGE LORENZO

Below More mutual respect on the rostrum

SAN MARINO GP

MISANO WORLD CIRCUIT

ROUND 13
September 4

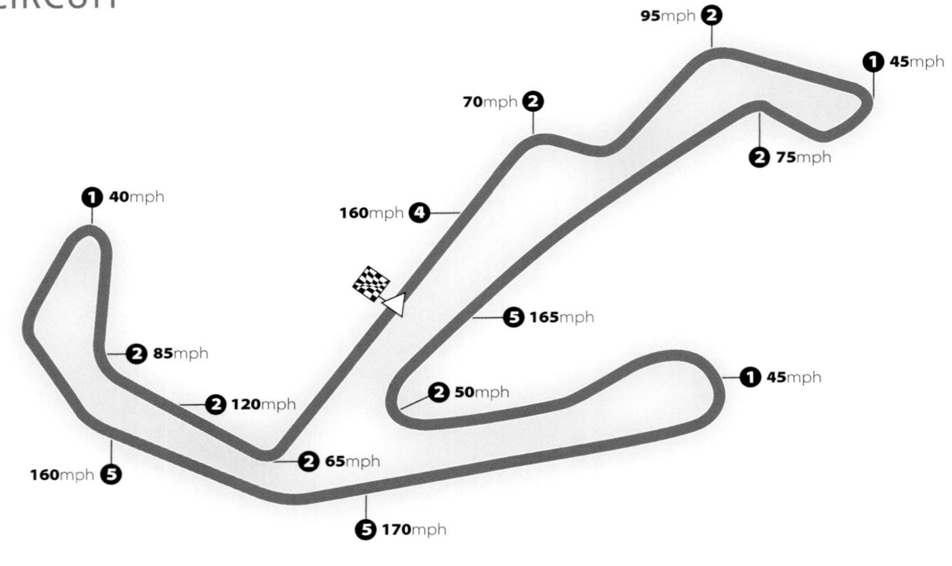

RACE RESULTS

CIRCUIT LENGTH 2.626 miles
NO. OF LAPS 28
RACE DISTANCE 73.529 miles
WEATHER Dry, 28°C
TRACK TEMPERATURE 35°C
WINNER Jorge Lorenzo
FASTEST LAP 1m 33.906s, 100.662mph, Jorge Lorenzo (Record)
PREVIOUS LAP RECORD 1m 34.340s, 99.435mph, Dani Pedrosa, 2010

QUALIFYING

	Rider	Nationality	Team	Qualifying	Pole +	Gap
1	Stoner	AUS	Repsol Honda Team	1m 33.138s		
2	Lorenzo	SPA	Yamaha Factory Racing	1m 33.258s	0.120s	0.120s
3	Pedrosa	SPA	Repsol Honda Team	1m 33.318s	0.180s	0.060s
4	Spies	USA	Yamaha Factory Racing	1m 33.947s	0.809s	0.629s
5	Simoncelli	ITA	San Carlo Honda Gresini	1m 33.990s	0.852s	0.043s
6	Dovizioso	ITA	Repsol Honda Team	1m 34.026s	0.888s	0.036s
7	Edwards	USA	Monster Yamaha Tech 3	1m 34.054s	0.916s	0.028s
8	Bautista	SPA	Rizla Suzuki MotoGP	1m 34.360s	1.222s	0.306s
9	Barbera	SPA	Mapfre Aspar Team	1m 34.592s	1.454s	0.232s
10	Aoyama	JPN	San Carlo Honda Gresini	1m 34.637s	1.499s	0.045s
11	Rossi	ITA	Ducati Team	1m 34.676s	1.538s	0.039s
12	Abraham	CZE	Cardion AB Motoracing	1m 34.727s	1.589s	0.051s
13	Crutchlow	GBR	Monster Yamaha Tech 3	1m 34.791s	1.653s	0.064s
14	De Puniet	FRA	Pramac Racing Team	1m 34.870s	1.732s	0.079s
15	Hayden	USA	Ducati Team	1m 34.955s	1.817s	0.085s
16	Capirossi	ITA	Pramac Racing Team	1m 35.502s	2.364s	0.547s
17	Elias	SPA	LCR Honda MotoGP	1m 36.167s	3.029s	0.664s

FINISHERS

1 JORGE LORENZO Said before the race that he felt he had his Mugello bike back. The race proved him right, although he hit the front early and held off the Hondas rather than having to hunt them down. Reduced Stoner's championship lead to 35 points.

2 DANI PEDROSA A little disappointed as the bike didn't feel as good at the start of the race as it had done in practice. Had trouble with the front tucking until the fuel load went down, then took advantage of Stoner fading and put in a demon pass on the fastest corner of the track.

3 CASEY STONER Had the bike to win but simply ran out of strength at half-distance. Three nights with little sleep after Indianapolis got the blame, along with the neck injury from Assen that had recurred, preventing him from training properly: 'I'm just worn out.'

4 MARCO SIMONCELLI Overcame both fears about fuel consumption and his old rival Dovizioso to win the three-way fight for fourth on the last lap. Could have been even better if he hadn't selected the wrong engine map off the start, after which he had a lot of ground to make up. Did so with his usual élan and a good hard pass on Rossi.

5 ANDREA DOVIZIOSO In trouble with fuel consumption all weekend, and after Sunday's warm-up discovered he'd have to turn the power down even further to finish the race. Understandably demotivated, as he knew he couldn't fight for the podium, and then had to cope with being beaten by Simoncelli for the first time this season.

6 BEN SPIES Took a while to get used to a big change to the front of the bike, put in after warm-up, and then to get past Rossi. Ben reached the two Italians, trying a major outbraking move on the last lap at the Quercia left-hander – as did Dovi and Simoncelli – but came off worst.

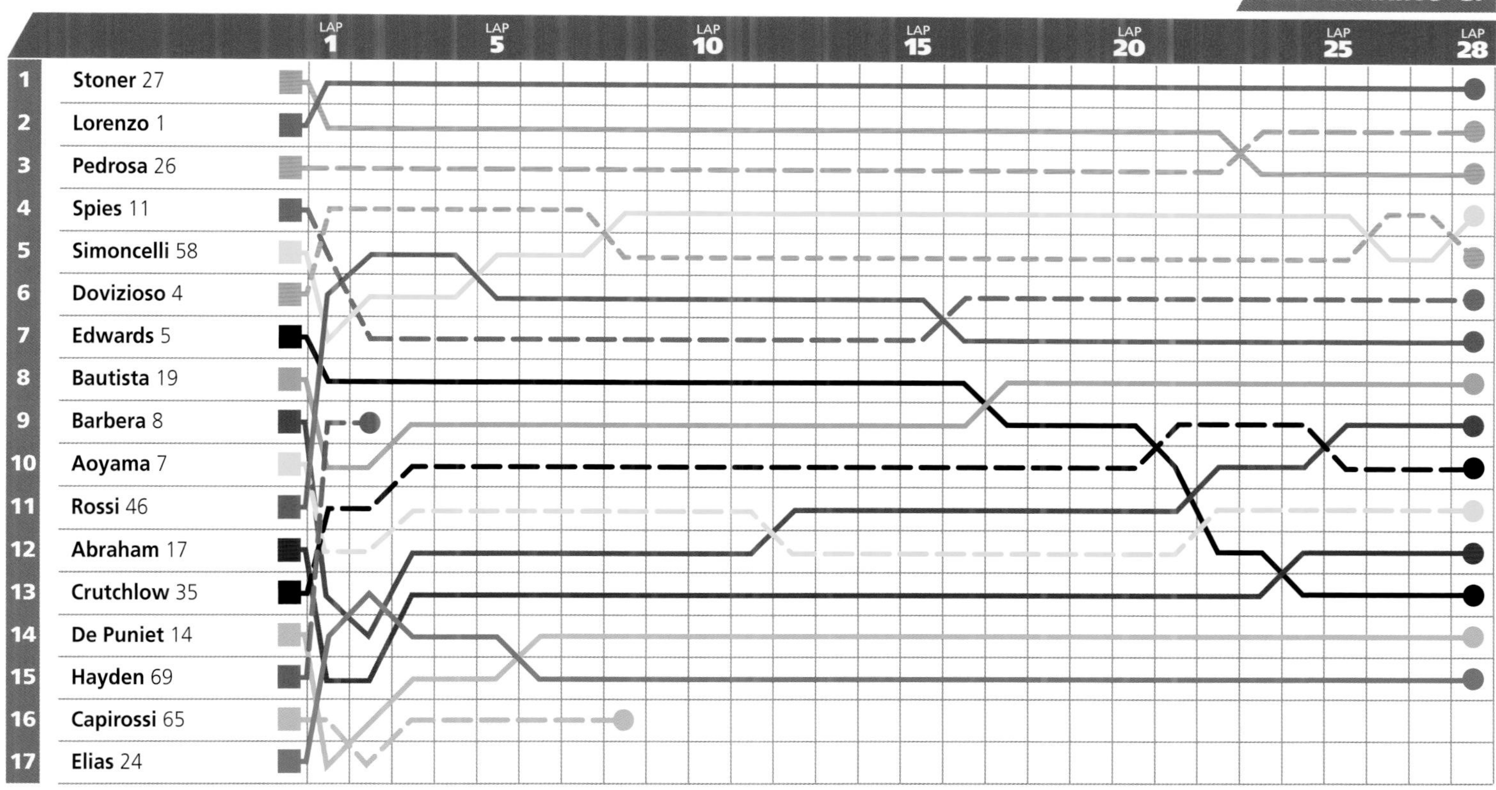

RACE

	Rider	Motorcycle	Race Time	Time +	Fastest Lap	Av Speed	B
1	Lorenzo	Yamaha	44m 11.877s		1m 33.906s	99.816mph	H/M
2	Pedrosa	Honda	44m 19.176s	7.299s	1m 33.965s	99.542mph	H/M
3	Stoner	Honda	44m 23.844s	11.967s	1m 34.224	99.368mph	H/M
4	Simoncelli	Honda	44m 29.230s	17.353s	1m 34.518s	99.167mph	H/M
5	Dovizioso	Honda	44m 29.267s	17.390s	1m 34.529s	99.166mph	H/M
6	Spies	Yamaha	44m 29.969s	18.092s	1m 34.581s	99.139mph	H/M
7	Rossi	Ducati	44m 35.580s	23.703s	1m 34.633s	98.931mph	H/M
8	Bautista	Suzuki	44m 42.555s	30.678s	1m 34.737s	98.674mph	H/M
9	Barbera	Ducati	44m 49.379s	37.502s	1m 34.836s	98.424mph	H/M
10	Crutchlow	Yamaha	44m 49.597s	37.720s	1m 34.920s	98.416mph	H/M
11	Aoyama	Honda	44m 51.425s	39.548s	1m 35.069s	98.349mph	H/M
12	Abraham	Ducati	44m 52.383s	40.506s	1m 35.352s	98.314mph	H/M
13	Edwards	Yamaha	45m 05.226s	53.349s	1m 35.375s	97.847mph	H/M
14	De Puniet	Ducati	45m 14.243s	1m 02.366s	1m 35.623s	97.522mph	H/M
15	Elias	Honda	45m 32.033s	1m 20.156s	1m 36.338s	96.887mph	H/M
NF	Capirossi	Ducati	15m 21.868s	20 laps	1m 36.423s	82.038mph	H/M
NF	Hayden	Ducati	3m 20.984s	26 laps	1m 36.633s	94.073mph	H/M

CHAMPIONSHIP

	Rider	Team	Points
1	Stoner	Repsol Honda Team	259
2	Lorenzo	Yamaha Factory Racing	224
3	Dovizioso	Repsol Honda Team	185
4	Pedrosa	Repsol Honda Team	150
5	Spies	Yamaha Factory Racing	135
6	Rossi	Ducati Team	133
7	Hayden	Ducati Team	105
8	Simoncelli	San Carlo Honda Gresini	93
9	Edwards	Monster Yamaha Tech 3	87
10	Aoyama	San Carlo Honda Gresini	82
11	Barbera	Mapfre Aspar Team MotoGP	69
12	Bautista	Rizla Suzuki MotoGP	57
13	Abraham	Cardion AB Motoracing	50
14	Elias	LCR Honda MotoGP	47
15	Crutchlow	Monster Yamaha Tech 3	45
16	De Puniet	Pramac Racing Team	29
17	Capirossi	Pramac Racing Team	29
18	Hopkins	Rizla Suzuki MotoGP	6
19	Akiyoshi	San Carlo Honda Gresini	3

7 VALENTINO ROSSI Rode a 'little crazy through the first three corners' to get from 11th on the grid to sixth place and the dice for fourth. Stayed with what he calls 'the second group' until half-distance when the tyres started sliding. One of his best races of the year but, as he reminded everyone, we're only talking about seventh place.

8 ALVARO BAUTISTA It was a measure of Suzuki's progress that eighth place was seen as a disappointment, especially after Alvaro qualified well in eighth. His race was compromised by a bad start and a slow first two laps. The special Rizla Micron livery looked smart, though.

9 HECTOR BARBERA Also finished where he qualified, like Bautista, but had to work for it. Tentative off the start, Hector lost four places in the first two laps before settling down to lap at the same pace he'd achieved in practice. Not a bad weekend.

10 CAL CRUTCHLOW After two crashes in qualifying, another finish to back up Indianapolis was needed. His first top-ten finish since Catalunya was Cal's reward for a physically tough race. Got involved with Aoyama and Barbera after a good start, only losing out to the Spaniard in the closing stages.

11 HIROSHI AOYAMA A tough race in conditions which Hiro said felt more like Malaysia than Europe. Lost touch with the group when he made a mistake on lap 11.

12 KAREL ABRAHAM As with fellow-rookie Crutchlow, this was another confidence-restoring ride. Resisted the temptation to put the softer rear tyre on for qualifying, instead concentrating on race set-up. Started the race well, then made a mistake which meant losing touch with the group in front.

13 COLIN EDWARDS He was shadowing Spies when he ran into serious arm pump – in both arms. This is a track where, says Colin, he always rides tensely. Also said he didn't know it was possible for arm pump to be that painful. Thought seriously about pulling in, but stuck it out to the flag.

14 RANDY DE PUNIET Lost whatever feeling with the bike he'd found at Indianapolis. Back to struggling round with no feeling from the front.

15 TONI ELIAS Another race totally compromised by the lack of front-end feel. Chased settings all weekend to no avail. Started well, but when the raindrops abated and the pace went up he couldn't follow.

NON-FINISHERS

LORIS CAPIROSSI A clutch problem off the line stretched the chain and in turn resulted in damage to the rear sprocket. Came in to change the wheel but retired soon afterwards. Definitely not the way Loris wanted to end his last GP in Italy, after announcing his retirement.

NICKY HAYDEN Managed a racing lap of Misano for the first time, and then some more, but failed to finish, falling on the final corner of the last lap: a couple of small bumps set the front off and that was it. The one saving grace, he hoped, was that he might have saved some engine mileage – assuming, of course, it hadn't ingested any gravel.

ARAGON GP
MOTORLAND ARAGON
ROUND 14
September 18
alpinestars
RACING AHEAD
SHINDENGEN
NGK
SPARK PLUGS
TERMIGNONI
BRIDG
HONDA
One HEAR

AUSSIE GRIT

Casey Stoner reasserted his authority again as the rest struggled to keep up with the factory Hondas

It was a strange weekend. While the action on Sunday was less than stunning, there was enough weirdness going on to keep everyone's attention. First, a loss of power at the track on Friday meant that the afternoon's free practice was cancelled and replaced by an extended Saturday morning session. Then there was the continuing saga of the Ducati chassis, which gave rise to a new first – the sight of Valentino Rossi starting the race from pit lane.

What was certain was that the Bologna boys had turned up with yet another new chassis, at least part of which was aluminium, not carbon fibre. It can also be stated categorically, mainly thanks to a bit of inadvertent espionage by Italian TV, that the Aragon chassis was not the full twin-beam design seen in the drawings photographed at Misano. The aluminium parts appeared to be the steering head and two short beams with four short legs running down to the mounting points on each cylinder head. This was not a remaking of the 'shoebox' chassis in a different material; it looked like Ducati had gone to longer frame members to try to engender the flex and feeling that Rossi and the other Desmosedici pilots had been missing. The team tried to confuse things by painting the bare metal black during Thursday night, but it definitely had the look of an interim measure.

The complication was that Ducati's changing chassis designs from Germany onwards had eaten up their allowance of six engines. Rossi took his sixth at Misano and used it with the new chassis,

Arai
antoniolupi
35
MONSTER ENERGY
STANLEY
YAMAHA

meaning that motor number six had had its engine-mounting lugs machined to accept both the original 11.1 chassis and the new one. Older engines would have to have their seals broken to enable machining of the mounting blanks, so it was inevitable that Valentino would have to use at least one new engine before the end of the season. Once he'd qualified down in 13th it was decided that this would be a good time to take the penalty for going over the six-engine allowance.

And so Valentino followed the field round on the warm-up lap, then came down pit lane and stopped at the exit, hard up against the pit wall, to give himself a good line through the left-hand bend in the exit road. Rossi made it as high as ninth place by lap seven, but that was as good as it got. Like many of the field, he ran into tyre problems. The rear had spun from the second lap onwards and destroyed the tyre. 'I never see a Bridgestone like this,' he said after the race.

None of which affected Casey Stoner in the slightest. He had one of those weekends where his domination was reminiscent of Mick Doohan at his best. The Aussie started from pole, set the fastest lap fourth time round and won by over eight seconds. The only sour note was struck by sponsor Repsol's special livery, rolled out in anticipation of the team's 100th GP victory. The oil company commissioned artist and fashion designer David Delfin, who apparently took his inspiration from superheroes. That translated into a bright orange design scattered with stars and what looked like

Opposite Cal Crutchlow in Turn 13 with Motorland's giant wall looming behind him

Above Rossi prepares to start from pit lane ten seconds after the rest of the field

Below Andrea Dovizioso crashed out on the first lap and put his championship third place in danger

Above Toni Elias and Loris Capirossi walk away from their crash, but it would put Loris out of the next race

Below Rossi's new chassis can be seen at the nose of the tank and the black-painted arms below it

Opposite Dani Pedrosa tried hard, but he couldn't close in on Casey Stoner

felt-tip marker numbers. Suffice to say, it wasn't greeted with universal praise. Unlike Casey's flawless race, which added nine points to his championship lead thanks to his team-mate Dani Pedrosa following him home at a respectful distance, with reigning champion Jorge Lorenzo, the only man with a chance of the title, in third.

Lorenzo had to get past his fast-starting team-mate Ben Spies and a combative Marco Simoncelli to secure his rostrum finish. He was aided by Spies's tyre woes and Simoncelli running off-track while lying third. Jorge's attitude at the end of the race seemed to be that at least he'd got on the rostrum this time. 'We couldn't get more than a podium' were his actual words, while refusing to give up on his championship hopes despite what was now a 44-point deficit.

For the crowd, race-day entertainment came via another impressive ride from Alvaro Bautista on the much-improved Suzuki and the Rossi/Aoyama/Crutchlow dice for ninth. That was won by Cal, another step in rebuilding the confidence that evaporated after his Silverstone crash, as Valentino's rear tyre gave him problems. Rossi's pre-race optimism was noticeably absent afterwards. 'Looks like we don't fix a lot,' he revealed. 'Very difficult race... expect a bit better pace. I am not able to be fast.' And back again to 'Looks like after a lot of races we don't fix nothing.'

Even Nicky Hayden felt it necessary to mention a lack of direction in Ducati's development. He was an amazing 25 seconds slower over race distance

than the previous year, while Stoner's times were within a second of each other – and he wasn't pressured this year like he was last time. This, remember, was the track where Stoner finally found how to make the Ducati work for him and took his first victory of 2010. That wasn't going to improve the mood at Ducati, especially as their ex-rider's points lead meant the possibility of Casey being more than 50 points ahead after Phillip Island, and therefore being crowned World Champion at home in Australia on his 26th birthday, with two races still left. Large helping of *schadenfreude*, anyone?

'I DON'T MIND WHEN THE BIKE SLIDES AROUND A LITTLE'
CASEY STONER

YOU CAN'T ALWAYS GET WHAT YOU WANT

There were lots of complaints about tyre wear rates after the race. This was unusual, as Bridgestone normally have to field moans about how long their rubber takes to warm up rather than how long it lasts.

Bridgestone's explanation was that the weather on race day was much cooler and windier than for qualifying; nevertheless, Stoner set a new lap record on just his fourth lap of the race, indicating, Bridgestone pointed out, strong tyre warm-up performance. He then ran consistently in the 1m 49s bracket over the first half of the race. His pace meant that he finished over eight seconds clear of Dani Pedrosa, whose best effort was also below the previous lap record.

Throughout the race, tyre management proved very important as wear rate on the surface was relatively high. Off the racing line the tarmac was dirty and this always leads to increased tyre wear, especially for those in battles further down the field who cannot always stick to the ideal and clean line.

Masao Azuma, Bridgestone's Chief Field Engineer, said: 'Conditions for the race today were completely different from the rest of the weekend as the track was much cooler and there was a strong wind blowing down the main straight. This meant that the situation for the tyres and bike set-ups was very different. Even though our tyre compound options were the same this time as at Aragon last year, because the track conditions were different this year so was tyre behaviour. It is a prime illustration of the balance between warm-up performance and durability – warm-up performance was clearly very good today in the cool conditions, with the top ten fastest riders all setting their best times within the first six laps, and Casey's lap record coming on lap four. Conversely, it was also clear that tyre wear was a key factor for some riders towards the end of the race, but this is the trade-off of achieving better warm-up performance, something the riders have been asking for this season.'

Above Ben Spies was one of several riders to find that his softer-than-usual tyres wouldn't last

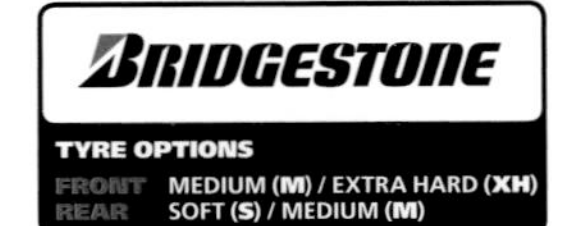

ARAGON GP

MOTORLAND ARAGON

ROUND 14
September 18

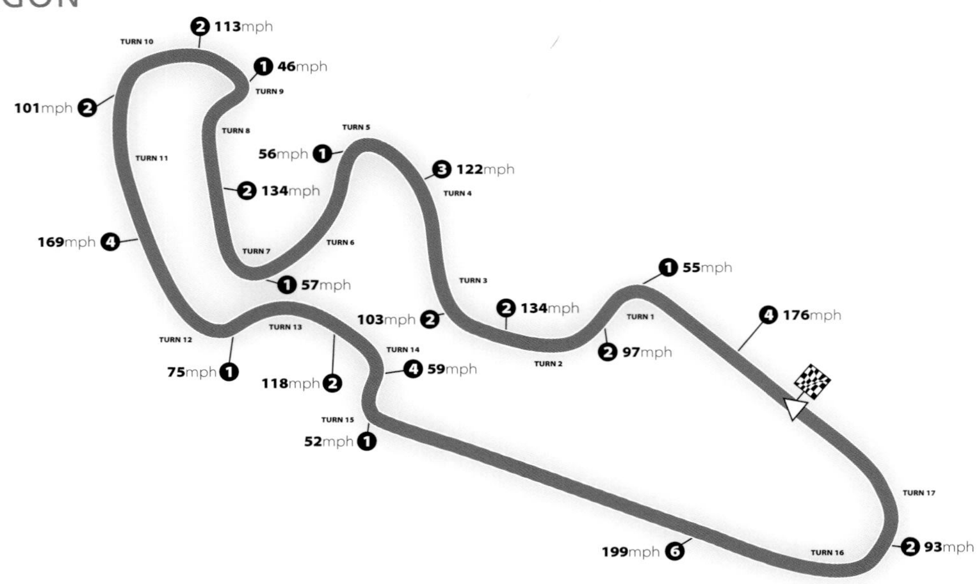

RACE RESULTS

CIRCUIT LENGTH 3.155 miles
NO. OF LAPS 23
RACE DISTANCE 72.565 miles
WEATHER Dry, 19°C
TRACK TEMPERATURE 26°C
WINNER Casey Stoner
FASTEST LAP 1m 49.046s, 104.142mph, Casey Stoner (Record)
PREVIOUS LAP RECORD 1m 49.521s, 102.795mph, Dani Pedrosa, 2010

QUALIFYING

	Rider	Nationality	Team	Qualifying	Pole +	Gap
1	Stoner	AUS	Repsol Honda Team	1m 48.451s		
2	Pedrosa	SPA	Repsol Honda Team	1m 48.747s	0.296s	0.296s
3	Spies	USA	Yamaha Factory Racing	1m 49.155s	0.704s	0.408s
4	Lorenzo	SPA	Yamaha Factory Racing	1m 49.270s	0.819s	0.115s
5	Dovizioso	ITA	Repsol Honda Team	1m 49.372s	0.921s	0.102s
6	Simoncelli	ITA	San Carlo Honda Gresini	1m 49.528s	1.077s	0.156s
7	Hayden	USA	Ducati Team	1m 49.752s	1.301s	0.224s
8	Abraham	CZE	Cardion AB Motoracing	1m 49.777s	1.326s	0.025s
9	Aoyama	JPN	San Carlo Honda Gresini	1m 49.813s	1.362s	0.036s
10	De Puniet	FRA	Pramac Racing Team	1m 49.826s	1.375s	0.013s
11	Bautista	SPA	Rizla Suzuki MotoGP	1m 49.883s	1.432s	0.057s
12	Crutchlow	GBR	Monster Yamaha Tech 3	1m 49.893s	1.442s	0.010s
13	Rossi	ITA	Ducati Team	1m 49.960s	1.509s	0.067s
14	Barbera	SPA	Mapfre Aspar Team	1m 49.976s	1.525s	0.016s
15	Edwards	USA	Monster Yamaha Tech 3	1m 50.105s	1.654s	0.129s
16	Capirossi	ITA	Pramac Racing Team	1m 50.752s	2.301s	0.647s
17	Elias	SPA	LCR Honda MotoGP	1m 51.073s	2.622s	0.321s

FINISHERS

1 CASEY STONER Another faultless performance. Started cautiously off pole but once his hard tyres were warmed up he quickly went to the front – fourth to first on lap one. Controlled the race with ease to take Repsol Honda's 100th Grand Prix win and what looked like a decisive 44-point lead in the championship.

2 DANI PEDROSA Knew from the start he couldn't match Stoner so concentrated on controlling the gap to Lorenzo in the closing laps. In trouble with his rear tyre from the start, losing tenths in the first sector and sliding 'all the time' in the second half of the race. Enjoyed the sliding, if not finishing second for three races in a row.

3 JORGE LORENZO Unable to replicate his times from practice but didn't suffer drop-off in tyre performance. Had to make up for a bad start, felt no confidence in the rear, but took the rostrum that evaded him last year – this was, he said, the best he could have done. Tried to stay optimistic about the championship.

4 MARCO SIMONCELLI Got up to third before his tyres started to go off around lap 10. Made a mistake and dropped back but was able to retake Spies – whose tyre, Marco observed, was in even worse shape. Knew he wouldn't be able to catch Lorenzo, so felt happy with fourth.

5 BEN SPIES Came out of the first corner in the lead but knew he couldn't keep the Repsols behind him. Thought he could fight for the final rostrum spot but after six or seven laps his rear tyre's grip dropped sharply and – unusually – kept dropping rather than staying at the new level. Left Ben unhappy that the chance of a good finish was lost.

6 ALVARO BAUTISTA Another whose race nearly ended in the first corner. Made up for poor qualifying with a strong showing and, unlike most, used the softer front tyre. In an entertaining fight with Hayden and Barbera until he broke away in the final laps. Reckoned he'd have done better if the track temperature had been as high as in practice.

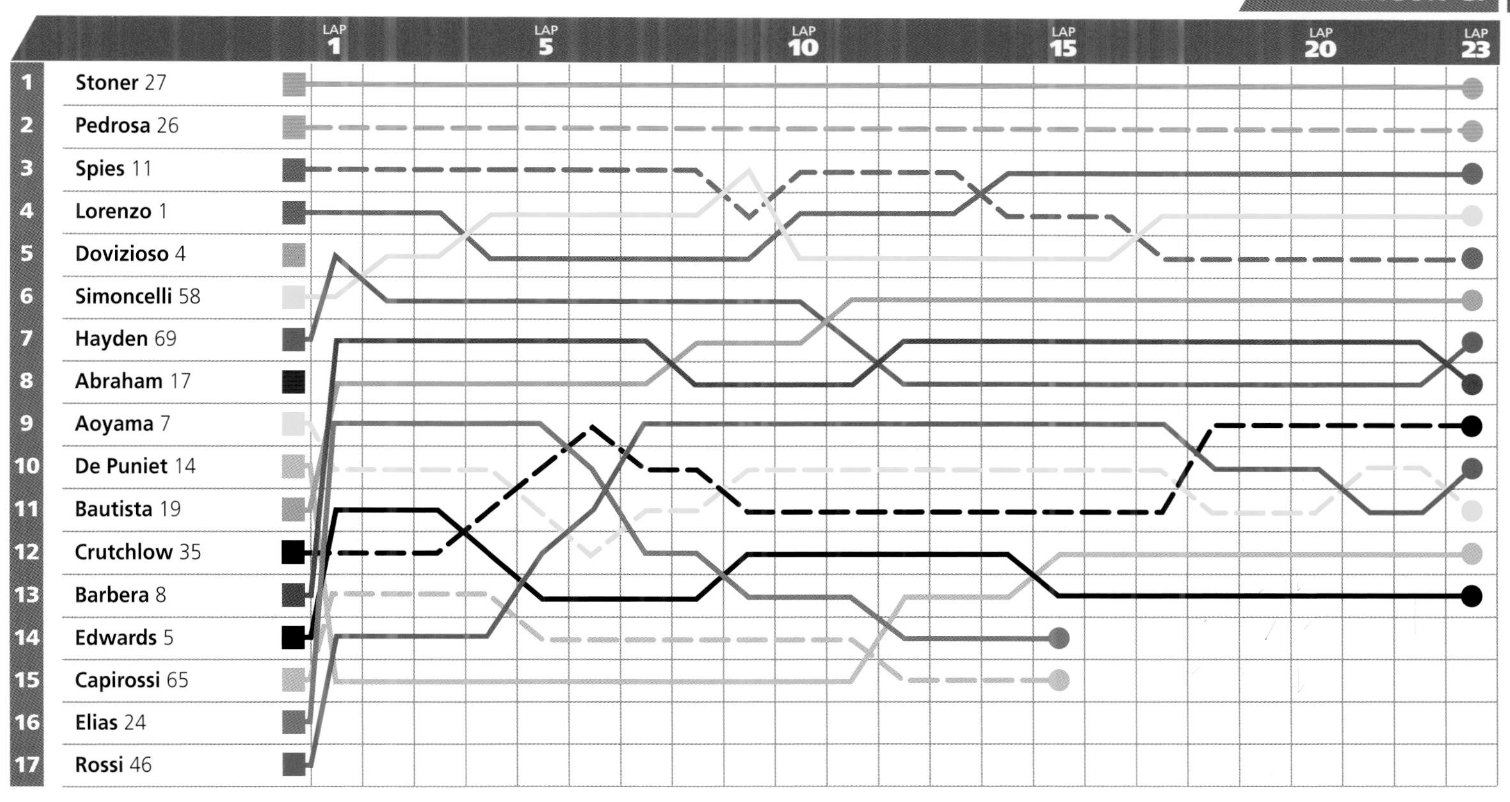

RACE

	Rider	Motorcycle	Race Time	Time +	Fastest Lap	Av Speed	
1	Stoner	Honda	42m 17.427s		1m 49.046s	102.965mph	XH/M
2	Pedrosa	Honda	42m 25.589s	8.162s	1m 49.454s	102.635mph	XH/M
3	Lorenzo	Yamaha	42m 31.636s	14.209s	1m 50.056s	102.392mph	XH/M
4	Simoncelli	Honda	42m 38.073s	20.646s	1m 49.650s	102.135mph	XH/M
5	Spies	Yamaha	42m 45.166s	27.739s	1m 49.593s	101.852mph	XH/M
6	Bautista	Suzuki	42m 47.800s	30.373s	1m 50.564s	101.747mph	M/M
7	Hayden	Ducati	42m 51.715s	34.288s	1m 50.685s	101.593mph	XH/M
8	Barbera	Ducati	42m 54.732s	37.305s	1m 50.807s	101.473mph	XH/M
9	Crutchlow	Yamaha	42m 57.079s	39.652s	1m 51.097s	101.381mph	XH/M
10	Rossi	Ducati	42m 57.259s	39.832s	1m 50.743s	101.374mph	XH/M
11	Aoyama	Honda	42m 57.424s	39.997s	1m 51.225s	101.368mph	M/M
12	De Puniet	Ducati	43m 12.144s	54.717s	1m 51.029s	100.792mph	XH/M
13	Edwards	Yamaha	43m 15.857s	58.430s	1m 51.600s	100.648mph	M/M
NF	Elias	Honda	28m 12.276s	8 laps	1m 51.863s	100.688mph	XH/M
NF	Capirossi	Ducati	28m 12.364s	8 laps	1m 51.627s	100.682mph	M/M
NF	Dovizioso	Honda					XH/M
NF	Abraham	Ducati					XH/M

CHAMPIONSHIP

	Rider	Team	Points
1	Stoner	Repsol Honda Team	284
2	Lorenzo	Yamaha Factory Racing	240
3	Dovizioso	Repsol Honda Team	185
4	Pedrosa	Repsol Honda Team	170
5	Spies	Yamaha Factory Racing	146
6	Rossi	Ducati Team	139
7	Hayden	Ducati Team	114
8	Simoncelli	San Carlo Honda Gresini	106
9	Edwards	Monster Yamaha Tech 3	90
10	Aoyama	San Carlo Honda Gresini	87
11	Barbera	Mapfre Aspar Team MotoGP	77
12	Bautista	Rizla Suzuki MotoGP	67
13	Crutchlow	Monster Yamaha Tech 3	52
14	Abraham	Cardion AB Motoracing	50
15	Elias	LCR Honda MotoGP	47
16	De Puniet	Pramac Racing Team	33
17	Capirossi	Pramac Racing Team	29
18	Hopkins	Rizla Suzuki MotoGP	6
19	Akiyoshi	San Carlo Honda Gresini	3

7 NICKY HAYDEN His first 'normal' race with the 11.1 version of the Ducati. Started well but was soon in trouble with the inevitable rear-tyre problems. As early as the third lap he noticed a drop in grip and couldn't load the bike like he wanted in corners, with particular problems in the long final corner.

8 HECTOR BARBERA Probably the best start of his MotoGP career, from 14th to sixth half-way round lap one. Bautista got away, so diced with Hayden for the honour of being first Ducati home – not helped when he saw Nicky's pit board showing a different number of laps with two left to go. Confused, he let Hayden back, then ran wide after re-passing.

9 CAL CRUTCHLOW In the top ten for the first time since Catalunya. A really good race, after losing places when he locked the front at the first corner and dropped to 12th. Caught and passed Aoyama, then joined by Rossi, these three providing the race's best entertainment. Pleased to be able to make up in the corners what he lost on the straights.

10 VALENTINO ROSSI Used a new chassis with aluminium parts. Had to start from pit lane for exceeding the allowance of six engines per season. Reached the Hayden dice before rear-tyre wear hit and he dropped back to battle with Crutchlow and Aoyama in the later stages.

11 HIROSHI AOYAMA Couldn't find the grip on Sunday that he'd had in practice, but rode confidently in the fight with Rossi and Crutchlow.

12 RANDY DE PUNIET Ran off-track on the first lap, avoiding Abraham's crash, after which he passed a couple of riders and was closing on the group in front when he made another mistake and lost all the time he'd gained.

13 COLIN EDWARDS A horrible way to mark his 150th start in Grand Prix racing. Spent practice playing with weight distribution to try to find grip in the corners to make up for lack of top end. Made another big change after warm-up but tyre grip dropped off dramatically after five laps.

NON-FINISHERS

TONI ELIAS Another great start from the back of the grid, after which the usual lack of grip made itself felt and Toni dropped back through the field. Crashed when hit by Capirossi on the exit of the chicane.

LORIS CAPIROSSI Touched Elias at the exit of the chicane, Turn 14, on lap 15, and the two crashed. Loris again dislocated the shoulder he'd originally injured at Assen. He was also concussed, which made him a serious doubt for the Japanese GP.

ANDREA DOVIZIOSO Crashed at the second corner of the first lap, yet another victim of cold-tyre syndrome. Remained third in the championship, but Pedrosa closed the gap to 15 points.

KAREL ABRAHAM Also crashed at the second corner of the first lap, landing heavily on his shoulder, and was then clipped on the head by his bike's back wheel. Diagnosed with concussion and spent the night in hospital, putting his participation in the next race in doubt.

JAPANESE GP

TWIN-RING MOTEGI

ROUND 15

October 2

STRANGE DAYS INDEED

Dani Pedrosa won as Jorge Lorenzo kept his championship hopes alive

After all the hysteria, a tweet from a Japanese journalist summed up the mood as the first bikes went out on track: 'Normal MotoGP FP1 started in Motegi and to be normal means special for Japan.' In retrospect, 'normal' is not a word that could be applied to the 2011 Japanese Grand Prix. The race featured more incidents than seemed possible or probable, with only two of the first seven men home not taking an off-track excursion or suffering a ride-through penalty. In the stands, fans wore T-shirts and waved placards thanking 'the MotoGP family' for coming to Japan. There was still some paranoia among the riders but everyone turned up, as did the top brass of all the Japanese companies.

Although Honda own Motegi, there was a good deal of pan-Japanese solidarity in evidence. As part of Yamaha's 50th year of racing celebrations, the foyer of Honda's magnificent museum played host to four historic Yamaha racers. They were paraded on Sunday morning, with Norick Abe's dad, Mitsuo, riding his son's old 500. Honda's top management were there in even greater force than usual. The President of the Honda Motor Company and the President of HRC were at the track for the whole weekend, further evidence of the importance the Japanese industry as a whole placed on the GP and demonstrating that the country was open for business as usual.

HRC were assuredly open for business. A Honda had never won at Motegi in the 800cc era and, almost unbelievably, the factory team, Repsol Honda, had never won at the Twin Rings. After free practice, the three Repsol bikes were at the top of the timing screens, and it took a superhuman effort from Jorge Lorenzo in qualifying to split the trio. The chances of a Repsol

one–two–three disappeared before the lights went out, however. Andrea Dovizioso, third on the grid, moved early, setting off a chain reaction that saw Marco Simoncelli, directly behind him, and Cal Crutchlow also jump the start. For Dovi, still without a contract for 2012, the drive-through penalty ruined his chances of a rostrum place or better, at the only track on the calendar where he's had a pole position and where he was runner-up last year. To really make his afternoon gloomy, Andrea went into pit lane while leading and then lost out to Simoncelli in the post-penalty fight for fourth.

Valentino Rossi's chances also disappeared on the first lap. There were definite signs of hope from the way the bike was responding, although they may have been amplified by the relatively simple nature of the Motegi circuit's challenges. Vale's race was over at the first left-hander behind the pits. Moving left as Lorenzo was moving right they touched, Rossi then hitting Ben Spies's Yamaha with his front brake lever and going down. Spies was sent careering across the gravel trap and fell but, unlike Rossi, the American was able to continue.

The three Repsol Hondas did head the field for the next three laps, although Dovizioso knew all too well that he wouldn't be there for long. Stoner was leading on lap five when the after-effects of the earthquake mugged him. One of the bumps left on the back straight by the 'quake set off a tank-slapper violent enough to all but shake Casey's hands off the bars. It also shook the brake pads away from the discs, so when he went for the lever there wasn't any response. A second grab pinged the back wheel in the air and almost shot the Aussie over the handlebars. He ran into the gravel at high speed, and did well to avoid the wall

Above *Déjà vu* for Ben Spies who again had to come back from last place at Motegi

Below Stoner battles with Nicky Hayden as he fights back from his run-on

Opposite Dovizioso closes in on Toni Elias after his stop-and-go penalty

DOCTORGLASS
24
GIVI
viar
elf
HONDA
Arai
DUCATI
GENERALI
riello ups
69
TIM
Enel
riello ups

and rejoin. Next time round Dovizioso took his penalty. All these dramas left Dani Pedrosa in the lead, being pursued doggedly by Jorge Lorenzo. Alvaro Bautista found himself in third, the Suzuki not looking out of place at the sharp end of the season, with Nicky Hayden in close attendance.

It took Stoner six laps to catch the pair disputing third. His pass on Hayden led immediately to Nicky being towed into Turn 1 far too hot and taking a trip through the gravel. Bautista was relegated to fourth on the same lap but, although the rostrum was out of his reach, the Spanish rider knew he had to keep pressing to fend off the Dovizioso/Simoncelli dice which was closing on him. Three laps later he lost the front in the left-hander after the underpass, at the end of the lap. It was difficult to know what to feel – happy that the team had shown their bike was competitive, or terminally depressed because the best finish for years was within their grasp at a time when the factory's continuing participation in the sport hung in the balance.

Honda were happy, though. Pedrosa controlled the race perfectly, Lorenzo only managing to show him a wheel once, and Dani was obviously well aware of the significance of his win. The new, outgoing, post-injury

Above Honda's circuit played host to part of Yamaha's celebrations of 50 years of racing

Below Casey Stoner, on the kerb and off the side of the bike, as he closes in on Alvaro Bautista's Suzuki

Opposite Marco Simoncelli's crew prepare to tell him the bad news about his penalty for jumping the start

LOCAL HERO

The presence of 44-year-old Shinichi Ito on the grid as a wild card was not just a reward for his years of service as GP rider, tester and Suzuka Eight Hour winner, it was also a gesture of solidarity. Ito is from Miyagi, the area most affected by the earthquake and the tsunami that followed.

He lost friends, family members and neighbours in the March disasters, as well as his business. His house then became a rescue centre because it was the only place with power, thanks to the solar panels on its roof. He came out of retirement to race the Eight Hour and won. 'I hope I can bring some courage to East Japan,' he said, after the President and Vice-President of HRC made a point of visiting his pit on Friday.

Shinichi's objective was to take the chequered flag, and he achieved it, although not without problems. 'I had a physical problem after Friday's crash, so the first part of the race was difficult for me. I reminded myself about the main reason for participating and I knew I could not give up.' HRC again made a point of thanking him formally.

All of which contrasted with the attitude of some other racers who persisted in believing some of the outlandish stories about radiation danger. Lorenzo's refusal to shower with tap water, using bottled water instead, was the prime example. The Italian media, noticeable by its absence, still managed to print photos of Simoncelli in pit lane with a Geiger counter under the headline 'Race of Fear.' The Japanese response was to thank people for coming, although the occasional T-shirt did take a dig at 'the paranoid' and 'superstition' – strong stuff by ultra-polite Japanese standards.

The funniest story concerned one of the Geiger counter-wielding teams, who were surprised to find that the background radiation at home in Italy was higher than at Motegi, and that the radiation count in a plane at high altitude was way above both. Which, of course, is what anyone who'd done any research on the subject had been saying all along.

personality was in evidence when he walked into the post-race press conference and demanded a round of applause from his audience. Not only was this Honda's first win at Motegi since Tamada's victory in 2004, it was the factory team's first ever win here. It was also Spain's 400th Grand Prix victory.

Dani had some personal reasons for feeling chuffed. 'I'm really happy because at this track I've had a mix of good and bad results and some bad injuries, so to come back one year later and win at Honda's track is great,' he said, referring to the crash that so blighted the end of last season and the beginning of this one for him. It also gave Pedrosa the full set of victories in every class at the Twin Rings. Lorenzo described Dani's riding as 'inspired', and managed to draw some satisfaction from taking four points out of Stoner's championship lead, reducing it to 40 points. Casey wasn't happy with third, of course: he never is if he doesn't win when he thinks he could. Lorenzo might just have postponed the inevitable, but chances are he'd deprived Stoner of the opportunity to clinch the title at his home race on his 26th birthday.

'THE RACE WAS VERY WEIRD AT THE BEGINNING'
DANI PEDROSA

JAPANESE GP

TWIN-RING MOTEGI

ROUND 15

October 2

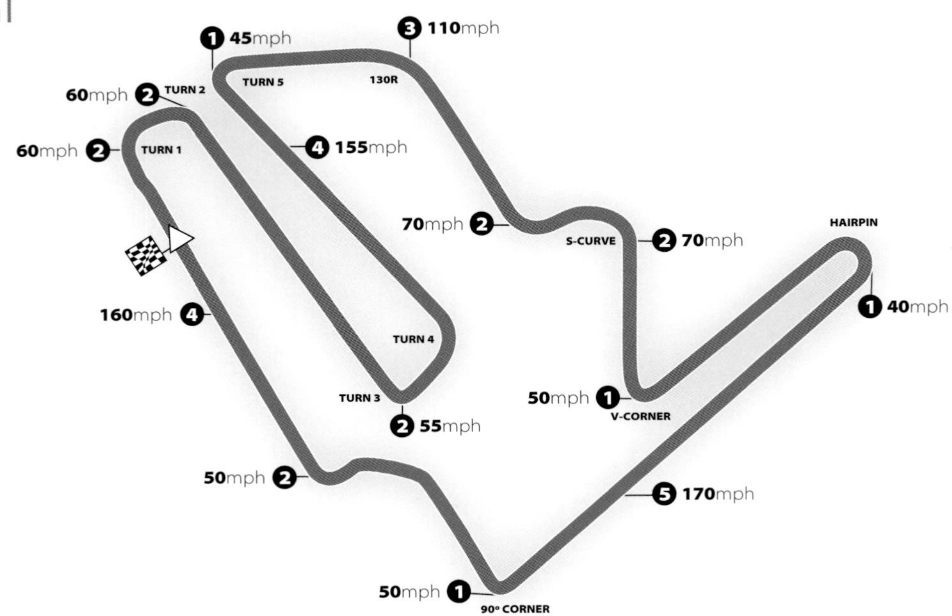

RACE RESULTS

CIRCUIT LENGTH 2.983 miles
NO. OF LAPS 24
RACE DISTANCE 71.597 miles
WEATHER Dry, 19°C
TRACK TEMPERATURE 29°C
WINNER Dani Pedrosa
FASTEST LAP 1m 46.090s, 101.221mph, Dani Pedrosa (Record)
PREVIOUS LAP RECORD 1m 47.091s, 100.288mph, Casey Stoner, 2008

QUALIFYING

	Rider	Nationality	Team	Qualifying	Pole +	Gap
1	Stoner	AUS	Repsol Honda Team	1m 45.267s		
2	Lorenzo	SPA	Yamaha Factory Racing	1m 45.523s	0.256s	0.256s
3	Dovizioso	ITA	Repsol Honda Team	1m 45.791s	0.524s	0.268s
4	Pedrosa	SPA	Repsol Honda Team	1m 45.966s	0.699s	0.175s
5	Spies	USA	Yamaha Factory Racing	1m 46.042s	0.775s	0.076s
6	Simoncelli	ITA	San Carlo Honda Gresini	1m 46.211s	0.944s	0.169s
7	Rossi	ITA	Ducati Team	1m 46.467s	1.200s	0.256s
8	Bautista	SPA	Rizla Suzuki MotoGP	1m 46.586s	1.319s	0.119s
9	Barbera	SPA	Mapfre Aspar Team	1m 46.694s	1.427s	0.108s
10	Hayden	USA	Ducati Team	1m 46.763s	1.496s	0.069s
11	Aoyama	JPN	San Carlo Honda Gresini	1m 46.811s	1.544s	0.048s
12	Crutchlow	GBR	Monster Yamaha Tech 3	1m 46.818s	1.551s	0.007s
13	De Puniet	FRA	Pramac Racing Team	1m 46.917s	1.650s	0.099s
14	Edwards	USA	Monster Yamaha Tech 3	1m 47.165s	1.898s	0.248s
15	Abraham	CZE	Cardion AB Motoracing	1m 47.922s	2.655s	0.757s
16	Elias	SPA	LCR Honda MotoGP	1m 48.169s	2.902s	0.247s
17	Akiyoshi	JPN	LCR Honda MotoGP	1m 48.367s	3.100s	0.198s
18	Cudlin	AUS	Pramac Racing Team	1m 48.962s	3.695s	0.595s
19	Ito	JPN	Honda Racing Team	1m 49.971s	4.704s	1.009s

FINISHERS

1 DANI PEDROSA Third win of the year, thanks in part to others' misfortunes, but Dani's riding was, in Lorenzo's words, 'inspired'. The Spaniard has now won in all three classes at Motegi and – amazingly – took the first ever win for the Repsol Honda team in the top class here.

2 JORGE LORENZO Only denied pole by Stoner's final qualifying laps. Lucky to come out of the first-lap fairing bashing unscathed, but then rode with all his old skill and verve to take four points out of Casey's championship lead.

3 CASEY STONER Looked odds-on for another win but was completely compromised by a run-on at the end of the back straight after a frightening high-speed tank-slapper knocked his brake pads back. It wasn't a mistake and only a very good save kept him in the race. He rejoined in seventh. Not happy.

4 MARCO SIMONCELLI Suckered into moving before the lights went out by Dovizioso. When the ride-through penalties had been served he chased Andrea down and, after a few scary moments, put in a good clean pass three laps from home. Knew he should have been on the rostrum, but happy to have beaten his old rival.

5 ANDREA DOVIZIOSO Instigated the rash of false starts – first time he'd ever jumped the start. Leading when he came in for his ride-through, then powered through the field from tenth with Marco in close attendance. The only top man to use the softer rear tyre, losing a little performance in the last five laps, and beaten by Simoncelli.

6 BEN SPIES Recovered from severe food poisoning only to endure a carbon copy of his race a year ago: punted off-track on the first lap, rejoined dead last, then climbed through the field to a top-ten finish. Lap times suggest he could have been fighting for the rostrum but for the collision.

7 NICKY HAYDEN Happier with the bike than in recent races and, despite getting a nudge from Rossi in Turn 1, found himself fighting for third when the dust settled. Tried to follow Stoner when he came past but got into the first corner of lap 12 way too hot, running off-track and rejoining in 12th place.

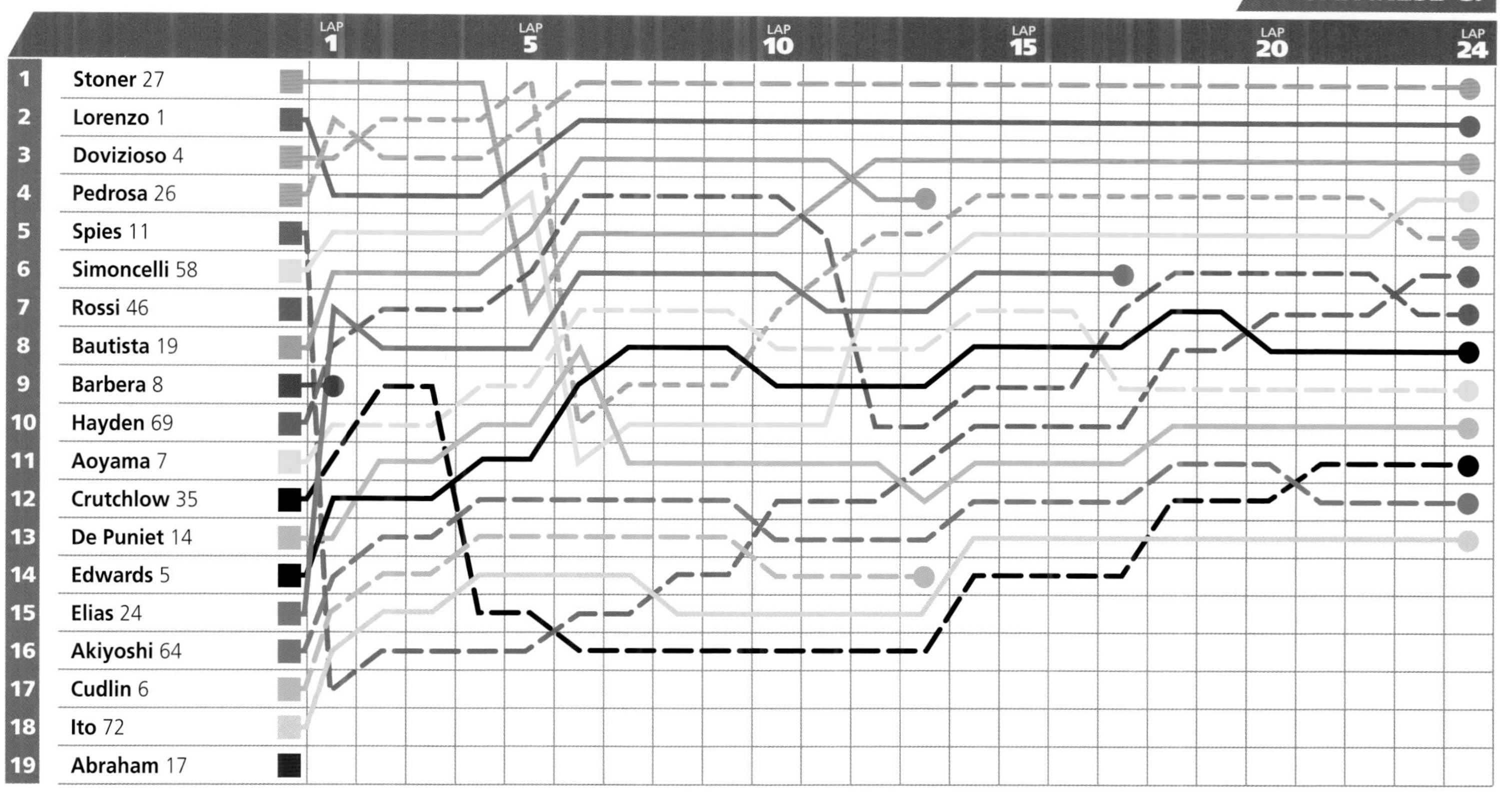

RACE

	Rider	Motorcycle	Race Time	Time +	Fastest Lap	Av Speed	B
1	Pedrosa	Honda	42m 47.481s		1m 46.090s	100.392mph	H/M
2	Lorenzo	Yamaha	42m 54.780s	7.299s	1m 46.398s	100.108mph	H/M
3	Stoner	Honda	43m 05.861s	18.380s	1m 46.193s	99.679mph	H/M
4	Simoncelli	Honda	43m 11.031s	23.550s	1m 46.484s	99.480mph	H/M
5	Dovizioso	Honda	43m 11.172s	23.691s	1m 46.114s	99.474mph	H/S
6	Spies	Yamaha	43m 25.085s	37.604s	1m 46.715s	98.943mph	H/S
7	Hayden	Ducati	43m 26.648s	39.167s	1m 47.098s	98.884mph	H/S
8	Edwards	Yamaha	43m 32.504s	45.023s	1m 47.434s	98.662mph	H/M
9	Aoyama	Honda	43m 36.555s	49.074s	1m 47.788s	98.509mph	H/M
10	De Puniet	Ducati	43m 46.503s	59.022s	1m 48.092s	98.137mph	H/S
11	Crutchlow	Yamaha	44m 01.445s	1m 13.964s	1m 47.638s	97.581mph	H/S
12	Akiyoshi	Honda	44m 09.190s	1m 21.709s	1m 48.850s	97.296mph	H/S
13	Ito	Honda	44m 13.862s	1m 26.381s	1m 49.633s	97.124mph	H/S
NF	Elias	Honda	30m 50.565s	7 laps	1m 47.951s	98.660mph	H/S
NF	Bautista	Suzuki	23m 26.728s	11 laps	1m 47.153s	99.249mph	H/S
NF	Cudlin	Ducati	23m 53.901s	11 laps	1m 48.798s	97.369mph	H/S
NF	Barbera	Ducati	1m 57.120s	23 laps	1m 57.120s	91.699mph	H/S
NF	Rossi	Ducati					

CHAMPIONSHIP

	Rider	Team	Points
1	Stoner	Repsol Honda Team	300
2	Lorenzo	Yamaha Factory Racing	260
3	Dovizioso	Repsol Honda Team	196
4	Pedrosa	Repsol Honda Team	195
5	Spies	Yamaha Factory Racing	156
6	Rossi	Ducati Team	139
7	Hayden	Ducati Team	123
8	Simoncelli	San Carlo Honda Gresini	119
9	Edwards	Monster Yamaha Tech 3	98
10	Aoyama	San Carlo Honda Gresini	94
11	Barbera	Mapfre Aspar Team MotoGP	77
12	Bautista	Rizla Suzuki MotoGP	67
13	Crutchlow	Monster Yamaha Tech 3	57
14	Abraham	Cardion AB Motoracing	50
15	Elias	LCR Honda MotoGP	47
16	De Puniet	Pramac Racing Team	39
17	Capirossi	Pramac Racing Team	29
18	Akiyoshi	LCR Honda MotoGP	7
19	Hopkins	Rizla Suzuki MotoGP	6
20	Ito	Honda Racing Team	3

8 COLIN EDWARDS Slightly surprised to be top satellite rider again, after a race he wasn't terribly pleased with. Felt he never had the pace at any time during the weekend and then took too long to get past Aoyama.

9 HIROSHI AOYAMA Didn't live up to the promise of his Friday and Saturday form come race day, and thought the drop in track temperature might be to blame. Others felt the pressure of being involved in much of the commemorative activity related to the earthquake and tsunami might have distracted him.

10 RANDY DE PUNIET Tailing Elias and Aoyama but distracted by the board being shown for the ride-through penalties: he thought he was going to be called, which made him slow on the straight and then go wide at the first corner.

11 CAL CRUTCHLOW As well as being penalised for a jump start, Cal ran off-track when he nearly tagged Elias at Turn 3. Given those events, and the fact he wasn't in the best of health, he finished his fourth race in a row and at a pace that suggested eighth place wouldn't have been impossible.

12 KOUSUKE AKIYOSHI The Japanese Superbike Champion rode as a wild card for the LCR team. Happy with his race pace, if not his start, and loved putting on a show for the Japanese fans.

13 SHINICHI ITO The 44-year-old veteran became the oldest rider to take part in MotoGP. He's from Miyagi, the area most affected by the natural disasters in March, and his presence was symbolic of hope and respect.

NON-FINISHERS

TONI ELIAS By far his best race of the year. Qualified badly, as usual, but started well and didn't fade from seventh place. Fought back when Dovi passed him, but crashed on the brakes when he hit a bump at Turn 5 on lap 17.

ALVARO BAUTISTA Equalled his best qualifying of the year, avoided the first-lap mayhem and found himself in third place. Couldn't hold off the resurgent Stoner, though, and crashed while in fourth, trying to retain the gap to Dovizioso.

DAMIAN CUDLIN Riding in MotoGP for the first time as a substitute for the injured Capirossi on the recommendation of Sito Pons, for whom he rode as a replacement in Moto2. Did everything right until he crashed out of 12th place.

HECTOR BARBERA Crashed on lap 12 of the circuit where he was badly injured three years ago. This time it was less serious but still nasty: he suffered concussion and a broken collarbone.

VALENTINO ROSSI Enthusiastic about his chances after qualifying in seventh, but on the first lap he bounced off Lorenzo's Yamaha at Turn 3 and into Spies, catching his front brake lever and falling. Initial worries about a finger injury were soon dispelled.

NON-STARTERS

KAREL ABRAHAM Qualified but was ruled out of the race due to the concussion he suffered at Aragon.

LORIS CAPIROSSI Recovering from the shoulder reinjured at Aragon and did not travel to Japan. Replaced by Damian Cudlin.

AUSTRALIAN GP
PHILLIP ISLAND
ROUND 16
October 16
BRIDGESTONE
WORLD CHAMPION
FREIXENET
REPSOL
GAS
WORLD CHA

SUCH A PERFECT DAY

Stoner wrapped up the title as the factory Hondas dominated the top four and took the company's 60th constructors' championship

Casey Stoner has not been beaten at Phillip Island under the 800cc formula and he duly dominated again this year, making it five victories in a row at his home race. This time the win also clinched his second world title – and on a different make of bike from the first time, a feat only achieved by four other riders in the whole history of Grand Prix motorcycle racing. And it was his 26th birthday.

Coming into the weekend, he had no real expectation of being able to celebrate the championship in front of his home crowd. He would have had to win with Jorge Lorenzo, the only man with a mathematical chance of making Casey wait, finishing off the rostrum. Once again Lorenzo was heroic in practice and qualifying, putting his Yamaha second on the grid with only Stoner's Honda in front of him. But his prospects ended in Sunday morning warm-up when he crashed halfway through the final corner, after the bumpy surface set off a speed wobble. Jorge walked away and it seemed he was OK – until he pulled off his left glove, threw it on the ground and went straight to the medical centre. When his whole crew gathered outside, rather than working on the bike, it was obvious he wasn't going to race. Then the track marshals started searching for the discarded glove: Jorge had taken the tip off his left ring finger. To complete Yamaha's misery, Ben Spies had taken a big hit to the head and ribs when he crashed at Turn 3 in qualifying, and after warm-up he too decided he couldn't race.

Lorenzo's absence promoted Alvaro Bautista to the front row of the grid, something a Suzuki rider couldn't have dreamed of a year or two ago, and a measure of the progress the team has made. Long corners and cold tarmac were the GSV-R's nemesis and Phillip Island has

Above Jorge Lorenzo emerges from the medical centre and heads for a Melbourne hospital

Below The Aussie fans got what they came to see; a Stoner victory and his coronation

plenty of both. The rider who dominated at this track before the Stoner era was less happy. Valentino Rossi endured another horrible qualifying session, ending up 11th on the grid with only three riders behind him, the absence of both factory Yamahas and Aspar Ducati's replacement rider, Damian Cudlin, having reduced the grid to a thin 14 bikes. The paddock's biggest and best sponsored independent team also announced that they wouldn't be leasing a Ducati again in 2012, and instead would be running two bikes under the new CRT rules. When Aspar can't afford the going rate, it's pretty obvious that costs really have got out of hand.

The only problems Stoner encountered all weekend came from the track and the weather, not his opponents. TV pictures from the first day of practice showed a fleeting glimpse of one astonishing save in the final corner after the front end tucked. Casey wasn't the only one to complain about the state of the tarmac. Since the 2010 GP a large number of bumps had appeared, some big enough, according to Nicky Hayden, to force riders to pick a new line to avoid them. The good news was that the track would be resurfaced in 2012, but unfortunately not until December. The riders were not amused. Casey has not been shy in criticising circuits; in the case of Indianapolis his remarks about the Motor Speedway not being very interesting offended some delicate local sensibilities. He didn't hold back on the subject of his home track, either; no home-town bias there.

Having flattered to deceive, the weather decided to get nasty on race day. The 125s started and ended on a wet track and the wind was strong enough to bother the big bikes. Colin Edwards said it was simply a matter of survival: 'It was impossible to judge when a gust was

Above This entertaining dice for eighth was disrupted by the rain; Abraham, Crutchlow and Aoyama fell and only the Czech was able to remount

Above Valentino Rossi watches his Ducati barrel-roll into the grass at MG corner

Opposite Casey Stoner, double World Champion

Below Marco Simoncelli finished second, a career-best result, after a last-lap sort-out with Andrea Dovizioso

going to hit you from one lap to the next.' To add to the problems, it looked like rain was on the way. Sure enough, a few laps into the race a sprinkling of rain brought out the white flags, signifying that riders could swap to their wet-weather bikes if they wished. No-one took up the offer immediately.

Stoner pulled away from the fast-starting Hayden and the other factory Hondas of Pedrosa, Simoncelli and Dovizioso. That fight for the lower rostrum places resolved itself into another round of the season-long duel between Simoncelli and Dovizioso. Nicky, the best Ducati qualifier, faded with tyre woes; Dani, unhappy all weekend, had more trouble than most with the wind.

Valentino Rossi looked to be doing his usual trick of making up for poor qualifying with an aggressive start and steady progress. In the absence of the factory Yamahas, fifth place looked a distinct possibility, especially as he pushed past Hayden and Bautista right on half-distance. But as soon as he overtook the Spaniard, under brakes at MG, he slipped off. The curse of the Ducati front end had struck again – push hard, fall off. The progress that had been made at Motegi, a much simpler track, didn't carry across to the more complex problems of Phillip Island and Rossi was left repeating the now familiar mantra 'We work hard but we don't solve anything.' An interesting development was Jerry Burgess

telling Australian TV that it was possible the rider wasn't providing the right feedback. The first external sign of some tension in the camp, perhaps?

Inevitably the rain came, just four laps from the flag, but only at one corner. Bautista came round Hayshed as normal only to hit a wall of rain at Lukey Heights. He fell, as did Abraham, Crutchlow and Aoyama, the latter two simultaneously. The conditions allowed Dovizioso to jump across a big gap and take second off Simoncelli, only to lose out to a final charge reminiscent of the early-season Marco. Two riders, Hayden and Capirossi, gambled on changing bikes but the rain was gone as quickly as it had arrived.

Stoner had a worrying few moments but won, to the joy of his fellow countrymen and, at last, for the man himself. Standing on the bike in *parc fermé*? Grinning from ear to ear on the rostrum? Throwing his kneesliders to the crowd? That wasn't normal behaviour for Casey, but it was truly heartwarming to see from someone who doesn't always give the impression of enjoying his job. He also went to the medical centre to check up on Lorenzo – again, not something a rider usually does. Stoner has undoubtedly proved himself the best of the 800cc era. Let's hope he keeps enjoying his achievements.

'I DON'T THINK I COULD FIT MORE THINGS IN TODAY!'
CASEY STONER

EXALTED COMPANY

Casey Stoner's second world title gave him entry to a very exclusive club – the one for champions who have won the top title in motorcycle racing on different makes of motorcycle. The list of members is very short: Geoff Duke, Giacomo Agostini, Eddie Lawson, Valentino Rossi and now Casey Stoner.

Duke won on Norton and Gilera, Ago on MV Agusta and Yamaha, Steady Eddie on Yamaha and Honda, and the Doctor on Honda and Yamaha. Casey's 2007 title win was on a Ducati, the company's first world championship in GPs. Of the five, only Lawson won titles in consecutive years on different bikes – 1988 for Yamaha and the following season with Honda.

Casey joined the MotoGP class in 2006 on an LCR Honda. He qualified on pole for his second race, then finished on the rostrum in his third. Only Freddie Spencer has started from pole at a younger age, and that second place in Turkey made Stoner the youngest Australian ever to stand on the MotoGP rostrum.

When he became World Champion in 2007 he won ten races, scored points in every round and was only off the rostrum four times. He was also one of the youngest ever winners of the premier class, at just 21 years of age. This year Casey's victory at Silverstone was the first time a Honda rider had won three races in a row since Rossi in 2003, while the win at Laguna Seca, his fifth of the year, was a new record for Honda riders in MotoGP. His tenth pole of the year, at Motegi, gave him the record for number of poles by any rider in the MotoGP era.

It's also interesting to note what the form book says. All the other men who won on two makes of bike also won more than two titles. Duke was champion in 1951, '53, '54 and '55; Ago every year from 1967 to '72 on MV, and then again in '75 on Yamaha; Lawson's titles came in 1984, '86 and '88 with Yamaha and '89 on a Honda; Valentino won on Hondas from 2001 to '05, and then in '08 and '09 with Yamaha. It doesn't look like Casey's finished yet.

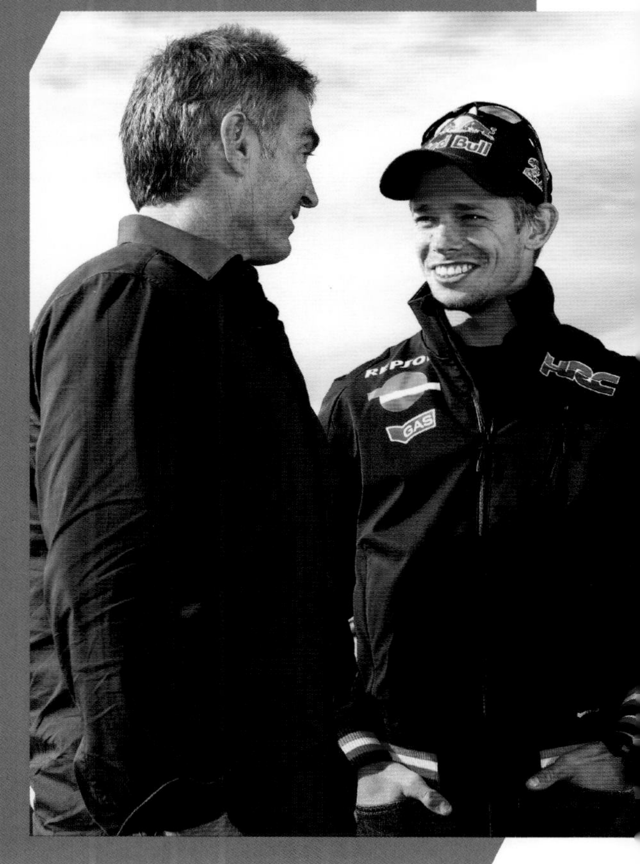

AUSTRALIAN GP

PHILLIP ISLAND

ROUND 16

October 17

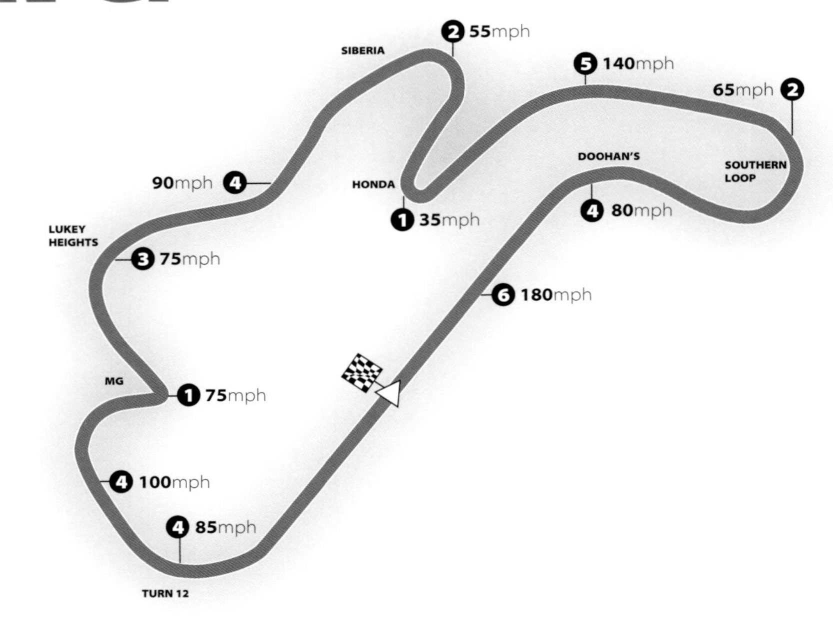

RACE RESULTS

CIRCUIT LENGTH 2.760 miles
NO. OF LAPS 27
RACE DISTANCE 74.620 miles
WEATHER Dry, 14°C
TRACK TEMPERATURE 26°C
WINNER Casey Stoner
FASTEST LAP 1m 30.629s, 106.506mph, Casey Stoner
LAP RECORD 1m 30.059s, 110.482mph, Nicky Hayden, 2008

QUALIFYING

	Rider	Nationality	Team	Qualifying	Pole +	Gap
1	Stoner	AUS	Repsol Honda Team	1m 29.975s		
2	Lorenzo	SPA	Yamaha Factory Racing	1m 30.448s	0.473s	0.473s
3	Simoncelli	ITA	San Carlo Honda Gresini	1m 30.599s	0.624s	0.151s
4	Bautista	SPA	Rizla Suzuki MotoGP	1m 30.714s	0.739s	0.115s
5	Dovizioso	ITA	Repsol Honda Team	1m 30.780s	0.805s	0.066s
6	Hayden	USA	Ducati Team	1m 30.792s	0.817s	0.012s
7	Spies	USA	Yamaha Factory Racing	1m 30.835s	0.860s	0.043s
8	Pedrosa	SPA	Repsol Honda Team	1m 30.871s	0.896s	0.036s
9	Edwards	USA	Monster Yamaha Tech 3	1m 31.237s	1.262s	0.366s
10	Capirossi	ITA	Pramac Racing Team	1m 31.583s	1.608s	0.346s
11	De Puniet	FRA	Pramac Racing Team	1m 31.635s	1.660s	0.052s
12	Aoyama	JPN	San Carlo Honda Gresini	1m 31.889s	1.914s	0.254s
13	Rossi	ITA	Ducati Team	1m 31.980s	2.005s	0.091s
14	Crutchlow	GBR	Monster Yamaha Tech 3	1m 32.023s	2.048s	0.043s
15	Abraham	CZE	Cardion AB Motoracing	1m 32.054s	2.079s	0.031s
16	Elias	SPA	LCR Honda MotoGP	1m 32.503s	2.528s	0.449s
NQ	Cudlin	AUS	Mapfre Aspar Team	1m 36.666s	6.691s	4.163s

FINISHERS

1 CASEY STONER Won the race from pole to clinch his second world title. He only had to finish sixth with Lorenzo absent, but Casey doesn't do things that way – he was never headed and set fastest lap. The only scare came with rain at the last corner late in the race, but he stayed on and remained undefeated at his home race, and all on his 26th birthday.

2 MARCO SIMONCELLI Simply couldn't bear the thought of finishing third – and behind Dovizioso – having been second for the whole race. Dovi mugged him when the rain arrived but Marco 'threw everything at him' to take his second rostrum of the year, and a career-best finish in MotoGP.

3 ANDREA DOVIZIOSO First visit to the podium since Brno. Lost touch with Simoncelli when Pedrosa came past, but jumped across a big gap to contest second when the rain arrived a few laps from the flag. Got past Marco but didn't have the grip to hold him off in the final corners of the last lap.

4 DANI PEDROSA An unpleasant weekend. Nearly overbalanced at the start and got away badly. Worked his way up to third but had scrubbed his front tyre badly and couldn't keep Dovi behind him, losing ground to the Italian in the fight for third in the championship. One of the few riders to use the softer rear tyre.

5 COLIN EDWARDS Best non-factory rider yet again, this time after a race he described as 'all about surviving'. First it was the gusting wind, then it was the rain, but Colin delivered – just like when conditions were difficult at Jerez and Silverstone.

6 RANDY DE PUNIET Went wide early on trying to catch Hayden and Edwards while in eighth, then rode well to get back up to the group containing Abraham, Aoyama and Crutchlow. Was the only one of the four to stay on his bike when the rain came, for easily his best finish of the year so far.

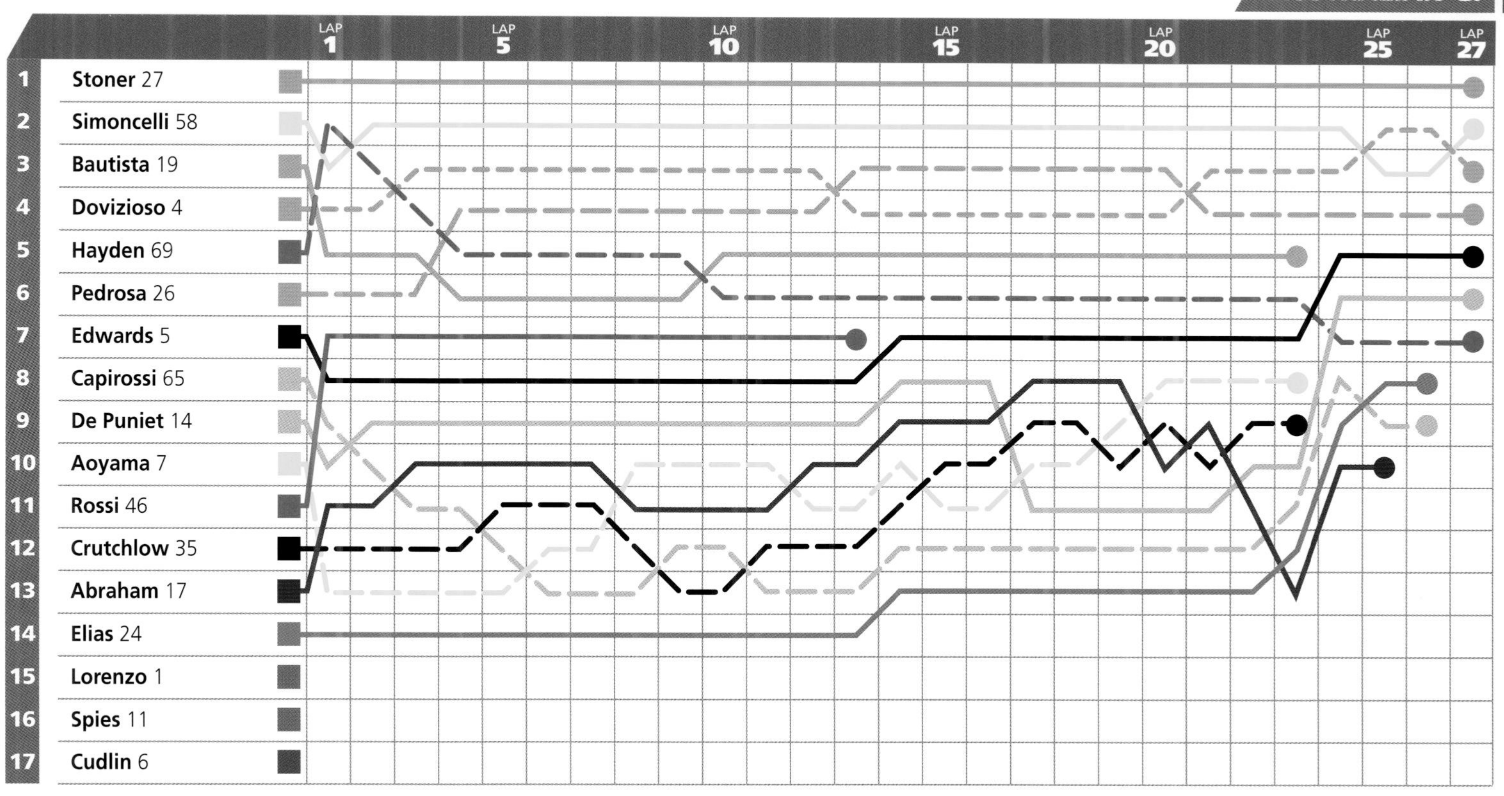

RACE

	Rider	Motorcycle	Race Time	Time +	Fastest Lap	Av Speed	
1	Stoner	Honda	42m 02.425s		1m 30.629s	106.506mph	S/H
2	Simoncelli	Honda	42m 04.635s	2.210s	1m 31.519s	106.413mph	S/H
3	Dovizioso	Honda	42m 04.879s	2.454s	1m 31.501s	106.403mph	S/H
4	Pedrosa	Honda	42m 15.585s	13.160s	1m 31.486s	105.954mph	S/M
5	Edwards	Yamaha	42m 33.311s	30.886s	1m 32.153s	105.218mph	S/M
6	De Puniet	Ducati	42m 51.225s	48.800s	1m 32.243s	104.485mph	S/H
7	Hayden	Ducati	43m 18.739s	1m 16.314s	1m 31.652s	103.379mph	S/H
8	Elias	Honda	42m 05.177s	1 lap	1m 33.189s	102.450mph	S/M
9	Capirossi	Ducati	42m 09.187s	1 lap	1m 32.695s	102.287mph	S/M
10	Abraham	Ducati	42m 45.142s	2 laps	1m 32.866s	96.975mph	S/H
NF	Bautista	Suzuki	35m 43.039s	4 laps	1m 31.619s	106.789mph	S/H
NF	Aoyama	Honda	35m 58.374s	4 laps	1m 32.916s	106.031mph	S/M
NF	Crutchlow	Yamaha	35m 58.593s	4 laps	1m 32.901s	106.020mph	S/M
NF	Rossi	Ducati	20m 09.118s	14 laps	1m 31.965s	106.980mph	S/H

CHAMPIONSHIP

	Rider	Team	Points
1	Stoner	Repsol Honda Team	325
2	Lorenzo	Yamaha Factory Racing	260
3	Dovizioso	Repsol Honda Team	212
4	Pedrosa	Repsol Honda Team	208
5	Spies	Yamaha Factory Racing	156
6	Simoncelli	San Carlo Honda Gresini	139
7	Rossi	Ducati Team	139
8	Hayden	Ducati Team	132
9	Edwards	Monster Yamaha Tech 3	109
10	Aoyama	San Carlo Honda Gresini	94
11	Barbera	Mapfre Aspar Team MotoGP	77
12	Bautista	Rizla Suzuki MotoGP	67
13	Crutchlow	Monster Yamaha Tech 3	57
14	Abraham	Cardion AB Motoracing	56
15	Elias	LCR Honda MotoGP	55
16	De Puniet	Pramac Racing Team	49
17	Capirossi	Pramac Racing Team	36
18	Akiyoshi	LCR Honda MotoGP	7
19	Hopkins	Rizla Suzuki MotoGP	6
20	Ito	Honda Racing Team	3

7 NICKY HAYDEN Best qualifying of the year. In trouble with lack of rear grip from the start, but the bike was fast and Nicky was close to the front for a time. Then the rear tyre blistered and he was just trying to make it to the finish. Decided to change bikes when it rained, having seen Bautista go down, and claimed another seventh place.

8 TONI ELIAS The Phillip Island weather exacerbated the problems Toni usually has with getting some heat into his tyres. Sure enough, he had edge-grip problems all race, but he stayed on the bike and profited from the crashes.

9 LORIS CAPIROSSI Back after missing Japan, due to aggravating his shoulder injury at Aragon. Gambled when the rain came and went into the pits to change bikes, only losing one place, but would probably have finished in front of Elias if he'd stayed out. Still a pleasing result given his physical condition.

10 KAREL ABRAHAM Tangled up with Crutchlow, Aoyama and de Puniet for most of the race and, like Cal and Hiro, crashed at Lukey Heights when the rain arrived but, unlike them, was able to get back on track and garner some valuable points in his fight with the Brit for the 'Rookie of the Year' title.

NON-FINISHERS

ALVARO BAUTISTA On the front row after Lorenzo's withdrawal, an amazing achievement for Suzuki on a track that used to spell poison for the GSV-R. Didn't get too good a start, lost ground on the leaders while fighting with Hayden, but looked safe in fifth when he hit the rain and slid off. Still, the best race of the year for Alvaro and the team.

HIROSHI AOYAMA Crashed hard once more in qualifying, and again in the race when he hit the rain. Made a decision over the weekend to move to the Castrol Honda team in World Superbike for the 2012 season.

CAL CRUTCHLOW Didn't enjoy qualifying at all but seemed to be having fun in the race, disputing eighth with Abraham, Aoyama and de Puniet. Fell at the same time as the Japanese rider when they ran into the localised rain at Lukey Heights with just three laps to go.

VALENTINO ROSSI Another bad qualifying, but a good start following a good warm-up promised a continuation of the progress made in Motegi. When he pushed to go past Bautista under brakes at the downhill MG corner, though, the front washed out. It turned out to be the same old story for the Ducati, despite the aluminium chassis parts.

NON-STARTERS

JORGE LORENZO Fell at the final corner in warm-up, severely damaging the ring finger of his left hand. Taken to Melbourne for plastic surgery.

BEN SPIES Fell at the very rapid Turn 3 in qualifying, suffering concussion and rib damage. Rode in warm-up but realised he couldn't maintain the required level of concentration.

DAMIAN CUDLIN Drafted in to replace Barbera, but suffered an enormous highside in practice which left him with a massive contusion on his hip, plus skin loss and bruising on his ribs. Tried to qualify but could only manage a couple of laps.

MALAYSIAN GP
SEPANG INTERNATIONAL CIRCUIT
ROUND 17
October 23
ADVANCE
ADVANCE

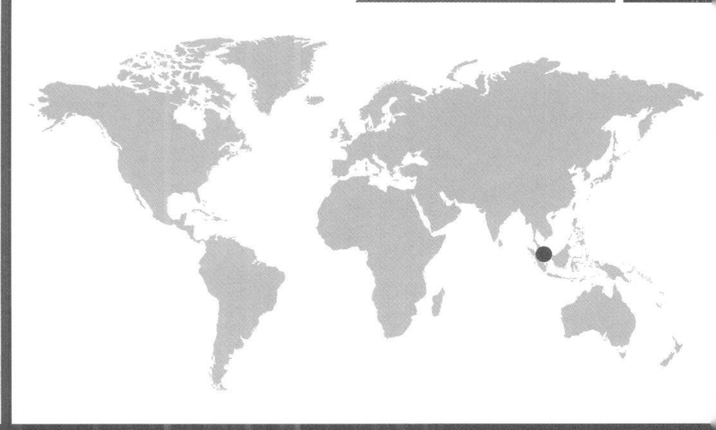

PARADISE LOST

Marco Simoncelli lost his life as a result of an accident on the second lap. The race was abandoned

It is easy to forget how dangerous motorcycle racing can be. The incident that cost Marco Simoncelli his life, and robbed the sport of one of its most endearing personalities, couldn't have been prevented or predicted.

TV pictures don't show the whole incident, but it seems that Marco lost the rear and lowsided. But instead of bike and rider sliding harmlessly to the outside of the corner, the rear tyre found some traction, maybe because Marco was still hanging on to the bars and trying to get it up off his knee, and he was fired back across the path of oncoming riders. Colin Edwards flung his machine to the right, but neither he nor Valentino Rossi could do anything to avoid the fallen bike and rider. Both men's bikes appeared to hit Marco and, horrifically, his helmet was sent rolling on to the grass. The red flag went out, medics were with Marco within seconds, but there was nothing they could do. Edwards suffered a dislocated shoulder. Those are the bare facts.

The sport lost a star, undoubtedly a future MotoGP race winner, probably a champion, and a racer whom the paying public adored. You will find a full obituary of Marco elsewhere in this book, but the fallout from this personal tragedy will go on affecting his family, his friends, his team and the whole paddock. What of Team Gresini, which also lost Daijiro Kato in 2003? And what will happen to their sponsor? What about Honda's plans for their factory bikes? Who can predict the effect on Colin Edwards's and Valentino Rossi's states of mind?

The death of a racer, of course, overshadows everything else that happens during a race weekend,

reducing to utter trivia such subjects as lap times and grid positions. However, there were some significant events before the tragedy of Sunday afternoon.

The factory Yamaha team were without Jorge Lorenzo after his Phillip Island accident, and Ben Spies also had to withdraw after two more crashes aggravated his injuries. Test rider Katsuyuki Nakasuga, drafted in to replace Lorenzo, would be the only man in factory colours on the grid. Despite the World, British and other domestic Superbike championships being over, Yamaha decided against giving a young hopeful a try-out. The policy of bringing in Japanese test riders, set at the start of the season, was adhered to. The planned test on the Monday after the race may also have had a bearing on that decision.

Another victim of earlier injury was John Hopkins. The American was taking a second wild-card ride for the Suzuki team after his heroics in the British

Above The Repsol Honda trio in *parc fermé* after qualifying

Below Race Direction's sombre post-race press conference

'SIC FOR ME WAS LIKE A YOUNGER BROTHER. SO STRONG ON TRACK AND SO SWEET IN THE NORMAL LIFE. I WILL MISS HIM A LOT.'

VALENTINO ROSSI

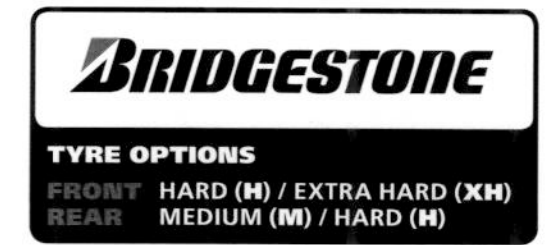

MALAYSIAN GP

SEPANG INTERNATIONAL CIRCUIT

ROUND 17

October 23

RACE RESULTS

CIRCUIT LENGTH 3.447 miles
NO. OF LAPS 20
RACE DISTANCE 68.940 miles
WEATHER Dry, 31°C
TRACK TEMPERATURE 46°C
WINNER N/A
FASTEST LAP N/A
LAP RECORD 2m 02.108s, 101.635mph, Casey Stoner, 2007

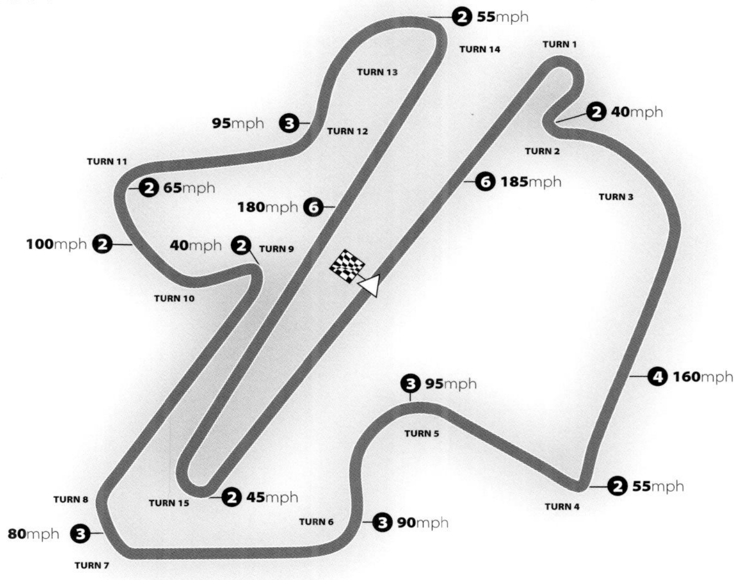

Superbike Championship. His GP ended early when the plates and screws holding the finger he hurt in the Czech Republic failed after the first day's practice.

The race was shaping up to be a Honda benefit. With the title settled the previous week, and Lorenzo's second place all but certain, attention was focusing on the fight for third between Dani Pedrosa and Andrea Dovizioso, whose departure for a satellite Yamaha ride in 2012 was adding some spice to the struggle. Dani took pole, only his second of the year; Dovi was in third, only his third front-row start of the season. As they sandwiched Casey, the Repsol Honda team had a monopoly of the front row for the first time since 1997 when Mick Doohan, Alex Criville, Takuma Aoki and Tady Okada filled what was then a four-man front row at Phillip Island. Behind them, Edwards was fourth on the grid, his best qualifying since Valencia in 2008, and Hayden was top Ducati rider in sixth. Rossi was ninth.

Off track, the speculation continued about whether Suzuki would or would not return to MotoGP in 2012, with Dorna CEO Carmelo Ezpeleta ramping up the temperature of his confrontation with the factories in an interview with the Spanish sports daily, *AS*. No longer, he said, would Dorna prop up teams who paid the exorbitant lease fees for satellite team bikes. In future, Dorna's support would be concentrated on CRT teams who build their own bikes. Ezpeleta's signals on this subject have previously been coded, but this time they were explicit and driven by the recent news of Aspar Martinez's team being unable, or unwilling, to pay the price of leasing Ducatis, Pramac downsizing to one bike for 2012, and two of the best-financed Moto2 teams, those of Stefan Bradl and Marc Marquez, deciding they couldn't afford to move to MotoGP.

Once the sad news was confirmed everyone just wanted to get to the airport and go home. All that was left was to marvel at the strength and dignity of Paolo Simoncelli, Marco's father. Ciao Super Sic.

QUALIFYING

	Rider	Nationality	Team	Qualifying	Pole +	Gap
1	Pedrosa	SPA	Repsol Honda Team	2m 01.462s		
2	Stoner	AUS	Repsol Honda Team	2m 01.491s	0.029s	0.029s
3	Dovizioso	ITA	Repsol Honda Team	2m 01.666s	0.204s	0.175s
4	Edwards	USA	Monster Yamaha Tech 3	2m 02.010s	0.548s	0.344s
5	Simoncelli	ITA	San Carlo Honda Gresini	2m 02.105s	0.643s	0.095s
6	Hayden	USA	Ducati Team	2m 02.172s	0.710s	0.067s
7	Aoyama	JPN	San Carlo Honda Gresini	2m 02.254s	0.792s	0.082s
8	Bautista	SPA	Rizla Suzuki MotoGP	2m 02.332s	0.870s	0.078s
9	Rossi	ITA	Ducati Team	2m 02.395s	0.933s	0.063s
10	Crutchlow	GBR	Monster Yamaha Tech 3	2m 02.756s	1.294s	0.361s
11	De Puniet	FRA	Pramac Racing Team	2m 02.939s	1.477s	0.183s
12	Capirossi	ITA	Pramac Racing Team	2m 03.077s	1.615s	0.138s
13	Abraham	CZE	Cardion AB Motoracing	2m 03.438s	1.976s	0.361s
14	Barbera	SPA	Mapfre Aspar Team	2m 03.619s	2.157s	0.181s
15	Elias	SPA	LCR Honda MotoGP	2m 03.646s	2.184s	0.027s
16	Spies	USA	Yamaha Factory Racing	2m 03.678s	2.216s	0.032s
17	Nakasuga	JPN	Yamaha Factory Racing	2m 04.072s	2.610s	0.394s

VALENCIAN GP
CIRCUITO RICARDO TORMO
ROUND 18
November 6

THE FINAL COUNTDOWN

Casey Stoner signed off a near-perfect season with the closest finish of the 800cc era

This was always going to be a strange weekend, and it turned out to be by turns moving, exhilarating and just plain weird.

What to make of the sight of Paris Hilton on the rostrum after her sponsored 125 rider, Maverick Viñales, became the youngest-ever rider to win back-to-back GPs – and in his rookie season as well? Or Fausto Gresini in floods of tears as his rider, Michele Pirro, won the Moto2 race? And then Pirro himself, eloquent despite his limited English, explaining that he couldn't celebrate his first GP victory.

The memory of Gresini's lost rider, Marco Simoncelli, was everywhere. Every bike had his number 58 on it somewhere. Valentino Rossi wore a special helmet and Kevin Schwantz led the memorial lap on Marco's bike. After which, in accordance with the Simoncelli family's wishes, there was a thunderous fireworks display. Much more fitting for Marco than a minute's silence.

There was a horrible reminder of the dangers of racing when Rossi, Hayden, Bautista and de Puniet went down in a maelstrom of sparks and flailing limbs at the first corner of the MotoGP race; then there was the relief of seeing them all walk away – in Rossi's case with unmistakable 'WTF?' body language. Bautista had tagged the back of Dovizioso's Honda as the field braked, his Suzuki sliding across the track and scooping up both factory Ducatis and de Puniet's Pramac Ducati. Replays showed that Dovi had moved slightly to his right, across Bautista's line, but he was in front. It was a racing incident, the sort of thing that will happen if people insist on racing motorcycles. And it was wet, with the rain never quite going away. The Desmosedici warms up its tyres quickly and similar conditions at Jerez showed what could happen.

Above The first-turn pile-up that eliminated Rossi, Hayden, de Puniet and Bautista

Below Jorge Lorenzo turned up at Valencia but had to do media work rather than ride

'I TOOK RISKS I HAVEN'T TAKEN ALL SEASON'

CASEY STONER

With the removal of the Ducatis at the first corner, it looked like the show was over and that the crowd would be deprived of a race. Casey Stoner had been over a second faster than the rest in qualifying, on a track where small gaps are hard to close. Double that second, at least, for a true comparison with tracks like Catalunya or Silverstone. So it was no surprise to see the new World Champion open up a lead at the rate of a second a lap over the first six laps; he was more than 10 seconds in front after 13 laps. Behind him, Dovizioso and Pedrosa scrapped, not only over the other rostrum places but for third overall in the championship, with Ben Spies right behind them. It was spitting with rain on some part of the circuit for the whole race, and as the Circuito Ricardo Tormo has variable grip at the best of times, conditions couldn't have been worse. Andrea Dovizioso has always excelled in these tricky situations and he controlled Pedrosa superbly. Any time Dani got in front, Andrea pushed straight back to second place.

The other fight was for Rookie of the Year. Cal Crutchlow and Karel Abraham went at it hammer and tongs from the start. Loris Capirossi looked to be catching the pair in his final GP. Loris has ridden in an astonishing 41 per cent of all Grand Prix events that have ever been held. Typically, he forsook his usual number, 65, in favour of Marco Simoncelli's 58, with the express permission of the family.

When the rain became serious, eight laps from home, both Pedrosa and Capirossi decided discretion was the better part of valour. That coincided with Ben Spies attacking Dovizioso and Stoner also deciding he didn't fancy falling off. He then selected neutral, ran wide

Right Loris Capirossi carried Marco Simoncelli's number in his 328th and final GP

Opposite Kevin Schwantz prepares to lead the tribute to Simoncelli on Marco's bike

Right Cal Crutchlow leads Karel Abraham in the fight for Rookie of the Year

Below Andrea Dovizioso leads Dani Pedrosa and Ben Spies before the rains came

and locked the rear when he found first gear. It was enough for Spies to take the lead. That was on lap 27 of 30. Both Ben and Casey said later that at this point their main concern was staying on their bikes. Some time before the flag they appeared to decide it might be worth taking a few chances. In Casey's case it was halfway round the last lap, when he realised he'd closed the gap on the American on the back straight and thought he might do what he hadn't done all year – take a big risk.

Stoner got right up to Spies on the brakes for the last corner, then put the power down perfectly. His drive had to be perfect, said Casey, or he wouldn't have won. He ran a wide line to use a small patch of newer

tarmac with much more grip, and took the victory by fifteen-thousandths of a second. Both men came out of the corner in first gear with, in Ben's words, the bike 'twisted all the way back and grabbing gears'. Casey didn't think Honda's seamless-shift gearbox had helped much; in fact, he thought its tendency to make the bike carry the front wheel was a hindrance. Stoner's first act in *parc fermé* was to apologise to Spies, who took the defeat philosophically. 'Power,' he said, summing up the situation nicely.

Casey was fulsome in his praise of Ben's riding but did observe that he, Casey Stoner, probably deserved to win as he'd led 95 per cent of the race. Ben was just happy to end what he called 'a horrendous month' with a podium finish.

The rookie's dispute was also settled on the last lap in favour of Crutchlow after Abraham made an error and ran off track. Cal's fourth place was the best finish by a British rider in the MotoGP era. Two MotoGP debutants, both in their 30s – Katsuyuki Nakasuga, Yamaha's factory tester, and American Superbike Champion Josh Hayes – brought their Yamahas home after a weekend in which neither made a mistake under very tricky circumstances. They also had the satisfaction of beating five regular MotoGP riders.

So the 800cc era of MotoGP ended as it had started, with Casey Stoner powering past a Yamaha. On the first lap of the 2007 Qatar race he ripped past Valentino Rossi's M-1 on the front straight. On the last lap of the 2011 Valencian GP Ben Spies was the victim on the run to the flag.

Bring on the 1,000s.

THE 800cc YEARS

The 800cc formula for MotoGP arrived for the 2007 season and lasted for five years and 88 races. The tables on this page, compiled by Dr Martin Raines, clearly show that the dominant bike of the era was the Yamaha M-1 and the dominant rider was Casey Stoner.

Stoner won the first and last 800cc titles, for Ducati and Honda respectively, while Yamaha took all three titles in between, with Rossi (twice) and Lorenzo. Both constructors' and teams' titles went the same way as the riders' championship each year. Stoner won a staggering 37.5% of all 800cc races, started from pole in the same number and was on the podium in 66%. Rossi's percentages are 16% of pole positions, 24% of wins and 54.5% podium finishes.

The idea of the 800s was to get away from the 210mph-plus top speeds of the 990cc bikes and increase safety margins. It didn't quite happen like that. The 800s were like giant 250s, requiring lots of corner speed and lean angle. By the end of 2011 the 800s were lapping just as fast as the 990s on most tracks despite being slightly slower in a straight line.

For 2012, MotoGP goes up to a full 1,000cc but without any increase in the fuel allowance for factory bikes. Not everyone is convinced there will be much difference in the racing, although the extra torque of the new bikes might allow riders to adopt a more 'point and squirt' style. There again, putting the power the 800s generate down on the tarmac is already a big enough challenge. The most significant change is likely to come from the completely new generation of Bridgestone tyres.

RIDER	WINS
Casey Stoner	33
Valentino Rossi	21
Jorge Lorenzo	17
Dani Pedrosa	13
Chris Vermeulen	1
Ben Spies	1
Andrea Dovizioso	1
Loris Capirossi	1

RIDER	PODIUMS
Casey Stoner	58
Valentino Rossi	48
Dani Pedrosa	48
Jorge Lorenzo	44
Andrea Dovizioso	16
Nicky Hayden	8
Chris Vermeulen	6
Colin Edwards	6
Ben Spies	6
Loris Capirossi	5
Toni Elias	5
Marco Melandri	4
John Hopkins	4
Marco Simoncelli	2
Randy de Puniet	2
Alex de Angelis	1
Alex Barros	1

RIDER	POLES
Casey Stoner	33
Jorge Lorenzo	18
Dani Pedrosa	15
Valentino Rossi	14
Colin Edwards	3
Marco Simoncelli	2
Ben Spies	1
Andrea Dovizioso	1
Nicky Hayden	1
Chris Vermeulen	1

MANUFACTURER	WINS
Yamaha	39
Ducati	24
Honda	24
Suzuki	1

VALENCIAN GP

CIRCUITO RICARDO TORMO

ROUND 18

November 6

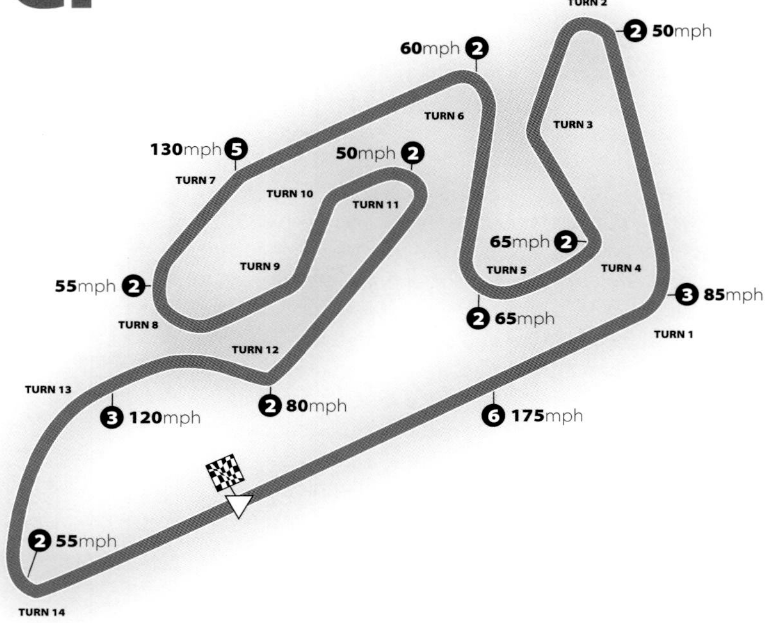

RACE RESULTS

CIRCUIT LENGTH 2.488 miles
NO. OF LAPS 30
RACE DISTANCE 74.640 miles
WEATHER Mixed, 17°C
TRACK TEMPERATURE 16°C
WINNER Casey Stoner
FASTEST LAP 1m 34.167s, 92.535mph, Andrea Dovisioso
LAP RECORD 1m 32.582s, 96.767mph, Casey Stoner, 2008

QUALIFYING

	Rider	Nationality	Team	Qualifying	Pole +	Gap
1	Stoner	AUS	Repsol Honda Team	1m 31.861s		
2	Pedrosa	SPA	Repsol Honda Team	1m 32.875s	1.014s	1.014s
3	Spies	USA	Yamaha Factory Racing	1m 33.057s	1.196s	0.182s
4	De Puniet	FRA	Pramac Racing Team	1m 33.118s	1.257s	0.061s
5	Bautista	SPA	Rizla Suzuki MotoGP	1m 33.443s	1.582s	0.325s
6	Rossi	ITA	Ducati Team	1m 33.478s	1.617s	0.035s
7	Hayden	USA	Ducati Team	1m 33.656s	1.795s	0.178s
8	Dovizioso	ITA	Repsol Honda Team	1m 33.824s	1.963s	0.168s
9	Barbera	SPA	Mapfre Aspar Team	1m 34.186s	2.325s	0.362s
10	Abraham	CZE	Cardion AB Motoracing	1m 34.265s	2.404s	0.079s
11	Crutchlow	GBR	Monster Yamaha Tech 3	1m 34.329s	2.468s	0.064s
12	Capirossi	ITA	Pramac Racing Team	1m 34.671S	2.810s	0.342s
13	Elias	SPA	LCR Honda MotoGP	1m 34.680s	2.819s	0.009s
14	Aoyama	JPN	San Carlo Honda Gresini	1m 34.838s	2.977s	0.158s
15	Nakasuga	JPN	Yamaha Factory Racing	1m 35.999s	4.138s	1.161s
16	Hayes	USA	Monster Yamaha Tech 3	1m 36.042s	4.181s	0.043s

FINISHERS

1 CASEY STONER Took his season's tally of wins to ten, the same as when he was champion in 2007. Led from the start, but backed off when the rain intensified and caught by Spies. Decided to get home safely but changed his mind halfway round the last lap, closing on the brakes at the last corner and getting perfect drive to win by a tiny margin.

2 BEN SPIES Shadowed Dovizioso and Pedrosa and, once past them, caught Stoner when the Aussie missed a gear. Had to judge how hard to push in deteriorating conditions in the final laps. Took risks but couldn't break the tow, and was out-dragged to the line. Phlegmatic about the result, but admitted it was a good end to a horrible month.

3 ANDREA DOVIZIOSO Very happy to beat Pedrosa and clinch third in the championship in his last race with Honda, the company he's been with for ten years. Impressive on a track he's never liked after a big crash at the end of qualifying, and tactically clever with the softer front tyre, not letting Dani (who used the harder option) lead him for any significant time.

4 CAL CRUTCHLOW The best result by a British rider in the MotoGP era, clinching the Rookie of the Year title after a spirited fight with Abraham. They swapped fifth place repeatedly, not slowing when the rain came down eight laps from home, and both passed Pedrosa on the last lap, but Karel tagged Cal's rear and ran off-track.

5 DANI PEDROSA Wasn't happy with his riding: he 'tensed up' and was worse in the wetter final laps. Didn't appear too worried about conceding third overall to Dovizioso, especially if the alternative was another broken collarbone.

6 KATSUYUKI NAKASUGA Yamaha's test rider was pleasantly surprised with his finishing position in his first MotoGP, riding as Jorge Lorenzo's replacement. Not only did he fulfil the test rider's primary function – not crashing – but he beat a couple of MotoGP regulars as well.

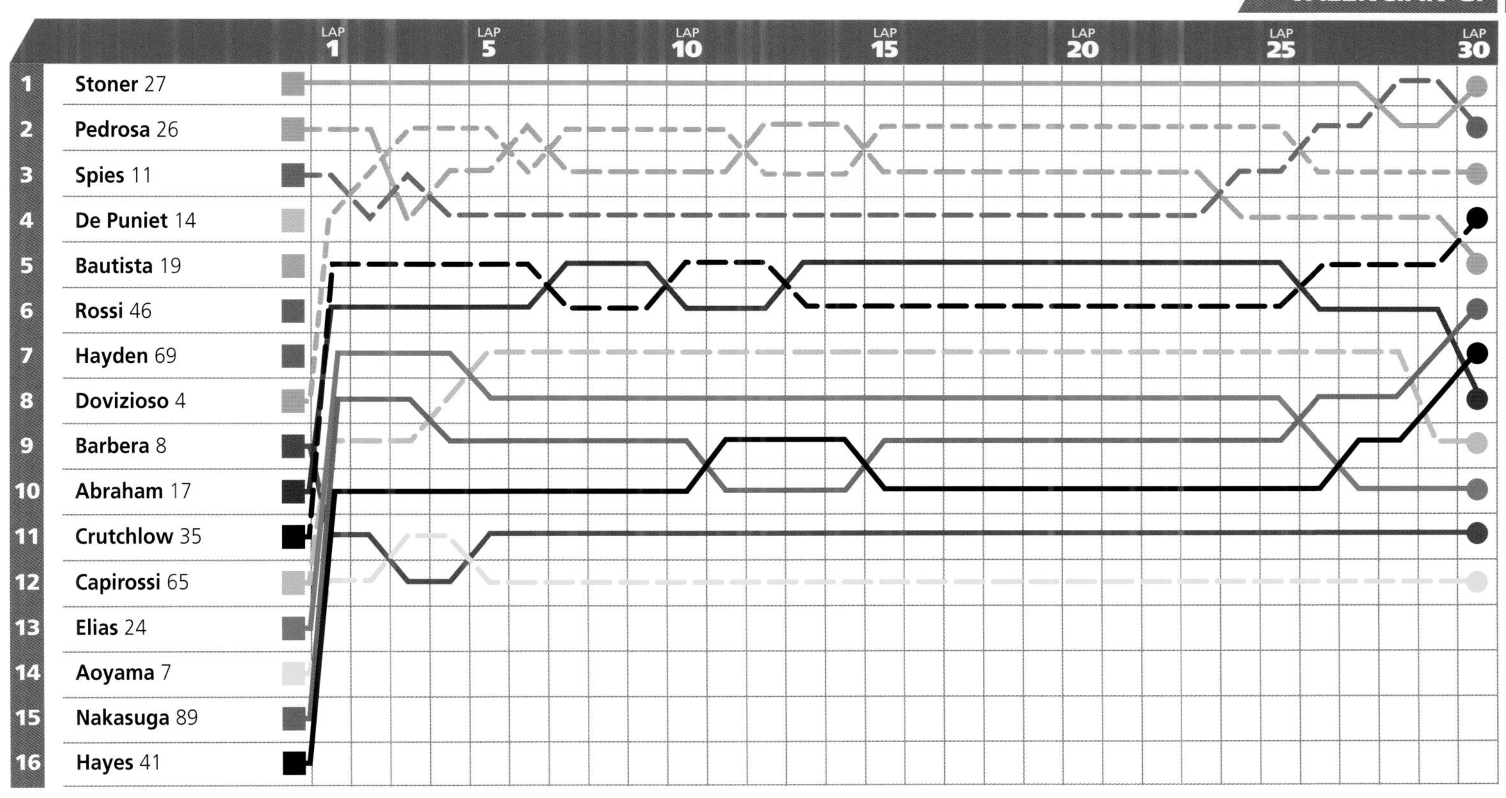

RACE

	Rider	Motorcycle	Race Time	Time +	Fastest Lap	Av Speed	B
1	Stoner	Honda	48m 18.645s		1m 34.259s	92.724mph	M/M
2	Spies	Yamaha	48m 18.660s	0.015s	1m 34.442s	92.724mph	M/M
3	Dovizioso	Honda	48m 24.581s	5.936s	1m 34.167s	92.535mph	S/M
4	Crutchlow	Yamaha	48m 27.363s	8.718s	1m 35.015s	92.446mph	M/M
5	Pedrosa	Honda	48m 27.966s	9.321s	1m 34.214s	92.427mph	S/M
6	Nakasuga	Yamaha	48m 42.463s	23.818s	1m 35.668s	91.969mph	S/M
7	Hayes	Yamaha	48m 51.763s	33.118s	1m 35.721s	91.677mph	S/M
8	Abraham	Ducati	48m 56.597s	37.952s	1m 34.997s	91.526mph	M/M
9	Capirossi	Ducati	49m 07.598s	48.953s	1m 35.267s	91.184mph	S/M
10	Elias	Honda	49m 11.146s	52.501s	1m 35.201s	91.074mph	S/M
11	Barbera	Ducati	49m 25.164s	1m 06.519s	1m 35.152s	90.644mph	S/M
12	Aoyama	Honda	49m 27.405s	1m 08.760s	1m 35.142s	90.576mph	S/M
NF	De Puniet	Ducati					S/M
NF	Bautista	Suzuki					S/M
NF	Rossi	Ducati					S/M
NF	Hayden	Ducati					S/M

CHAMPIONSHIP

	Rider	Team	Points
1	Stoner	Repsol Honda Team	350
2	Lorenzo	Yamaha Factory Racing	260
3	Dovizioso	Repsol Honda Team	228
4	Pedrosa	Repsol Honda Team	219
5	Spies	Yamaha Factory Racing	176
6	Simoncelli	San Carlo Honda Gresini	139
7	Rossi	Ducati Team	139
8	Hayden	Ducati Team	132
9	Edwards	Monster Yamaha Tech 3	109
10	Aoyama	San Carlo Honda Gresini	98
11	Barbera	Mapfre Aspar Team MotoGP	82
12	Crutchlow	Monster Yamaha Tech 3	70
13	Bautista	Rizla Suzuki MotoGP	67
14	Abraham	Cardion AB Motoracing	64
15	Elias	LCR Honda MotoGP	61
16	De Puniet	Pramac Racing Team	49
17	Capirossi	Pramac Racing Team	43
18	Nakasuga	Yamaha Factory Racing	10
19	Hayes	Monster Yamaha Tech 3	9
20	Akiyoshi	LCR Honda MotoGP	7
21	Hopkins	Rizla Suzuki MotoGP	6
22	Ito	Honda Racing Team	3

7 JOSH HAYES The US Superbike Champion was meant to ride in the post-race test here but found himself replacing Colin Edwards on the Tech 3 Yamaha. It's difficult to imagine a more difficult debut: first time on the bike, first time with carbon brakes and Bridgestone tyres, and all on a treacherous track. He impressed everyone.

8 KAREL ABRAHAM Spent the whole race dicing with Crutchlow, not just for fifth place but the Rookie of the Year title too. Lost out on the last lap when the pair passed Pedrosa and Karel went for an optimistic move on Cal, touching the Brit's rear tyre with his front and running off-track.

9 LORIS CAPIROSSI The paddock's longest-serving rider bowed out after a 22-year career with a top-ten finish. He was closing on the Abraham/Crutchlow dice when the rain came but decided not to risk spoiling his finale. Carried Marco Simoncelli's number 58 rather than the 65 he's always used.

10 TONI ELIAS Got his now-usual rocket start, avoiding the first-corner mayhem, but again, as usual, had problems with rear grip and suffered when the track got wetter and his more-than-respectable pace slowed.

11 HECTOR BARBERA Handicapped not just by his shoulder and rib injuries from Japan but also by a clutch that was slipping for the first couple of laps. Had a lonely race, not what he wanted at the track closest to his home town.

11 HIROSHI AOYAMA Definitely not the result Hiro wanted for his final MotoGP race. Chronic chatter completely destroyed any confidence he had in the front of the bike, an extreme example of the problems he'd suffered all year.

NON-FINISHERS

RANDY DE PUNIET Just when it seemed Randy's luck had turned, with his strongest showing of the year in practice and qualifying, he crashed at the first corner of the race through no fault of his own.

ALVARO BAUTISTA Tagged the back of Dovizioso's Honda on the run down to the first corner and fell, his Suzuki sliding across the track and skittling three other bikes.

VALENTINO ROSSI Devastated not to be able to wear a Super Sic T-shirt on the lap of honour. Like his team-mate, a victim of the domino effect that put four bikes on the floor at the first corner.

NICKY HAYDEN Taken out at the first corner. Took a big hit to his right hand, and although X-rays showed no damage on Sunday, by Tuesday he was diagnosed with a broken scaphoid and radius, so was unable to take part in the tests of the 1,000cc 2012 bike.

NON-STARTERS

COLIN EDWARDS Recovering from a shoulder operation to repair the damage done in the crash at Malaysia. Replaced by Josh Hayes.

JORGE LORENZO Did not risk the repair to the finger he hurt in Australia, as his runner-up spot in the championship was secure. Replaced by Katsuyuki Nakasuga. Did not take part in the testing session for 1,000cc bikes on the Tuesday and Wednesday after the race.

WORLD CHAMPIONSHIP CLASSIFICATION

MotoGP

	Rider	Nation	Motorcycle	QAT	ESP	POR	FRA	CAT	GBR	NED	ITA	GER	USA	CZE	IND	RSM	ARA	JPN	AUS	MAL	VAL	Points
1	**Stoner**	AUS	Honda	25	–	16	25	25	25	20	16	16	25	25	25	16	25	16	25	–	25	350
2	**Lorenzo**	SPA	Yamaha	20	25	20	13	20	–	10	25	20	20	13	13	25	16	20	–	–	–	260
3	**Dovizioso**	ITA	Honda	13	4	13	20	13	20	16	20	13	11	20	11	11	–	11	16	–	16	228
4	**Pedrosa**	SPA	Honda	16	20	25	–	–	–	–	8	25	16	–	20	20	20	25	13	–	11	219
5	**Spies**	USA	Yamaha	10	–	–	10	16	–	25	13	11	13	11	16	10	11	10	–	–	20	176
6	**Simoncelli**	ITA	Honda	11	–	–	11	10	–	7	11	10	–	16	4	13	13	13	20	–	–	139
7	**Rossi**	ITA	Ducati	9	11	11	16	11	10	13	10	7	10	10	6	9	6	–	–	–	–	139
8	**Hayden**	USA	Ducati	7	16	7	9	8	13	11	6	8	7	9	2	–	9	9	9	–	–	132
9	**Edwards**	USA	Yamaha	8	–	10	3	–	16	9	7	6	8	8	9	3	3	8	11	–	–	109
10	**Aoyama**	JPN	Honda	6	13	9	8	–	7	8	5	1	6	7	7	5	5	7	–	–	4	98
11	**Barbera**	SPA	Ducati	4	10	–	7	5	5	4	9	5	7	6	–	7	8	–	–	–	5	82
12	**Crutchlow**	GBR	Yamaha	5	8	8	–	9	–	2	–	2	–	–	5	6	7	5	–	–	13	70
13	**Bautista**	SPA	Suzuki	–	–	3	4	4	11	5	3	9	–	–	10	8	10	–	–	–	–	67
14	**Abraham**	CZE	Ducati	3	9	–	6	6	9	–	4	4	5	–	–	4	–	–	6	–	8	64
15	**Elias**	SPA	Honda	–	7	5	5	3	8	6	1	–	3	5	3	1	–	–	8	–	6	61
16	**De Puniet**	FRA	Ducati	–	–	6	–	–	4	–	2	3	–	4	8	2	4	6	10	–	–	49
17	**Capirossi**	ITA	Ducati	–	5	4	–	7	6	–	–	–	4	3	–	–	–	–	7	–	7	43
18	**Nakasuga**	JPN	Yamaha	–	–	–	–	–	–	–	–	–	–	–	–	–	–	–	–	–	10	10
19	**Hayes**	USA	Yamaha	–	–	–	–	–	–	–	–	–	–	–	–	–	–	–	–	–	9	9
20	**Akioshi**	JPN	Honda	–	–	–	–	–	–	3	–	–	–	–	–	–	–	4	–	–	–	7
21	**Hopkins**	USA	Suzuki	–	6	–	–	–	–	–	–	–	–	–	–	–	–	–	–	–	–	6
22	**Ito**	JPN	Honda	–	–	–	–	–	–	–	–	–	–	–	–	–	–	3	–	–	–	3

CONSTRUCTOR

	Motorcycle	QAT	ESP	POR	FRA	CAT	GBR	NED	ITA	GER	USA	CZE	IND	RSM	ARA	JPN	AUS	MAL	VAL	Points
1	**Honda**	25	20	25	25	25	25	20	20	25	25	25	25	20	25	25	25	–	25	405
2	**Yamaha**	20	25	20	13	20	16	25	25	20	20	13	16	25	16	20	11	–	20	325
3	**Ducati**	9	16	11	16	11	13	13	10	8	10	10	8	9	9	9	10	–	8	180
4	**Suzuki**	–	6	3	4	4	11	5	3	9	–	–	10	8	10	–	–	–	–	73

TEAM

	Motorcycle	QAT	ESP	POR	FRA	CAT	GBR	NED	ITA	GER	USA	CZE	IND	RSM	ARA	JPN	AUS	MAL	VAL	Points
1	**Repsol Honda Team**	38	20	38	25	25	25	28	28	38	36	25	36	31	25	36	38	–	36	528
2	**Yamaha Factory Racing**	30	25	20	23	36	–	35	38	31	33	24	29	35	27	30	–	–	30	446
3	**Ducati Team**	16	27	18	25	19	23	24	16	15	19	19	8	9	15	9	9	–	–	271
4	**San Carlo Honda Gresini**	17	13	9	19	10	7	10	16	11	6	23	11	18	18	20	20	–	4	232
5	**Monster Yamaha Tech 3**	13	8	18	3	9	16	11	7	8	8	8	14	9	10	13	11	–	22	188
6	**Pramac Racing Team**	–	5	10	–	7	10	–	2	3	4	7	8	2	4	6	17	–	7	92
7	**Mapfre Aspar Team Moto**	4	10	–	7	5	5	4	9	5	7	6	–	7	8	–	–	–	5	82
8	**Rizla Suzuki MotoGP**	–	6	3	4	4	11	5	3	9	–	–	10	8	10	–	–	–	–	73
9	**Cardion AB Motoracing**	3	9	–	6	6	9	–	4	4	5	–	–	4	–	–	6	–	8	64
10	**LCR Honda MotoGP**	–	7	5	5	3	8	6	1	–	3	5	3	1	–	–	8	–	6	61

Moto2
CHAMPIONSHIP

Anleihe
Windreich AG
Windenergie seit 1999
65%

GERMANY CALLING

The second year of the Moto2 formula produced great racing, an epic confrontation for the title, and improved lap times

In the end it was a weird way to win the title. Stefan Bradl found out he was Moto2 World Champion after the third free practice session for the final GP of the year. The only man who could stop him, Marc Marquez, wasn't fit to ride after his big accident in Malaysia. Bradl, from Bavaria, was the first German World Champion since Dirk Raudies won the 125s in 1993. And it wasn't just the rider who was German – his Viessmann Kiefer Racing team and Kalex chassis are also from Germany.

The Kalex chassis was first used last year by just one team, Sito Pons's outfit, so Kiefer were the second customer – though more teams will be using Kalex chassis in 2012. Before they came to Moto2, Kalex had built only one motorcycle chassis. That's an impressive learning curve. As in 2010, the most numerous design on the grid was the Suter, with the British-built FTR not far behind. Reigning champions Moriwaki returned, as did the lone TSR-chassis bike (badged as a Motobi) plus in-house designs from Tech 3 and – early on – MZ. The only maker that dropped out over the close season was Bimota. FTR had ended the first year as the chassis to have but a new, stiffer Suter and the Kalex immediately took the upper hand in 2011.

Bradl started the year with a run of five consecutive pole positions and won four of the first six races. After the British GP – his first wet-weather win – he was 82 points clear of Marc Marquez, but that win proved to be his last. This was the point at which his championship lead was extended to its maximum.

Marquez, meanwhile, crashed out of the first three races, but his season got going when won his fourth race, Le Mans, and set the fastest lap. If young Marquez's 125 championship season in 2010 had been impressive, his first year in Moto2 – as a rookie on four-strokes – was

Above Andrea Iannone dives inside Simone Corsi's FTR

Top right Scott Redding was one of the pre-season favourites but struggled with the new Suter chassis

Above right Bradley Smith rode hard in his first Moto2 season; three rostrums and a fastest lap were his reward

astonishing, leading no less an authority than 1993 500cc World Champion Kevin Schwantz to say he was the fastest man out there. It's true that his team were able to afford to test extensively and he got any chassis upgrades first, but there was no doubt that Schwantz was right.

After Silverstone, Marquez won three in a row, then took second at Brno, and then won another three on the bounce – six wins in seven races. By this point, after Aragon, Bradl's lead was down to six points. The German camp was rattled. However, Aragon was the last race that Marquez won. He did take the championship lead at Motegi but relinquished it next time out.

Then there were two crucial incidents during the three 'flyaway' races. The first was in Australia. Marquez crashed early on during free practice and spent nearly all the session in his pit while the bike was rebuilt. He got out just before the flag and crossed the line 30 seconds after the chequered flag went out. He didn't slow down, trying to squeeze in another lap at racing speed. Going into the fastest corner on the track, turn three, he tailgated Thai rider Ratthapark Wilairot and a terrifying incident resulted. It was reminiscent of a couple of incidents that have had awful implications, but, amazingly, neither man suffered serious injury. Race Direction punished Marquez by adding a minute to his qualifying time, thus demoting him to the back of the grid. In the race, he came through to third, just behind Bradl, and the German retook the championship lead.

1 – QATARI GP

Moto2 is meant to be all about wheel-to-wheel racing but no one told that to Stefan Bradl (Viessmann Kalex) at Qatar. The young German ran away from the opposition to beat runner-up Andrea Iannone (Speed Master Suter) by 4.3 seconds.

'Unbelievable!' said Bradl. 'We were competitive from the start of free practice, everything seemed easy!'

While Bradl made the race his own for his second Moto2 win, Iannone charged through from 16th on the grid to attack Thomas Lüthi (Interwetten Suter) and Yuki Takahashi (Gresini Moriwaki), who were disputing second. Iannone knifed past the pair in his usual thrillingly vicious style but couldn't get rid of the Swiss and the Japanese. Finally Iannone made the break, but there was nothing he could do about Bradl.

Takahashi held third during the closing stages but lost two places in the final laps when he came under attack from Lüthi and then Alex de Angelis (JIR Motobi).

Several fancied runners fell by the wayside, including second-fastest qualifier Marc Marquez (Repsol Suter) and Scott Redding (Marc VDS Suter), who had starred in pre-season testing.

2 – SPANISH GP

Andrea Iannone (Speed Master Suter) proved faster and tougher than his Moto2 rivals to win from the fourth row and take the championship lead. In tricky, damp conditions, the Italian enjoyed barging his way through the pack to take the lead shortly after halfway.

Thomas Lüthi (Interwetten Suter) and Simone Corsi (Ioda Racing FTR) completed the podium with rookie Bradley Smith (Tech 3) beating Qatar winner and Jerez pole-sitter Stefan Bradl (Viessmann Kiefer Kalex) in an entertaining duel for fourth place.

Smith led the first lap, before Corsi and then Lüthi took over, Lüthi building a one-second advantage by lap nine. But Iannone was already on the charge, moving into second on lap seven, chased by Corsi, Smith and Yuki Takahashi (Gresini Racing Moto2-Moriwaki). Three laps later Takahashi crashed at Ferrari, the fastest corner on the track.

Once in front, Iannone quickly built a winning advantage, while Lüthi gave up the chase after saving several nasty slides. 'It was difficult but fun passing people – and I touched a few,' smiled Iannone.

Local favourite Marc Marquez (Repsol Suter) was running strongly in the second group when he was rammed out of the race by Jules Cluzel (Forward Racing Suter).

3 – PORTUGUESE GP

Stefan Bradl (Viessmann Kiefer Kalex) took the lead in the Moto2 championship with a brilliant 0.147s victory over Julian Simon (Mapfre Suter). Bradl kept his head in tricky conditions, with the track still damp in places from morning rainfall.

Thomas Lüthi (Interwetten Suter) was the first rider to have a go at Bradl – the Swiss took the lead on lap four, then slid off a few corners later. Next it was Kenan Sofuoglu (Technomag Suter), but the Turk slipped back, later to fall. Then it was Simon, who closed the gap down to a few tenths, just as Andrea Iannone (Speed Master Suter) arrived on the scene.

Iannone had made a typically spectacular charge through the pack, coming through from the fifth row. The Italian grabbed the lead, only to slide off at the chicane. He remounted to finish 13th. That put Bradl back into the lead. On the last lap Simon never quite got close enough to attempt a pass.

Takahashi crossed the line six seconds back, ending a sad and emotional weekend for the Japanese star who had lost his brother Koki in a road accident in Japan the previous weekend.

Eleven men crashed, including Marc Marquez (Repsol Suter) who took out Scott Redding (Marc VDS Suter).

4 – FRENCH GP

Marc Marquez (Repsol Suter) went into his fourth Moto2 race having crashed out of the previous three races – not an easy call for a teenage rookie. But the reigning 125 World Champion proved his talent at Le Mans, coming from behind to win the race by almost two seconds.

World Championship leader Stefan Bradl (Viessmann Kiefer Kalex) again started from pole, as he had in every race so far. He then made the early running, holding off strong challenges from Thomas Lüthi (Interwetten Suter), Yuki Takahashi (Gresini Moriwaki) and Julian Simon (Mapfre Suter). But the young German lost side grip and slipped back as Marquez was closing, having come through from ninth on lap one.

It took Marquez a while to pick his way into the lead, but once he was out front he quickly left his pursuers behind, setting the fastest lap of the race on the way.

'In the beginning the feeling was not so good – it was scary on cold tyres,' he said. 'But then I found my confidence.'

Takahashi won the four-way contest for second, just ahead of Bradl, Lüthi and Simon.

Left Four-stroke debutant Bradley Smith had an impressive season

Below left Alex de Angelis was again unstoppable at Phillip Island

Below At Silverstone Stefan Bradl celebrates his first wet-weather win

5 – CATALAN GP

It seemed like there were two Moto2 races. The first was all about Stefan Bradl (Kiefer Kalex) riding to another perfectly composed victory, his third from five races. The 21-year-old German, who led all but the second lap, never put a wheel wrong, despite immense pressure from the rabble behind him.

The second race was a very different affair – the usual braying Moto2 pack, brawling for position with the inevitable carnage. Julian Simon (Mapfre Suter), who briefly led Bradl, was a second behind the German with eight laps to go when a hard-charging Kenan Sofuoglu (Technomag Suter) rammed him from behind. Simon went down, Sofuoglu ran him over in the gravel trap and then also crashed. Simon suffered a broken right tib and fib.

Even scarier was the lap six accident which had Thomas Lüthi (Interwetten Suter) highsiding out of the pack battling for second. The group was so tight that he took Yuki Takahashi (Gresini Moriwaki) with him and impeded Bradley Smith, who set fastest lap. Luckily both men walked – or rather, staggered – away.

The Simon/Sofuoglu incident promoted Le Mans winner Marc Marquez (Repsol Suter) to second and put Aleix Espargaro (Pons Kalex) into third for his first GP podium.

6 – BRITISH GP

Stefan Bradl ran away with the Moto2 race just as Stoner ran away with the MotoGP event. It was another faultless ride from the German, who (again like Stoner) made it four wins from the first six races.

Bradl (Viessmann Kalex) led from the start to extend his series lead to an amazing 62 points ahead of Simone Corsi. Stefan had two riders come past him but neither could better his pace for long. Scott Redding (Marc VDS Racing Team-Suter) led for three laps but soon slipped backwards. Mattia Pasini (Ioda Racing Project-FTR) passed Bradl on lap six, then fell the next lap.

The only man in Bradl's league was Briton Bradley Smith (Tech 3), who gave the sodden crowd something to cheer about as he came through from 28th on the grid to finish second, the rookie's first Moto2 podium result. Michele Pirro (Gresini Moriwaki) won the contest for the final podium position, crossing the line five seconds down on Smith and five ahead of last year's Silverstone winner Jules Cluzel (Forward Racing-Suter).

'I focused on myself and my own race and didn't care what the others were doing,' said Bradl.

7 – DUTCH TT

The track was only damp at the start, but everyone started on rain tyres. The race was a humdinger, with four different leaders vying for the win as the track dried out and tyres began to degrade.

Marc Marquez (Repsol Suter) won after overcoming his lack of wet-weather confidence to get the better of Kenan Sofuoglu (Technomag Suter) and Bradley Smith (Tech 3).

Smith and Sofuoglu were the main men during the mid-stages of the race, Sofuoglu looking as scary as ever compared with Smith's neat, safe riding. Marquez took the lead with a breathtaking outside move through the 150mph right/left flick at Ramshoek and that was that.

'Usually in the rain I never get the feeling, but step by step the team has helped me,' said Marquez. 'The last laps were really tough as it rained more but by then the tyres looked destroyed.'

Former World Supersport champ Sofuoglu stayed on to finish second for his first Moto2 podium, 2.4 seconds behind Marquez, while Smith was third, for his second consecutive podium, a further four seconds back.

Exactly one third of the 29 starters crashed, including Kenny Noyes (Avintia STX FTR) and runaway world title leader Stefan Bradl (Viessmann Kalex).

8 – ITALIAN GP

Marc Marquez (Repsol Suter) won his third Moto2 victory by just seven hundredths of a second after a titanic battle with Stefan Bradl (Viessmann Kalex) and Bradley Smith (Tech 3). The lead changed throughout, Marquez and Bradl the main men, Smith only enjoying the briefest whiff of first place.

On the final lap Bradl also muscled his way past Smith but the World Championship leader couldn't quite close enough to attack Marquez.

'Early on my feeling wasn't so good, but step by step it got better,' said Marquez. His win took five points out of Bradl, who still led by 52 points, despite his Assen DNF.

Smith – running a modified Tech 3 chassis – was knocked back from first to third in the last two laps but was nevertheless delighted with his first dry-track Moto2 podium.

Andrea Iannone (Speed Master Suter) came through from 14th on the grid to catch the lead group, but by then he had burned his tyres. He finished fifth behind Alex de Angelis (JIR Motobi).

9 – GERMAN GP

Marc Marquez (Repsol Suter) made it three wins in a row, the rookie coming out on top of a tense duel with local hero Stefan Bradl (Viessmann Kalex). Marquez's fourth win of the year inched him closer to Bradl in the points chase, but the 21-year-old German could still win the title if he finished second to the 18-year-old in the last eight races.

Marquez and Bradl weren't alone in this race until the last five laps when they pulled a gap on Alex de Angelis (JIR Motobi) and Thomas Lüthi (Interwetten Suter), who had been with them for much of the race. De Angelis got between Marquez and Bradl on several occasions, but never made it into the lead. On the penultimate lap Lüthi fell victim to Randy Krummenacher (Kiefer Kalex), who had a brilliant ride from 15th, often lapping faster than the leaders.

Marquez moved in for the kill when Bradl struggled with rear grip in the late stages. 'Before the race I knew we could make the difference at the end because we were very strong on used tyres,' he said.

10 – CZECH REPUBLIC GP

Andrea Iannone won the best race in any GP class so far this year. The Italian came out on top of a vicious four-man skirmish for his first victory since May's Spanish GP. He came from behind to overhaul Marc Marquez, Stefan Bradl and Alex de Angelis.

Bradl led most of the first half of the race, after surviving a first-lap collision with Marquez, who was looking for a fourth consecutive win to take another chunk out of the German's points lead. During the final laps Bradl (Viessmann Kalex), Iannone (Speed Master Suter) and Marquez (Repsol Caixa Suter) kept swapping the lead, Iannone passing both his rivals in one corner with three laps to go. Marquez got back in front on the penultimate lap, after colliding with Iannone, but on the last lap it was Iannone who proved the hardest man. He crossed the line 0.16 seconds ahead of Marquez, with Bradl a further 0.24 seconds down and de Angelis just 0.08 behind the winner.

'It feels great to win again,' said Iannone after coming back from a disastrous series of races. 'During the summer break we analysed all the data from all the races and from pre-season testing and decided to go back to a completely standard Suter set-up.'

11 – INDIANAPOLIS GP

There were many turning points in 2011, and Indy was one of them. Marquez had beaten Bradl at the previous four races, but the German knew that if he just kept finishing on the podium he had a good chance of fending off his teenage rival.

At Indy Bradl (Viessmann Kalex) struggled with front-end feel and ended up crashing in qualifying, which put him way back in 22nd on the grid. Meanwhile Marquez (Repsol Suter) qualified on pole and rode to his fourth win from five races. Bradley Smith (Tech 3) was first in front, then Simone Corsi (Ioda FTR), with Marquez shadowing the Italian before sweeping ahead into the first turn. From there the Spaniard took off, and he was five seconds clear at half-distance.

Meanwhile Bradl was staging a spirited comeback. Down in 19th at the end of the first lap, he had fought his way up to tenth by half-distance and kept making forward progress to cross the line in sixth spot.

Corsi dropped out of the group battling for the lesser podium finishes after surviving a big moment, leaving Smith, Scott Redding (Marc VDS), Andrea Iannone (Speed Master Suter), Esteve Rabat (Blusens FTR) and Pol Espargaro (Tuenti FTR) in the running. At the finish it was Espargaro in second, just ahead of Rabat to complete the first all-Spanish Moto2 top three.

12 – SAN MARINO GP

Who can stop Marc Marquez? The Spanish teenager continued his relentless and remarkable progress at Misano, coming out on top of a typically frantic Moto2 confrontation to score his fifth win in six races. This latest success further reduced the gap to series leader Stefan Bradl, who had been 82 points ahead of him after June's British GP. After Misano Bradl's advantage was 23 points.

Once again Marquez (Repsol Suter) seemed to have it all worked out. After surviving several slides in the early stages he zeroed in on the leading trio of pole-sitter Bradl (Viessmann Kalex), Andrea Iannone (Speed Master Suter) and Scott Redding (Marc VDS Suter), who had led the early stages. Marquez was in the thick of this group for a while, leading three laps in the mid-stages of the race, before making his winning move with six laps to go.

Try as he might Bradl couldn't go with his big rival but at least he did get the better of Iannone in the final two laps. Redding finished fourth, just ahead of fellow Brit Bradley Smith (Tech 3)

'I made some mistakes and nearly crashed, but after that I improved my confidence with the bike,' said Marquez. 'I'm very happy with this victory because Bradl was so strong in qualifying.'

The following week, in Malaysia, it was Marc's turn to be on the wrong end of someone else's mistake. When marshals failed to show yellow flags at a corner hit by a localised downpour, Marc, and others, slid off at speed. His helmet took a big hit and he woke next day with double vision in one eye. He didn't race. Bradl did, and came second.

The question now was whether Marquez would be fit for the last race of the year so he could try to overcome his rival's 23-point lead? The answer, after lots of indecision, was 'no'. So Stefan Bradl became World Champion somewhere between third free practice and qualifying.

Neither of the two championship protagonists managed to dominate the end of the season. Instead Suter riders Andrea Iannone and Tom Lüthi finally came to terms with the much stiffer 2011 chassis, and Alex de Angelis once again ruled at Phillip Island.

The surprise of 2011 was that no FTR rider won a race. The Buckingham-based constructor's best rider was Simone Corsi, who scored points in every race bar two but only stood on the rostrum twice. Class rookie Pol Espargaro, of whom much was hoped, also had two top-three finishes and fellow Moto2 debutant Esteve Rabat had one.

Pre-season favourite Scott Redding had a disappointing year, although, like other Suter runners, he found some speed at the end of the year. British fans were able to cheer Bradley Smith's run of three rostrums in the middle of the season.

It seems odd now that there was ever any controversy about the switch to Moto2. The grid is oversubscribed, lap and race records set by the 250s are being equalled or beaten after just two seasons, and spectators love the action. Is it a class that can train riders for MotoGP like the 250s used to? That's still an open question, but the top three in this year's championship – Bradl, Marquez and Iannone – will be in MotoGP sooner rather than later. Then we'll know.

Opposite Marc Marquez and Andrea Iannone skate their Suters into the first turn at Aragon

Right 'It felt like the end of the world, but I am still here,' said Iannone after ending his winless run at Brno

Below The contenders: Marc Marquez bears the scars of his Sepang crash; Stefan Bradl practises his thousand-metre stare

13 – ARAGON GP

This was another edge-of-the-seat Moto2 conflict, with more passing manoeuvres than it's possible to record. The action all the way through the pack was thrilling and sometimes scary but in the end the result was the same: Marc Marquez dug deep during the final stages and ran away with it.

Until three-quarters distance the Repsol Suter rider had been in the thick of the battle with Andrea Iannone (Speed Master Suter), Stefan Bradl (Viessmann Kalex), Scott Redding (Marc VDS Suter), Simone Corsi (Ioda FTR) and Alex de Angelis (JIR Motobi).

Marquez and Iannone did most of the running until Iannone ran wide and gave the teenage rookie a break. Marquez didn't waste it and steadily eked out a margin while the rest of the leading group went at each other.

'Some of the passes were at the limit, but it was a nice battle,' said Marquez.

Iannone beat Corsi and de Angelis for second place, the trio separated by half a second. Aleix Espargaro (Pons Kalex) was fourth, with just 3.5 seconds separating him from 15th finisher Redding.

Marquez's sixth win in seven races moved him to within six points of Bradl, who finished eighth after his rear tyre moved on the rim. 'I can forget about the championship now – I don't want to think about it any more,' said a gloomy Bradl.

14 – JAPANESE GP

After June's British GP Marc Marquez had been 82 points down on Moto2 leader Stefan Bradl. At Motegi the Spanish teenager moved into the points lead – surely one of the sport's all-time greatest comebacks.

But this time Marquez (Repsol Suter) didn't actually win the race. He battled long and hard with Andrea Iannone (Speed Master Suter), the Italian prevailing. The pair swapped the lead several times and Iannone had a real fright mid-race when his engine died momentarily, briefly losing him the lead once more.

'I was quite scared,' said Iannone after his third win of 2011. 'But the engine came back and I was able to recover quite quickly.'

Thomas Lüthi (Interwetten Suter) won a fearsome four-man quarrel for third place, just beating former championship leader Bradl (Viessmann Kalex), Simone Corsi (Ioda FTR) and Alex de Angelis (JIR Motobi).

15 – AUSTRALIAN GP

This was title hopeful Stefan Bradl's big chance to get some points back on Marc Marquez, who had swept into the title lead at Motegi but was demoted to the back of the Phillip Island grid for dangerous riding in practice. He rammed luckless Thai rider Ratthapark Wilairot after the flag came out to end free practice. Both riders were very lucky to escape serious injury.

But no. Bradl (Viessmann Kalex) and Alex de Angelis (JIR Motobi) dominated the front of the race but once again the real star was the teenage Spaniard who staged a remarkable charge, from 38th to 16th on lap one, to tenth on lap four and finally to third at the flag.

Bradl and de Angelis had a thrilling duel, trading the lead several times until the San Marino rider took the lead on the final lap. Bradl immediately counter-attacked, but collided with de Angelis and nearly fell. So de Angelis won his second consecutive Phillip Island Moto2 race 1.3 seconds ahead of Bradl, who was five seconds ahead of Marquez (Repsol Suter) who just fended off surprise package Claudio Corti (Italtrans Suter).

'Every lap I was on the limit, but at the end my rear tyre dropped off a lot so I couldn't go for de Angelis and Bradl,' said Marquez, suggesting he may have won if he'd had more grip!

16 – MALAYSIAN GP

If Marc Marquez had been lucky to avoid injury, and a more serious punishment, for his Australian error, fate caught up with him in Malaysia. He crashed in FP1 on a wet corner because the marshals had not displayed rain flags. Concussion kept him out of the race.

Bradl went into the race with a three-point advantage, so if he could win, he would secure the title, while even second place would give Marquez a final chance in the Valencia finale.

The German took the lead from pole-sitter Thomas Lüthi (Interwetten Suter) on lap one and quickly opened a one-second lead over the Swiss, the pair of them getting well clear of the brawling pack. But by half-distance Lüthi had closed Bradl down and took the lead with two laps to go. Bradl stuck right with him, though, only for the red flags to come out after Axel Pons (Pons Kalex) had crashed.

It was Lüthi's first win since his final 125 victory in 2006. 'I was lucky the flags came out, but I think I could have beaten him anyway,' said the former 125 champ.

Bradl thought otherwise. 'I already had my plan to overtake him on the last lap, but we should look at the positives – hopefully I can win the title at Valencia.' Bradl would need 13th place at the final race to take the crown.

Pol Espargaro (Tuenti FTR) took third, just ahead of Alex de Angelis (JIR Motobi) who had staged a brilliant charge from 15th on lap one.

Above Michele Pirro, emotional winner for Team Gresini at Valencia

Above right At Sepang Tom Lüthi finally won an intermediate-class race

17 – VALENCIAN GP

Gresini Moriwaki rider Michele Pirro won the Moto2 finale, giving team boss Fausto Gresini something to smile (and cry) about. But it was another hairy race for Gresini, who saw his other Moto2 rider Yuki Takahashi take the lead only to suffer the most almighty highside in the tricky conditions. Gresini – already grief-stricken following the death of MotoGP rider Marco Simoncelli – had just returned from the medical centre, where Takahashi was undergoing check-ups, in time to see Pirro win the race. He slumped over the pit wall, crying his eyes out.

'I felt like I had Marco riding with me,' said former 125 GP and World Supersport rider Pirro, who won by six seconds.

Mika Kallio (Marc VDS Suter) and Dominique Aegerter (Technomag Suter) fought a long duel for second and third in a race blighted by many crashes. Anthony West (MZ) won a rough battle for fourth with Kenny Noyes (Avintia FTR) and Yonny Hernandez (Blusens FTR).

Stefan Bradl (Viessmann Kalex), who was crowned world champ when Marc Marquez (Repsol Suter) was deemed unfit to ride due to his Sepang injuries, was one of many crashers.

CHAMPIONSHIP STANDINGS

	Rider	Nat	Team	Motorcycle	Points
1	Stefan Bradl	GER	Viessmann Kiefer Racing	Kalex	274
2	Marc Marquez	SPA	Team Catalunya Caixa Repsol	Suter	251
3	Andrea Iannone	ITA	Speed Master	Suter	177
4	Alex de Angelis	RSM	JIR Moto2	Motobi	174
5	Thomas Lüthi	SWI	Interwetten Paddock Moto2	Suter	151
6	Simone Corsi	ITA	Ioda Racing Project	Suter	127
7	Bradley Smith	GBR	Tech 3 Racing	Tech 3	121
8	Dominique Aegerter	SWI	Technomag-CIP	Suter	94
9	Michele Pirro	ITA	Gresini Racing Moto2	Moriwaki	84
10	Esteve Rabat	SPA	Blusens-STX	FTR	79
11	Yuki Takahashi	JPN	Gresini Racing Moto2	Moriwaki	77
12	Aleix Espargaro	SPA	Pons HP 40	Pons Kalex	76
13	Pol Espargaro	SPA	HP Tuenti Speed Up	FTR	75
14	Julian Simon	SPA	Mapfre Aspar Team Moto2	Suter	68
15	Scott Redding	GBR	Marc VDS Racing Team	Suter	63
16	Mika Kallio	FIN	Marc VDS Racing Team	Suter	61
17	Kenan Sofuoglu	TUR	Technomag-CIP	Suter	59
18	Randy Krummenacher	SWI	GP Team Switzerland Kiefer Racing	Kalex	52
19	Yonny Hernandez	COL	Blusens-STX	FTR	43
20	Max Neukirchner	GER	MZ Racing Team	MZ-RE Honda	42
21	Jules Cluzel	FRA	NGM Forward Racing	Suter	41
22	Anthony West	AUS	MZ Racing Team	MZ-RE Honda	40
23	Mike di Meglio	FRA	Tech 3 Racing	Tech 3	30
24	Mattia Pasini	ITA	Ioda Racing Project	FTR	28
25	Claudio Corti	ITA	Italtrans Racing Team	Suter	23
26	Xavier Simeon	BEL	Tech 3 B	Tech 3	23
27	Alex Baldolini	ITA	Desguaces La Torre G22	Moriwaki	18
28	Kenny Noyes	USA	Avintia-STX	FTR	11
29	Kev Coghlan	GBR	Aerosport de Castello	FTR	11
30	Ratthapark Wilairot	THA	Thai Honda Singha SAG	FTR	4
31	Ricard Cardus	SPA	QMMF Racing Team	Moriwaki	2
32	Axel Pons	SPA	Pons HP 40	Pons Kalex	1

125 CHAMPIONSHIP

GOODBYE RING-DING

The last 125cc championship went down to the final round, a fitting farewell to two-strokes; next year it's four-strokes in Moto3

Only one class has been included in World Championship Grand Prix motorcycle racing every year since the championship's inception in 1949. That is the 125cc class. Every year, that is, until next year. The 2011 season was the last hurrah of the 125 and the last time, for the foreseeable future, that we'll hear the zing of a two-stroke engine in a Grand Prix paddock. In 2012 we will be watching Moto3, powered by single-cylinder 250cc four-strokes.

So Nico Terol goes into the record books as the last 125 champion. Despite being a clear pre-season favourite, it took him until the last round of the year to dispose of the persistent Frenchman Johann Zarco. At times it looked as if Zarco didn't want to win a race, let alone the championship. He was beaten on the run to the line, came off worst in a dead-heat tie-breaker, and when he did cross the line first Race Direction handed him a penalty that put him back to sixth. Not an easy season, but Johann certainly livened things up.

As did the Rookie of the Year and reigning Spanish Champion, 16-year old Maverick Vinales. With no time served in the Red Bull Rookies or wild-card GP experience, Maverick (his real name) won his fourth race, started from pole in his sixth and did the grand slam of pole, win and the fastest lap in his seventh. His wins at the last two races of the year made him the youngest rider ever, across all classes, to take back-to-back wins. Maverick held off the challenge of the vastly experienced German, Sandro Cortese, for third overall. Some rookie.

As has been the case in the last few years of both 125s and 250s, you needed one of a small number of top-spec Aprilias to have a chance of a race win or pole, let alone the championship. The only non-Aprilias

on the grid were a couple of KTMs, the occasional wild-card Honda and two Mahindras. The giant Indian engineering company took over the Italian Engines Engineering team which has run under such names as Lambretta, Loncin and Malagutti in recent seasons. The first effect was increased reliability, as both bikes finished in the points four times. The highlight was pole position in the final race of the 125 era thanks to Danny Webb, who was brave enough to fit slicks in the last minutes of a damp session. That happened in front of the company's CEO, Anand Mahindra, at his first GP to unveil their Moto3 bike. In view of the size of India's domestic market – 11 million motorcycles sold in 2010 – and the country's successful Formula 1 debut, he promised that his company was in MotoGP for the long haul.

If it weren't for Maverick Vinales, the Rookie of the

Above Sandro Cortese won two races but this one crash cost him third place in the championship

Above right He's young, he's fast, and he's a winner: Maverick Vinales

Right German rider Jonas Folger took his maiden win at Silverstone

Opposite Maverick Vinales pounces on Nico Terol in France for his first win

1 – QATARI GP

Nicolas Terol (Bankia Aprilia) confirmed his status as favourite for the final 125 world title by destroying his rivals at Losail. The Spaniard – runner-up last year after suffering a mid-season injury – disappeared from his pursuers at the rate of more than a second a lap. In the end he eased off to win by 'just' 7.7 seconds.

'My motorbike was perfect,' said Terol who had dominated qualifying. 'But it was a difficult race because it's difficult to concentrate when you're alone.'

The battle for second was a four-way affair until Sandro Cortese (Intact Aprilia) split from the group with two laps to go, leaving Sergio Gadea (Paris Hilton Blusens Aprilia), Efren Vazquez (Avant Derbi) and Jonas Folger (Red Bull Aprilia) to fight for the final podium position. Gadea won the contest just ahead of Vazquez. Folger was fourth, half a second behind Gadea.

2 – SPANISH GP

Nico Terol won an internecine duel with Bankia Aspar team-mate Hector Faubel in tricky wet conditions. Terol made the running early on, but Faubel caught him at one-third distance.

At half-distance Faubel teetered past Terol at the Dry Sack Hairpin, both of them searching for grip. The Aprilia pair swapped the lead several more times before Faubel lost it on the brakes into Dry Sack on the final lap while readying himself for a last-gasp challenge. The former 250 and Moto2 rider regained the track (and nearly fell again in the process) to finish fifth.

Second place went to Jonas Folger (Red Bull Aprilia), with Johann Zarco (AirAsia Derbi) taking the final podium place. Two teenage Brits filled out the top five – Danny Kent (Red Bull Aprilia) and Taylor Mackenzie (Phonica Aprilia), son of 1980s and 1990s 500 GP star Niall Mackenzie.

3 – PORTUGUESE GP

Nico Terol (Bankia Aprilia) ran away with the race to maintain his 2011 unbeaten record. In so doing the Spaniard became the first rider to win the opening three 125 GPs since Masao Azuma in 1999.

Terol was in his own race. He rocketed away from pole and was never troubled, building an 8 second lead at one point, then easing his pace to cross the line 3.7 seconds ahead.

The contest for second and third places was a very different story, with Sandro Cortese (Intact Aprilia) winning a last-lap battle with Johann Zarco (AirAsia Derbi) and Maverick Vinales (Blusens Aprilia).

4 – FRENCH GP

Spectators might have believed they were watching a cat play with a mouse as Nico Terol apparently toyed with Maverick Vinales (Blusens Aprilia). But it was the mouse who had the last laugh, the 16-year-old passing the world championship leader at the final turn.

At the start, Terol made the break and seemed set for his fourth runaway win from four races. But Vinales – riding in only his fourth GP – hunted down his fellow Spaniard. On lap 12 Terol conceded first place and then the pair started swapping places. On the last lap Terol ran wide at the final left, which allowed Vinales to attack at the last turn.

'I kept attacking and it paid off,' said Vinales, who rides for the Spanish team 'sponsored' by Paris Hilton.

Efren Vazquez (AirAsia Aprilia) won a frantic battle for third.

5 – CATALAN GP

Nico Terol was awarded his fourth win of the year after getting beaten to the line by Johann Zarco. The 20-year-old Frenchman was judged to have elbowed Terol as they drifted onto the kerb exiting the final corner. Zarco's punishment – a 20 second penalty – put him sixth.

Until the last-corner incident the pair had enjoyed a thrilling battle on a track that was barely dry following morning rainfall. The majority of the grid chose slicks.

Le Mans winner Maverick Vinales (Blusens Aprilia) was the fastest man in the early stages after taking the lead from Terol. At one-third distance the battle became a three-way affair when Zarco caught up. As the pace got hotter, Vinales was the first to wave a white flag, settling for a safe third.

Zarco got in front of Terol with four laps to go, Terol retook the lead as they started the final lap but took an excessively defensive line into the final corner, which allowed Zarco to get alongside on the exit.

6 – BRITISH GP

German teenager Jonas Folger (Red Bull Aprilia) took advantage of the slithery conditions to score his first GP win, beating Johann Zarco (AirAsia Derbi). The pair enjoyed a duel for the lead through the puddles until Folger escaped to win by almost four seconds.

After a sometimes frantic contest for the final place on the podium Hector Faubel (Bankia Aprilia) came out on top. His team-mate and championship leader Nico Terol rode to a conservative eighth-place finish, the first time he'd finished outside the top three.

Maverick Vinales set the first pole position of his Grand Prix career in only his sixth race, but fell in the race after setting the fastest lap.

Folger's win moved him to second in the world championship, and pushed his fellow countryman Sandro Cortese from second down to fourth. Zarco moved from fifth to third overall.

7 – DUTCH TT

Spain keeps churning them out – Maverick Vinales scored his second GP victory in just seven races, not bad for a 16-year-old rookie who made his GP debut only three months previously.

The race was another thriller, with plentiful overtaking as the drizzle began to fall. Several riders wanted the race to be red-flagged, but Race Direction held its nerve and waited until two-thirds distance had been completed before they stopped it, allowing the result to stand.

After a steady first few laps Vinales was eighth, but he charged through to take the lead from Sandro Cortese (Intact Aprilia) just before half-distance.

'The first few laps were difficult because there was some rain falling, but then I was able to pick up the pace,' said Vinales.

Championship leader Nico Terol (Bankia Aprilia) missed the race after injuring his right hand in two practice falls.

8 – ITALIAN GP

Nico Terol (Bankia Aprilia) made up for missing the Assen race with a victorious comeback, passing Johann Zarco (AirAsia Derbi) in the final dash to the finish line. Twice outwitted by teenagers in previous races – by Maverick Vinales at Le Mans and by Zarco at Catalunya (though Zarco copped a penalty for over-enthusiastic use of his left elbow) – Terol had this one worked out.

Instead of setting the pace he let Zarco past at mid-distance, then stalked his prey until the chequered flag was unfurled, when he used his factory Aprilia's superior speed to draft past.

Zarco knew what was coming. 'Whatever I did, I knew his bike was faster,' said the Frenchman, whose fourth podium of 2011 moved him into second overall, 39 points behind Terol.

Maverick Vinales (Blusens Aprilia) was once again impressive, winning a thrilling three-way battle for third from Efren Vazquez and Hector Faubel.

9 – GERMAN GP

Conspiracy theorists will have a field day with this one. When Johann Zarco (AirAsia Derbi) powered past Hector Faubel (Bankia Aprilia) exiting the final corner, it seemed like the young Frenchman had won his first GP, six weeks after he crossed the line first at Catalunya, only to be penalised for elbowing Spaniard Nico Terol (Bankia Aprilia).

This time Race Direction declared a dead-heat but made Spaniard Faubel the winner because he had set the fastest lap. Bad luck for Zarco, or the Spanish Inquisition?

The race was a classic, positions changing every other corner within the leading group, which started out as an eight-man freight train and was gradually whittled down to Zarco, Faubel and pole-sitter Maverick Vinales (Blusens Aprilia) who finished third, three-tenths down. Points leader Terol was fourth.

'This win is incredible for me,' said Faubel. 'The race was very, very crazy, always pass, pass, pass!'

10 – CZECH REPUBLIC GP

Sandro Cortese won a thrilling last-corner battle with Johann Zarco for the 125 win, the German's first victory in 109 GP starts. Cortese and Frenchman Zarco were out on their own after early leader Nico Terol (Bankia Aprilia) went out with a sick engine at half-distance.

Zarco (AirAsia Derbi) did all the running until Cortese (Intact Aprilia) nipped ahead at the start of the penultimate lap. Zarco counter-attacked on the final lap but nearly crashed.

'I can't believe it!' said Cortese. 'I lost my feeling for racing at the start of this season, so to get back to the front and win is unbelievable.'

Zarco's finish moved him to within just 12 points of Terol. Alberto Moncayo (Aprilia) scored his first podium in third, after coming out on top of a frantic battle with four other riders.

Impressive British rookie Danny Kent (Red Bull Aprilia) was handed his team-mate Jonas Folger's top-spec RS125W after the German fell ill before the race. He made good use of it to qualify seventh, but fell in the race.

Left The top three of the season: Johann Zarco, Nico Terol and Maverick Vinales

Above The dead heat in Germany between Johann Zarco and Hector Faubel; Faubel was given the win because he set fastest lap

Below The final 125 pole, at Valencia, went to Danny Webb on the Mahindra

Year would have been British teenager Danny Kent, plucked from the Red Bull Rookies by team owner Aki Ajo, who took Marc Marquez to the 2010 title. A fourth place in the wet in Spain and a brace of sixths when he was given the top A-spec bike – as opposed to the W-spec production version – underlined his potential.

The season played out to plan. The top teams, Ajo and Aspar, fought out the wins with only Vinales and the consistency of Cortese getting in the way. For Jorge 'Aspar' Martinez, it was another triumph. Terol is a product of his race school at the Valencia circuit, and although the team has won before, this felt like a home victory. Add in Aspar's 1988 title as a rider in the 125 class (and three in the defunct 80cc class) and you understand why it was important for them to say goodbye to the 125s with another title.

11 – INDIANAPOLIS GP

Two weeks after his bitter DNF at Brno, Nico Terol (Bankia Aspar) put his championship back on track by destroying his rivals at Indy. While the Spaniard got into the lead and disappeared, a growing battle for the runner-up spot developed behind him.

Early leader Johann Zarco (AirAsia Derbi) was often at the forefront of this group until he nearly crashed in the closing stages, which shifted the contest for second place to Maverick Vinales (Blusens Aprilia) and Sandro Cortese (Intact Aprilia). The pair swapped the position several times in the closing laps, the teenage Spaniard crossing the line just in front of the German, with Terol's team-mate Sergio Gadea right behind.

Zarco finished a distant fifth, drafting past his team-mate Efren Vazquez on the run to the chequered flag. British teenager Danny Kent (Red Bull Derbi) had also been in the group until he ran off-track. He recovered to 13th.

12 – SAN MARINO GP

Johann Zarco did it again. For the fourth time this year the up-and-coming Frenchman snatched defeat from the jaws of victory. This time Zarco – who was so near but so far from victory at Catalunya, Sachsenring and Brno – finally looked like he had done enough to beat Nico Terol (Bankia Aprilia) after a frantic final few corners. But as he came out of the final turn he sat up to look over his shoulder, waving frantically as Terol passed him on the line to win by 0.22 seconds.

'I made a big mistake,' said a distraught Zarco.

Terol was happy to accept this gift of win, his seventh of the year, and increase his championship advantage over Zarco to 31 points. Zarco's AirAsia Derbi team-mate Efren Vazquez took the final podium place, five seconds down on the leaders and four seconds ahead of Brno winner Sandro Cortese (Intact Aprilia), who just beat Terol's team-mate Hector Faubel for fourth.

13 – ARAGON GP

Nico Terol (Bankia Aprilia) waltzed his way to his eighth win of 2011 to take one more step towards the final 125 world title.

Terol led from start to finish, building an unbeatable lead, while team-mate and pole-sitter Hector Faubel fought a desperate duel for second with Johann Zarco (AirAsia Derbi). The confrontation went down to the last corner, where Faubel shot past Zarco, lost the front and crashed. That incident promoted Maverick Vinales (Blusens Aprilia) to third.

The frantic five-way punch-up for fourth place ended in favour of Efren Vazquez (AirAsia Derbi), after much bump and grind between the Spaniard and Luis Salom (RW Aprilia), Danny Kent (Red Bull Derbi Aprilia), Sandro Cortese (Intact Aprilia) and Alberto Moncayo (Aprilia). Kent was riding the A-spec Red Bull Aprilia for the last time, having qualified in fifth place for three races in a row.

14 – JAPANESE GP

At last! After a run of six second-place finishes in nine races, Frenchman Johann Zarco (AirAsia Derbi) finally won his first GP victory. Once again the race was a duel between Zarco and points leader Nico Terol (Bankia Aprilia), the pair leaving Terol's team-mate Hector Faubel behind in the early stages.

'It feels great to finally win – I was worried it might never happen,' said Zarco, whose Motegi pace was too much for Terol, the points leader happy for a safe second rather than a win-it-or-bin-it battle for first.

Faubel finished third. Teenage rookie Maverick Vinales (Blusens Aprilia) was a brilliant fourth, having started from pit lane after his chain snapped on the warm-up lap.

15 – AUSTRALIAN GP

The 125 grid was thrown into chaos by a pre-race downpour, but only Adrian Martin chose wets for the race. Martin (Bankia Aprilia) tore into the lead but as the track dried he went backwards, until he had to pit for slicks. Sandro Cortese (Intact Aprilia) took the risks in the tricky conditions and was rewarded with a runaway win.

Of title duellists Nico Terol (Bankia Aprilia) and Johann Zarco (AirAsia Derbi), Zarco got the best of the conditions, finishing third, just behind Luis Salom (RW Aprilia). Points leader Terol was more cautious, slipping to 16th before recovering to sixth when more rainfall brought out the red flags. Zarco's result trimmed Terol's championship lead to just 25 points.

125 MILESTONES

1949
Swiss GP, Berne
Italian Nello Pagani (above) won the first 125 GP riding a Mondial. Pagani went on to become the first 125cc World Champion.

1952
Ulster GP, Clady
Cecil Sandford (GBR) wins to become the first non-Italian 125cc World Champion. This was also the first title for MV Agusta.

1959
Italian GP, Monza
Ernst Degner gave MZ their first GP win, the first in the 125 class by a two-stroke.

1963
DDR GP, Sachsenring
New Zealander Hugh Anderson (Suzuki) won to become the first rider to win the 125 world title on a two-stroke.

1965
Isle of Man TT
Phil Read takes the first win in the class for Yamaha.

1969
Germany, Hockenheim
Dave Simmonds takes Kawasaki's first GP win on his way to the title, the last time a Briton won the 125 crown.

1970
Belgian GP, Spa
Angel Nieto, the most successful rider in the class, takes his first win on a Derbi.

1979
Dutch TT, Assen
Angel Nieto (Minarelli) took the last of 11 wins in a row, the longest winning streak in 125s.

1987
San Marino GP, Misano
Fausto Gresini (Garelli) equals Nieto's sequence of 11 consecutive wins.

1988
Spanish GP, Jarama
Jorge 'Aspar' Martinez wins the first race under the new rule allowing only single-cylinder machines on his way to the title.

1990
British GP, Donington
Loris Capirossi (Honda) wins his first GP and goes on to become the youngest ever champion, a record that still stands.

1991
Czech GP, Brno
Alessandro Gramigni gives Aprilia their first ever GP win and goes on to become their first champion the following year.

1996
Czech GP, Brno
Valentino Rossi (Aprilia) wins his first GP. The following year he would equal the record of 11 wins in a season.

2008
British GP, Donington
Scott Redding (Aprilia) wins at the age of just 15 years and 170 days to become the youngest ever GP victor.

2011
Catalan GP, Catalunya
Nico Terol's win is the last in a run of 14 podium finishes, equalling the record set by multiple World Champion Carlo Ubbiali (MV Agusta) in the 1950s.

16 – MALAYSIAN GP

Johann Zarco (AirAsia Derbi) kept his title dream alive with a great ride to third place from 15th on the grid, while championship leader Nico Terol (Bankia Aprilia) faltered in the steamy 35-degree heat.

Zarco, who had crashed in qualifying, stormed through to fifth on the first lap to get with the leading group. Twice Terol tried to go away at the front, but both times Maverick Vinales (Blusens Aprilia), Sandro Cortese (Intact Aprilia), Hector Faubel (Bankia Aprilia) and Zarco went with him.

Vinales was the strongest at the end, winning by a fraction from Cortese, with Zarco third and Faubel fourth. Terol suffered heat exhaustion during the late stages, almost crashed on the final lap, crossed the line in fifth place and collapsed after stopping on the slowdown lap. He recovered in the medical centre.

17 – VALENCIAN GP

Ringa-dinga-ding and then they were gone. The last two-stroke Grand Prix was won by Spaniard Maverick Vinales, the diminutive teenage sensation joined on the historic podium by his team's 'sponsor', Paris Hilton. But the real history man was runner-up Nico Terol, who secured the final 125 crown after his only rival, Johann Zarco (AirAsia Derbi), had crashed out.

Maverick (Blusens Aprilia) deserved his fourth victory, fought out in neither-one-thing-nor-the-other weather, spots of rain falling throughout the 24 laps. He enjoyed a battle royal – a fitting end for the often thrilling 125s – with Bankia Aspar team-mates Nico Terol and Hector Faubel. In the end, Maverick was bravest, Terol simply wanting to celebrate his title from the podium.

'This is like a dream,' said Terol. 'I pushed so hard every race and now this is the best moment of my life.'

CHAMPIONSHIP STANDINGS

	Rider	Nat	Team	Motorcycle	Points
1	Nicolas Terol	SPA	Bankia Aspar Team	Aprilia	302
2	Johann Zarco	FRA	Avant-AirAsia-Ajo	Derbi	262
3	Maverick Vinales	SPA	Blusens by Paris Hilton Racing	Aprilia	248
4	Sandro Cortese	GER	Intact-Racing Team Germany	Aprilia	225
5	Hector Faubel	SPA	Bankia Aspar Team	Aprilia	177
6	Jonas Folger	GER	Red Bull Ajo MotorSport	Aprilia	161
7	Efren Vazquez	SPA	Avant-AirAsia-Ajo	Derbi	160
8	Luis Salom	SPA	RW Racing GP	Aprilia	116
9	Sergio Gadea	SPA	Bankia Aspar Team	Aprilia	103
10	Alberto Moncayo	SPA	Andalucia Banca Civica	Aprilia	94
11	Danny Kent	GBR	Red Bull Ajo MotorSport	Aprilia	82
12	Jakub Kornfeil	CZE	Ongetta-Centro Seta	Aprilia	72
13	Adrian Martin	SPA	Bankia Aspar Team	Aprilia	45
14	Miguel Oliveira	POR	Andalucia Banca Civica	Aprilia	44
15	Marcel Schrotter	GER	Mahindra Racing	Mahindra	36
16	Simone Grotzkyj	ITA	Phonica Racing	Aprilia	32
17	Louis Rossi	FRA	Matteoni Racing	Aprilia	31
18	Zulfahmi Khairuddin	MAL	AirAsia-Sic-Ajo	Derbi	30
19	Danny Webb	GBR	Mahindra Racing	Mahindra	24
20	Luigi Morciano	ITA	Team Italia FMI	Aprilia	23
21	Nicklas Ajo	FIN	TT Motion Events Racing	Aprilia	19
22	Alexis Masbou	FRA	Caretta Technology	KTM	18
23	Jasper Iwema	NED	Ongetta-Abbink Metaal	Aprilia	16
24	Taylor Mackenzie	GBR	Phonica Racing	Aprilia	15
25	Alessandro Tonucci	ITA	Team Italia FMI	Aprilia	12
26	Hiroki Ono	JPN	Caretta Technology	KTM	8
27	Manual Tatasciore	ITA	Phonica Racing	Aprilia	5
28	Harry Stafford	GBR	Ongetta-Centro Seta	Aprilia	5
29	Toni Finsterbusch	GER	Freudenberg Racing Team	KTM	4
30	Miroslav Popov	CZE	Ellegi Racing	Aprilia	3
31	John McPhee	GBR	Racing Steps Foundation KRP	Aprilia	3
32	Josep Rodriguez	SPA	Blusens by Paris Hilton Racing	Aprilia	3
33	Giulian Pedone	SWI	Phonica Racing	Aprilia	1
34	Sturla Fagerhaug	NOR	WTR-Ten10 Racing	Aprilia	1

RED BULL ROOKIES

PETER CLIFFORD

Above The Red Bull Rookies field was as crowded and competitive as ever; they'll be back in 2012 and will stay on two-stroke KTMs

Lorenzo Baldassarri clinched the fifth Red Bull MotoGP Rookies Cup at the last round in Misano. The 15-year-old Italian took the title after a thrilling season-long struggle with 16-year-old Australian Arthur Sissis that was only decided when the two rubbed shoulders during the final race and Sissis ran off the track.

It was an incredible season for Baldassarri, his first in the Rookies Cup, and he proved his ability throughout the 14 races at eight GPs across Europe. His lowest finish was 12th in the second race at the opening weekend in Jerez, when he recovered after getting tangled in an incident. Apart from that he never finished outside the top six; he was on the podium six times and scored two victories. Sissis had four wins in his seven appearances on the podium, the ex-speedway ace riding extremely strongly and producing a more dramatic season's racing. He lost by nine points in the final reckoning and it's not hard to pick out where he might have saved those vital numbers.

The first race in Jerez didn't see either of them on the podium because Sissis ran off the track early, trying to blitz things from the start. Race one went to Philipp Oettl after the 14-year-old German caught early leader Brad Binder and eased the 15-year-old South African aside at the crucial moment. Binder was the pre-season favourite and sat on pole for the opening weekend in Spain, but race two gave him a dose of the bad luck that was to dog his season. It rained and he hated the soaking wet track. Sissis romped away to victory, leaving Oettl to pick up second and lead the points going into the second weekend in Estoril.

Oettl couldn't defend that points lead, though, as he broke his collarbone testing his German Championship bike. Binder was on pole again, winning the first race but crashing in the second while leading. Sissis took the win in race two and, with his second-place finish from race one, also had the points lead as Baldassarri followed him home in both races.

A lousy weekend of weather in Silverstone put a big dent in the Sissis Rookies Cup effort as he struggled to ninth and seventh. Baldassarri was superb. A runaway leader in the first race, he was caught out as the track dried but still finished fourth, while 15-year-old Lukas Trautmann scored a great win for Austria. Baldassarri raced away with Sunday's even wetter and colder race to win by 11 seconds from Trautmann. Third was Alain Techer; the 16-year-old Frenchman was starting to put together the fast, consistent rides that would see him third in the final points standings.

A wet track which then dried provided a different challenge at Assen and produced a fabulous battle between Sissis and Baldassarri. The Italian made a mistake in race one and seemed to have handed it to the Australian, but he came back with an incredible burst to snatch victory at the line. Race two in the Netherlands started with rain tyres on a damp track, and the Dunlops were shredded again as the circuit dried. Baldassarri and Sissis overcame a fine effort from 15-year-old German Florian Alt to ensure that the last

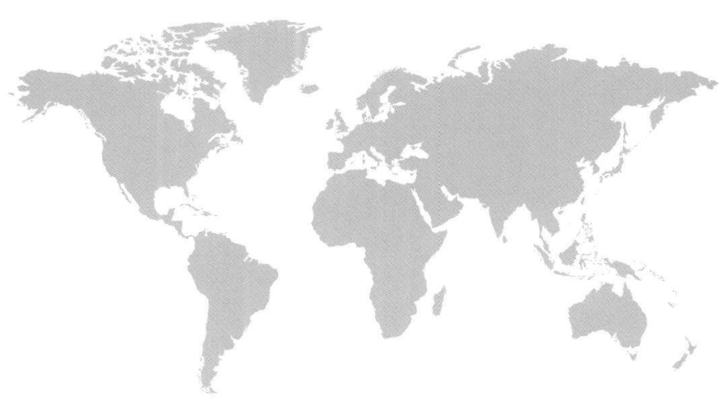

DOWN TO THE WIRE

laps were theirs alone, with the Australian grabbing the win this time.

The single race at Mugello went to Sissis, who opened up his points lead over Baldassarri, who took fourth place. The Italian failed to get past Tomas Vavrous and Aaron España at the final corner, a hint of the close-fighting difficulties that would threaten his Rookies Cup challenge in the remaining five races.

Sissis had overcome his dislike of the wet weather which had blunted his Silverstone effort and looked stronger every weekend. Then luck dealt him a blow in Germany, a technical problem leaving him with no points from race one. Philipp Oettl had got back on his bike at Silverstone, but he only really showed complete recovery from his broken collarbone at the Sachsenring. He took pole there and won the first race ahead of Binder and Scott Deroue, the 15-year-old Dutchman who was part of a sensational 12-man battle for the lead, showing how much he had improved after racing at the back of the field in Jerez. Baldassarri had not been able to fight his way out of the group and finished sixth. He had similar difficulties in race two but still left Germany with the points lead as arch rival Sissis crashed out at the penultimate corner. He clipped the rear of Florian Alt's bike, bidding for the win. That went to Techer ahead of Alt and Willi Albert, the 13-year-old German putting in the race of his year.

With zero points from the weekend, Sissis was thinking his season had hit its lowest point. He picked himself up and went to Brno, determined to forget Germany. Race one in the Czech Republic was stopped when it rained. American 14-year-old Joe Roberts won the restart brilliantly; Sissis was happy enough with the points for second that gave him a four-point advantage over Baldassarri. The Italian again struggled to fight his way to the front of the lead group and finished sixth.

Baldassarri had the same trouble in race two and it looked as if Sissis might seize a commanding points lead going into the single remaining race in Misano. The timing monitors showed 19 riders fighting for the lead at one stage but, when it counted, Sissis had the advantage: he led on the final lap and was not going to be caught. Then he crashed, three corners from the finish. The lead went to Baldassarri by six points, while Techer won from Vavrous and Deroue.

The showdown in Italy produced another classic. While Sissis and Baldassarri were thinking about the Rookies Cup they were also fighting for the win with Oettl and Alt. With four laps to go Sissis was battling hard with Baldassarri when he ran out of room, that slightest of slips handing the title to the Italian, who cruised home in third. Oettl, meanwhile, handed victory to Alt when he backed off early on the run to the line. That made it eight different race winners, while 16 of the 24 riders finished on the podium during another fabulous Rookies season.

Above Lorenzo Baldassarri won the Rookies Cup at his first attempt

Best Location and Exclusive Privileges

Situated at the heart of the action, either directly above the Pit Lane or in a smart village area, MotoGP VIP VILLAGE puts you as close as you can get to the world's top motorcycle racers.

Privileged Parking, excellent views, race coverage on closed-circuit TV, Pit Lane Walk, Paddock Tour, Service Road Tour and complimentary Official Programme on Sunday.

The MotoGP VIP VILLAGE Game will offer all guests the chance to win the possibility to view races from the pit wall, a service road tour and one of the many licensed MotoGP products.

Best Service and Excellent Cuisine

Hospitality is of the highest quality, from the buffet breakfast in the morning to gourmet lunch and afternoon petit fours, with a complimentary bar all day.

riders
RIDERS FOR HEALTH
BARRY COLEMAN
riders

MOTORCYCLES SAVE LIVES

In March, in a theatre in Oxford, some of the world's leading figures in the field of social change, in town for a conference, sat down to watch a film. The theatre was full. The film was about the life and times and work of the social enterprise that began here in our sport in the 1980s. It was about Riders for Health. The Riders people who were there – Andrea and me, for example – watched the film critically and a trifle nervously, conscious of the real possibility that we would look like idiots. Even if it weren't that bad, if we just looked a little bit lame, it promised to be memorably embarrassing. Maybe we would never ever quite live it down.

But then something happened that really was a surprise. In a way it was even more embarrassing than our worst fears. The audience rose as one to its feet and gave Riders for Health a long and very loud standing ovation. Riders! Little us! Imagine. And among the many very distinguished people who rose to his feet that day was the Archbishop Desmond Tutu, chief among those who brought the foul beast that was apartheid to its bitter end.

So, that's your sport. That's what it has done. I write this or something like it every year at this time so I might as well write it again: it's a fact that motorcycle racing is the only sport that has ever given rise to a sustained humanitarian movement. Some people are surprised by this. God knows what they think of motorcycle racing, but the chances are it's none too accurate and quite possibly – who knows? – none too flattering. But the truth is that Africa and our kind of racing were made for each other. For one thing, Africa, as you will have noticed, often provides a very uncertain environment. In Africa all your intentions and all your plans oft go awry. More often than not, in fact.

It's the same with racing. I'm often struck by the thoroughness and orderliness of the preparation for such a disorderly maelstrom as a Moto2 or MotoGP race. Especially Moto2. Computers (Riders has computers too), data (Riders has lots of data), financial calculation (Riders also has accountants), meticulous engineering (Riders has engineers) and all the rest. And then the lights go out.

Racing is a noisy but much more interesting and much more thrilling version of the real world: anything can

Left Zimbabwean health worker Solomon Mwembe gives advice to one of the women in his community

happen. But in Africa anything already has happened and does happen every day. People live on the edge out there, just as racers do, but not for fun. They live that way, in perpetual shortage of water, firewood and, of course, food because that's the way it is. And ill health is just another urgent threat, always hovering.

So maybe it's not so surprising that way back in the 1980s Africa didn't seem quite as scary to us as it did to many others, and maybe it's not such a surprise that more than 22 years later here we still are, hauling steadily onwards and upwards. We are used to the long haul and adversity doesn't really bother us. Think of the 125 rider who is riding his socks off for 27th place, falls down, wrecks his bike, breaks his collarbone and shows up two weeks later to see just what it would take to come 26th. His impossible dream. Well, that's in riders' and Riders' DNA. Can't help it. Just won't lie down. Preparation, strategy, frustration and coming back for more.

Since last year's report we've started a new programme, in Malawi, a small country but a surprisingly difficult one. We have worked there before, many years ago, as advisors to Save the Children. But now we are back, in our own right, slowly building a good working relationship with the Ministry of Health. Their health workers have terrible trouble getting around and they have a particular problem with what we call 'sample transport' – getting blood

'I AM SURE IF IT WAS NOT FOR MY MOTORCYCLE MY CLIENT WOULD HAVE DIED'

PETER, A COMMUNITY HEALTH WORKER FROM LUMUMBA, KENYA

Counterclockwise from top left

Archbishop Desmond Tutu speaking at the Skoll World Forum in Oxford, March 2011

Health workers at Riders' training academy in Harare learn how to handle their bikes safely over tough terrain

Solomon Mwembe rides to his next appointment in the Binga district of Zimbabwe

Sulayman Senghore, a Riders for Health technician, carries out a monthly service on Bubacarr Jallow's motorcycle

samples for HIV/AIDS testing from health centres to labs and getting the results back. We do that very thing already for ministries of health in Lesotho, Zambia and Zimbabwe, and the fact that samples actually get tested makes an almost unimaginable difference to those who want to know their status and would like to be put on anti-retroviral drugs. The turnaround time for such tests in Lesotho, with your favourite charity providing the motorcycle-based courier service, is slightly better than it would be in the United States. It's down to less than a week; it used to take three months – if you were very lucky.

Malawi has about 1.5 million people. Nigeria has one hundred times as many, and then some. As we go to press they have just told us that they would like sample transport there too. That's quite an impact, for a little organisation which thought, way back then, that it could probably figure out how to change chains and sprockets and the occasional bent gearchange lever in very difficult and unpredictable circumstances. I wonder why we thought we could do that?

Oh that's right. We're from motorcycle racing. It's what we do.

In some respects we're still waiting patiently, back there in 28th, for most of the world to understand what this really means, but we're used to it. And at least Desi gets it.

RIDERS IN NUMBERS

MotoGP is all about efficiency. Each team strains to get the absolute maximum performance from every euro they spend. Making sure that our work is also as cost-effective as possible is something that's crucial to Riders for Health. Now, as everyone's budgets are tightened, this is more important than ever.

We know we couldn't achieve what we do without the support of the motorcycle community. That is why Riders for Health has always focused on achieving the biggest possible impact from the money we spend in Africa. The income we receive from donations builds programmes that can support themselves, creating a lasting difference. And, by using low-cost, reliable motorcycles, Riders for Health is able to get hundreds of health workers across Africa on the road at the lowest cost.

VISITING MORE PEOPLE

A reliable motorcycle means a health worker can triple the number of villages they visit each month. Thanks to Riders for Health, health workers are now seeing four times as many people as before. They can protect against, and treat, diseases like malaria, measles, polio, HIV and cholera as well as helping provide sanitation and clean water and also helping to improve maternal health.

Before Riders

Under the Riders programme

TRAINING MORE RIDERS

To make sure that the impact of our work is long-lasting, training is at the heart of what we do. Since 2002, Riders for Health has trained over 2,000 local people in motorcycle riding, vehicle driving and basic maintenance at our training academy in Harare, Zimbabwe.

This year, Riders for Health opened a brand-new training school in Kisumu, Kenya. Already, more than 60 health workers have been trained how to ride safely and look after their motorcycles.

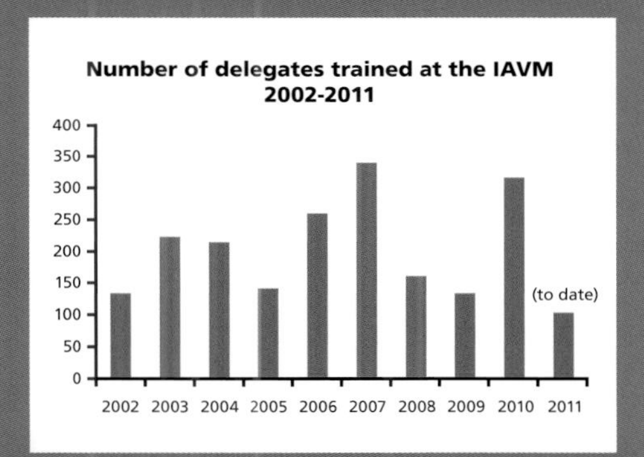

SAVING MORE LIVES

In the Gambia the number of immunisation campaigns the Ministry of Health has been able to run has increased dramatically since Riders for Health made sure that each health centre had all the vehicles it needed to reach every community.

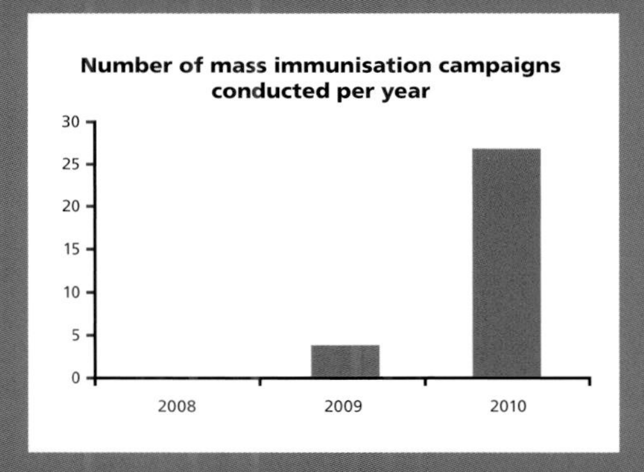

Thanks to the support of everyone involved in MotoGP, Riders for Health is able to reach more people across rural Africa with regular health care, saving millions of lives.